FAILED STATES

THE ABUSE OF POWER AND
THE ASSAULT ON DEMOCRACY

NOAM
CHOMSKY

HAMISH HAMILTON
an imprint of
PENGUIN BOOKS

HAMISH HAMILTON

Published by the Penguin Group
Penguin Books Ltd, 80 Strand, London WC2R 0RL, England
Penguin Group (USA) Inc., 375 Hudson Street, New York, New York 10014, USA
Penguin Group (Canada), 90 Eglinton Avenue East, Suite 700, Toronto, Ontario, Canada M4P 2Y3
(a division of Pearson Penguin Canada Inc.)
Penguin Ireland, 25 St Stephen's Green, Dublin 2, Ireland (a division of Penguin Books Ltd)
Penguin Group (Australia), 250 Camberwell Road,
Camberwell, Victoria 3124, Australia (a division of Pearson Australia Group Pty Ltd)
Penguin Books India Pvt Ltd, 11 Community Centre,
Panchsheel Park, New Delhi – 110 017, India
Penguin Group (NZ), cnr Airborne and Rosedale Roads, Albany, Auckland 1310, New Zealand
(a division of Pearson New Zealand Ltd)
Penguin Books (South Africa) (Pty) Ltd, 24 Sturdee Avenue,
Rosebank, Johannesburg 2196, South Africa

Penguin Books Ltd, Registered Offices: 80 Strand, London WC2R 0RL, England

www.penguin.com

First published in the United States of America by Metropolitan Books,
Henry Holt and Company, LLC 2006
First published in Great Britain by Hamish Hamilton 2006
2

The map on page 180, originally published by *Survival* (2001) of
the International Institute of Strategic Studies, appears courtesy of
Taylor & Francis Ltd, www.tandf.co.uk/journals

Printed in Great Britain by Clays Ltd, St Ives plc

A CIP catalogue record for this book is available from the British Library

ISBN-13: 978–0–241–14323–0
ISBN-10: 0–241–14323–3

Contents

Preface

The selection of issues that should rank high on the agenda of concern for human welfare and rights is, naturally, a subjective matter. But there are a few choices that seem unavoidable, because they bear so directly on the prospects for decent survival. Among them are at least these three: nuclear war, environmental disaster, and the fact that the government of the world's leading power is acting in ways that increase the likelihood of these catastrophes. It is important to stress the *government,* because the population, not surprisingly, does not agree. That brings up a fourth issue that should deeply concern Americans, and the world: the sharp divide between public opinion and public policy, one of the reasons for the fear, which cannot casually be put aside, that "the American 'system' as a whole is in real trouble—that it is heading in a direction that spells the end of its historic values [of] equality, liberty, and meaningful democracy."[1]

The "system" is coming to have some of the features of failed states, to adopt a currently fashionable notion that is conventionally applied to states regarded as potential threats to our security (like Iraq) or as needing our intervention to rescue the population from severe internal threats (like Haiti). Though the concept is recognized to be "frustratingly imprecise," some of the primary characteristics of failed states can be identified. One is their inability or unwillingness to protect their citizens from violence and perhaps even destruction. Another is their tendency to regard themselves as beyond the reach of domestic or international law, and hence free to carry out aggression and violence. And if they have democratic forms, they suffer from a serious "democratic deficit" that deprives their formal democratic institutions of real substance.[2]

Among the hardest tasks that anyone can undertake, and one of the most important, is to look honestly in the mirror. If we allow ourselves to do so, we should have little difficulty in finding the characteristics of "failed states" right at home. That recognition of reality should be deeply troubling to those who care about their countries and future generations. "Countries," plural, because of the enormous reach of US power, but also because the threats are not localized in space or time.

The first half of this book is devoted mostly to the increasing threat of destruction caused by US state power, in violation of international law, a topic of particular concern for citizens of the world dominant power, however one assesses the relevant threats. The second half is concerned primarily with democratic institutions, how they are conceived in the elite culture and how they perform in reality, both in "promoting democracy" abroad and shaping it at home.

The issues are closely interlinked, and arise in several contexts. In discussing them, to save excessive footnoting I will omit sources when they can easily be found in recent books of mine.[3]

Chapter 1

Stark, Dreadful, Inescapable

Half a century ago, in July 1955, Bertrand Russell and Albert Einstein issued an extraordinary appeal to the people of the world, asking them "to set aside" the strong feelings they have about many issues and to consider themselves "only as members of a biological species which has had a remarkable history, and whose disappearance none of us can desire." The choice facing the world is "stark and dreadful and inescapable: shall we put an end to the human race; or shall mankind renounce war?"[1]

The world has not renounced war. Quite the contrary. By now, the world's hegemonic power accords itself the right to wage war at will, under a doctrine of "anticipatory self-defense" with unstated bounds. International law, treaties, and rules of world order are sternly imposed on others with much self-righteous posturing, but dismissed as irrelevant for the United States—a long-standing practice, driven to new depths by the Reagan and Bush II administrations.[2]

Among the most elementary of moral truisms is the principle of universality: we must apply to ourselves the same standards we do to others, if not more stringent ones. It is a remarkable comment on Western intellectual culture that this principle is so often ignored and, if occasionally mentioned, condemned as outrageous. This is particularly shameful on the part of those who flaunt their Christian piety, and therefore have presumably at least heard of the definition of the hypocrite in the Gospels.[3]

Relying solely on elevated rhetoric, commentators urge us to appreciate the sincerity of the professions of "moral clarity" and "idealism" by the political leadership. To take just one of innumerable examples, the well-known scholar Philip Zelikow deduces "the new centrality of moral principles" in the Bush administration from "the administration's rhetoric" and a single fact: the proposal to increase development aid—to a fraction of that provided by other rich countries relative to the size of their economies.[4]

The rhetoric is indeed impressive. "I carry this commitment in my soul," the president declared in March 2002 as he created the Millennium Challenge Corporation to boost funding to combat poverty in the developing world. In 2005, the corporation erased the statement from its website after the Bush administration reduced its projected budget by billions of dollars. Its head resigned "after failing to get the program moving," economist Jeffrey Sachs writes, having "disbursed almost nothing" of the $10 billion originally promised. Meanwhile, Bush rejected a call from Prime Minister Tony Blair to double aid to Africa, and expressed willingness to join other industrial countries in cutting unpayable African debt only if aid was correspondingly reduced, moves that amount to "a death sentence for more than 6 million Africans a year who die of preventable and treatable causes," Sachs notes. When Bush's new ambassador, John Bolton, arrived at the United Nations shortly before its 2005 summit, he at once demanded the elimination of "all occurrences of the phrase 'millennium development goals'" from the document that had been carefully prepared after long negotiations to deal with "poverty, sexual discrimination, hunger, primary education, child mortality, maternal health, the environment and disease."[5]

Rhetoric is always uplifting, and we are enjoined to admire the sincerity of those who produce it, even when they act in ways that recall Alexis de Tocqueville's observation that the United States was able "to exterminate the Indian race . . . without violating a single great principle of morality in the eyes of the world."[6]

Reigning doctrines are often called a "double standard." The term is misleading. It is more accurate to describe them as a single standard, clear and unmistakable, the standard that Adam Smith called the "vile maxim of the masters of mankind: . . . All for ourselves, and nothing for other people." Much has changed since his day, but the vile maxim flourishes.[7]

The single standard is so deeply entrenched that it is beyond awareness. Take "terror," the leading topic of the day. There is a straightforward single standard: *their* terror against us and our clients is the ultimate evil, while *our* terror against them does not exist—or, if it does, is entirely appropriate. One clear illustration is Washington's terrorist war against Nicaragua in the 1980s, an uncontroversial case, at least for those who believe that the International Court of Justice and the UN Security Council—both of which condemned the United States—have some standing on such matters. The State Department confirmed that the US-run forces attacking Nicaragua from US bases in Honduras had been authorized to attack "soft targets," that is, undefended civilian targets. A protest by Americas Watch elicited a sharp response by a respected spokesman of "the left," *New Republic* editor Michael Kinsley, who patiently explained that terrorist attacks on civilian targets should be evaluated on pragmatic grounds: a "sensible policy [should] meet the test of cost-benefit analysis" of "the amount of blood and misery that will be poured in, and the likelihood that democracy will emerge at the other end"—"democracy" as defined by US elites, of course.[8]

The assumptions remain beyond challenge, even perception. In 2005, the press reported that the Bush administration was facing a serious "dilemma": Venezuela was seeking extradition of one of the most notorious Latin American terrorists, Luis Posada Carriles, to face charges for the bombing of a Cubana airliner, killing seventy-three people. The charges were credible, but there was a real difficulty. After Posada escaped from a Venezuelan prison, he "was hired by US covert operatives to direct the resupply operation for the Nicaraguan contras from El Salvador"—that is, to play a prominent role in Washington's terrorist war against Nicaragua. Hence the dilemma: "Extraditing him for trial could send a worrisome signal to covert foreign agents that they cannot count on unconditional protection from the US government, and it could expose the CIA to embarrassing public disclosures from a former operative." A virtual entry requirement for the society of respectable intellectuals is the failure to perceive that there might be some slight problem here.[9]

At the same time that Venezuela was pressing its appeal, over-whelming majorities in the Senate and House passed a bill barring US aid to countries that refuse requests for extradition—US requests, that is. Washington's regular refusal to honor requests from other coun-tries seeking extradition of leading terrorists passed without com-ment, though some concern was voiced over the possibility that the bill theoretically might bar aid to Israel because of its refusal to extra-dite a man charged with "a brutal 1997 murder in Maryland who had fled to Israel and claimed citizenship through his father."[10]

At least temporarily, the Posada dilemma was, thankfully, resolved by the courts, which rejected Venezuela's appeal, in violation of a US-Venezuelan extradition treaty. A day later, the head of the FBI, Robert Mueller, urged Europe to speed US demands for extradition: "We are always looking to see how we can make the extradition process go faster," he said. "We think we owe it to the victims of terrorism to see to it that justice is done efficiently and effectively." At the Ibero-American Summit shortly after, the leaders of Spain and the Latin American coun-tries "backed Venezuela's efforts to have [Posada] extradited from the United States to face trial" for the Cubana airliner bombing, but then backed down, after the US embassy protested the action. Washington not only rejects, or merely ignores, extradition requests for terrorists. It also uses the tool of presidential pardons for acceptable crimes. Bush I pardoned Orlando Bosch, a notorious international terrorist and as-sociate of Posada, despite objections by the Justice Department, which urged that he be deported as a threat to national security. Bosch resides safely in the United States, perhaps to be joined by Posada, in communi-ties that continue to serve as the base for international terrorism.[11]

No one would be so vulgar as to suggest that the United States should be subject to bombing and invasion in accord with the Bush II doctrine that "those who harbor terrorists are as guilty as the terror-ists themselves," announced when the government in Afghanistan asked for evidence before handing over people the United States ac-cused of terrorism (without credible grounds, as Robert Mueller later acknowledged). The Bush doctrine has "already become a de facto rule of international relations," writes Harvard international relations specialist Graham Allison: it revokes "the sovereignty of states that provide sanctuary to terrorists." Some states, that is, thanks to the exemption provided by the single standard.[12]

The single standard also extends to weapons and other means of destruction. US military expenditures approximate those of the rest of the world combined, while arms sales by thirty-eight North American companies (one of which is based in Canada) account for more than 60 percent of the world total. Furthermore, for the world dominant power, the means of destruction have few limits. Articulating what those who wish to see already knew, the prominent Israeli military analyst Reuven Pedatzur writes that "in the era of a single, ruthless superpower, whose leadership intends to shape the world according to its own forceful world view, nuclear weapons have become an attractive instrument for waging wars, even against enemies that do not possess nuclear arms."[13]

When asked why "should the United States spend massively on arms and China refrain?" Max Boot, a senior fellow at the Council on Foreign Relations, provided a simple answer: "we guarantee the security of the world, protect our allies, keep critical sea-lanes open and lead the war on terror," while China threatens others and "could ignite an arms race"—actions inconceivable for the United States. Surely no one but a crazed "conspiracy theorist" might mention that the United States controls sea-lanes in pursuit of US foreign policy objectives, hardly for the benefit of all, or that much of the world regards Washington (particularly since the beginning of the Bush II presidency) as the leading threat to world security. Recent global polls reveal that France is "most widely seen as having a positive influence in the world," alongside Europe generally and China, while "the countries most widely viewed as having a negative influence are the US and Russia." But again there is a simple explanation. The polls just show that the world is wrong. It's easy to understand why. As Boot has explained elsewhere, Europe has "often been driven by avarice" and the "cynical Europeans" cannot comprehend the "strain of idealism" that animates US foreign policy. "After 200 years, Europe still hasn't figured out what makes America tick." Others share these mental failings, notably those close by, who have considerable experience and therefore are particularly misguided. Of the countries polled, Mexico is among those "most negative" about the US role in the world.[14]

The course and outcome of a May 2005 review of the Non-Proliferation Treaty (NPT), to which we will return, illustrates the gravity of our responsibility for the persistence—and enhancement—of severe threats to our endangered species. A leading concern of participants in the NPT conference was Washington's intent to "remove the nuclear brakes," thereby "taking a big—and dangerous—step that will lead to the transformation of the nuclear bomb into a legitimate weapon for waging war." The potential consequences could not be more stark.[15]

RISKING ULTIMATE DOOM

The risk of nuclear destruction highlighted by Russell and Einstein is not abstract. We have already come close to the brink of nuclear war. The best-known case is the Cuban missile crisis of October 1962, when our escape from "nuclear oblivion" was nothing short of "miraculous," two prominent researchers conclude. At a retrospective conference in Havana in 2002, historian and Kennedy adviser Arthur Schlesinger described the crisis as "the most dangerous moment in human history." Participants at the conference learned that the dangers were even more severe than they had believed. They discovered that the world was "one word away" from the first use of a nuclear weapon since Nagasaki, as reported by Thomas Blanton of the National Security Archive, which helped organize the conference. He was referring to the intervention of a Russian submarine commander, Vasily Arkhipov, who countermanded an order to fire nuclear-armed torpedoes when his vessels were under attack by US destroyers, with consequences that could have been dreadful.[16]

Among the high-level planners who attended the Havana retrospective was Kennedy's defense secretary, Robert McNamara, who recalled in 2005 that the world had come "within a hair's breadth of nuclear disaster" during the missile crisis. He accompanied this reminder with a renewed warning of "apocalypse soon," describing "current US nuclear weapons policy as immoral, illegal, militarily unnecessary, and dreadfully dangerous." This policy creates "unacceptable risks to other nations and to our own" (both the risk of "accidental or inadvertent nuclear launch," which is "unacceptably high," and of nuclear attack by terrorists). McNamara endorsed the judgment of Clinton's defense secretary William Perry that "there is a greater than 50 percent probability of a nuclear strike on US targets within a decade."[17]

Graham Allison reports that the "consensus in the national security community" is that a "dirty bomb" attack is "inevitable," while an attack with a nuclear weapon is highly likely if fissionable materials—the essential ingredient—are not retrieved and secured. Reviewing the partial success of efforts to do so since the early 1990s, under the initiatives of Senators Sam Nunn and Richard Lugar, Allison describes the setback to these programs from the first days of the Bush administration. Bush planners put to the side the programs to avert "inevitable nuclear terror," as they devoted their energies to driving the country to war and then to efforts to contain somehow the catastrophe they created in Iraq.[18]

In the journal of the American Academy of Arts and Sciences, not given to hyperbole, strategic analysts John Steinbruner and Nancy Gallagher warn that the Bush administration's military programs and its aggressive stance carry "an appreciable risk of ultimate doom." The reasons are straightforward. Pursuit of total security by one state, including the right to wage war at will and "to remove the nuclear brakes" (Pedatzur), entails the insecurity of others, who are likely to react. The terrifying technology now being developed in Rumsfeld's transformation of the military "will assuredly diffuse to the rest of the world." In the context of "competition in intimidation," the action-reaction cycle creates a "rising danger, potentially an unmanageable one." If "the United States political system cannot recognize that risk and cannot confront the implications," they warn, "its viability will be very much in question."[19]

Steinbruner and Gallagher express hope that the threat the US government is posing to its own population and the world will be countered by a coalition of peace-loving nations—led by China! We have come to a pretty pass when such thoughts are expressed at the heart of the establishment. And what that implies about the state of American democracy—where the issues scarcely even enter the electoral arena or public discussion—is no less shocking and threatening, illustrating the democratic deficit mentioned in the preface. Steinbruner and Gallagher bring up China because of all the nuclear states it "has maintained by far the most restrained pattern of military deployment." Furthermore, China has led efforts in the United Nations to preserve outer space for peaceful purposes, in conflict with the United States, which, along with Israel, has barred all moves to prevent an arms race in space.

The militarization of space did not originate in the Bush administration. Clinton's Space Command called for "dominating the space dimension of military operations to protect US interests and investment," much in the way armies and navies did in earlier years. The United States must therefore develop "space-based strike weapons [enabling] the application of precision force from, to, and through space." Such forces will be needed, US intelligence and the Space Command agreed, because "globalization of the world economy" will lead to a "widening economic divide" and "deepening economic stagnation, political instability, and cultural alienation," thus provoking unrest and violence among the "have-nots," much of it directed against the United States. The space program fell within the framework of the officially announced Clinton doctrine that the United States is entitled to resort to "unilateral use of military power" to ensure "uninhibited access to key markets, energy supplies, and strategic resources."[20]

Clinton planners (STRATCOM) advised further that Washington should portray itself as "irrational and vindictive if its vital interests are attacked," including the threat of first strike with nuclear weapons against non-nuclear states. Nuclear weapons are far more valuable than other weapons of mass destruction, STRATCOM noted, because "the extreme destruction from a nuclear explosion is immediate, with few if any palliatives to reduce its effect." Furthermore, "nuclear weapons always cast a shadow over any crisis or conflict," extending the reach of conventional power. Again, the strategic doctrine is not new. For example, Carter's defense secretary Harold Brown called on

Congress to fund strategic nuclear capabilities because with them, "our other forces become meaningful instruments of military and political power," which must be available everywhere in the Third World because, "largely for economic reasons," there is "increased turbulence from within as well as intervention from the Soviet Union"—the latter more a pretext than a reason, a fact sometimes frankly recognized.[21]

Under the Bush administration, the threats have become even more serious. Bush planners extended Clinton's doctrine of control of space for military purposes to *"ownership"* of space, which *"may mean instant engagement anywhere in the world."* Top military commanders informed Congress in 2005 that the Pentagon is developing new space weaponry that would allow the United States to launch an attack "very quickly, with very short time lines on the planning and delivery, any place on the face of the earth," General James Cartwright, head of the Strategic Command, explained. The policy subjects every part of the globe to the risk of instant destruction, thanks to sophisticated global surveillance and lethal offensive weaponry in space—reciprocally endangering the people of the United States.[22]

The Bush administration has also broadened the first-strike option, and has increasingly blurred the line between conventional and nuclear weapons, thus heightening "the risk that the nuclear option will be used," military analyst William Arkin observes. Weapons systems now under development could "deliver a conventional payload precisely on target within minutes of a valid command and control release order," conforming to an air force doctrine that defines space superiority as "freedom to attack as well as freedom from attack." Weapons expert John Pike comments that the new programs allow the United States "to crush someone anywhere in the world on thirty minutes' notice with no need for a nearby air base," a substantial benefit given the regional antagonism aroused by the hundreds of US bases placed all over the world to ensure global domination. The national defense strategy that Rumsfeld signed on March 1, 2005, "enables us to project power anywhere in the world from secure bases of operation," recognizing "the importance of influencing events before challenges become more dangerous and less manageable," in accord with the preventive war doctrine. General Lance W. Lord, head of the Air Force Space Command, informed Congress that systems currently under development will allow the United States to "deliver a conventional payload precisely on target within minutes of a valid command and control release order"—and a nonconventional payload as well, needless to say.[23]

Not surprisingly, these actions have elicited concern, criticism, and reactions. Senior military and space officials of the European Union, Canada, China, and Russia warned that "just as the unleashing of nuclear weapons had unforeseen consequences, so, too, would the weaponization of space." As anticipated, Russia responded to Bush's vast increase in offensive military capacity by sharply increasing its own capacities, and has reacted to Pentagon leaks about militarization of space by announcing that it would "consider using force if necessary to respond." "Missile defense"—recognized on all sides to be a first-strike weapon—is a particularly severe danger to China. If the programs show any signs of success, China is likely to expand its offensive capacities to preserve its deterrent. China is already developing more powerful missiles with multiple nuclear warheads capable of reaching the United States, a policy called "aggressively defensive" by the Asia-Pacific editor for the world's leading military weekly. In 2004, the United States accounted for 95 percent of total global military space expenditures, but others may join if compelled to do so, vastly increasing the risks to everyone.[24]

US analysts recognize that current Pentagon programs "can be interpreted as a significant move by the United States toward weaponization of space [and that] there seems little doubt that space-basing of weapons is an accepted aspect of the Air Force transformation planning," developments that "are in the long term very likely to have a negative effect on the national security of the United States." Their Chinese counterparts agree that while Washington proclaims defensive intentions, "to China and to many other countries the construction of such a system looks more like the development of the Death Star spaceship in the *Star Wars* film series, [which can be used] to attack military and civilian satellites and targets anywhere on earth. . . . Space weapons are seen as 'first-strike' weapons rather than defensive arms, because they are vulnerable to countermeasures. Their deployment, therefore, could be seen as a sign of US intent to use force in international affairs." China and others may develop low-cost space weapons in reaction, so that US policy "could trigger an arms race in space." Furthermore, "to protect against the potential loss of its deterrent capability, China could also resort to building up its nuclear forces, which could in turn encourage India and then Pakistan to follow suit." Russia has already "threatened to respond to any country's deployment of space weapons—an act that could undermine the already fragile nuclear non-proliferation regime."[25]

Meanwhile the Pentagon is pondering a disturbing study by its leading academic consultant on the Chinese military, who has investigated Chinese-language military texts and interviewed their authors, drawing a conclusion that "has rattled many in Washington: China sees the US as a military rival." We must therefore abandon the idea that China is "an inherently gentle country" and recognize that the paranoid and devious Chinese may be quietly treading the path of evil.[26]

Former NATO planner Michael MccGwire reminds us that in 1986, recognizing the "dreadful logic" of nuclear weapons, Mikhail Gorbachev called for their total elimination, a proposal that foundered on Reagan's militarization of space programs ("Star Wars"). Western doctrine, he writes, "was explicitly premised on the credible threat of 'first use' of nuclear weapons, and that continues to be policy today." Russia had kept to the same doctrine until 1994, when it reversed its stand, adopting a "no first use" policy. But Russia reverted to NATO doctrine, and abandoned its call for abolition of nuclear weapons, in response to Clinton's expansion of NATO in violation of Washington's "categorical assurance" to Gorbachev that if he "would agree to a reunited Germany remaining in NATO, the alliance would *not* expand eastwards to absorb former members of the Warsaw Pact." In the light of earlier history, not to speak of strategic truisms, Clinton's violation of firm pledges posed a serious security threat to Russia, and "is the antithesis of the 'exclusion' principle underlying the concept of nuclear-weapons-free zones (NWFZ)." Clinton's violation of the assurances explains "why NATO resisted formalizing the de facto NWFZ encompassing central Europe from the Arctic to the Black

Sea." MccGwire goes on to point out that such formalization "was proposed by Belarus, Ukraine and Russia in the mid-1990s, but would have interfered with plans to extend NATO. Reverse reasoning explains why Washington supports the formation of an NWFZ in Central Asia. Should these former Soviet republics decide to join Russia in a military alliance, an NWFZ would deny Moscow the option of deploying nuclear weapons on their territory."[27]

"APOCALYPSE SOON"

The probability of "apocalypse soon" cannot be realistically estimated, but it is surely too high for any sane person to contemplate with equanimity. While speculation is pointless, reaction to the "stark and dreadful and inescapable" choice Einstein and Russell described definitely is not. On the contrary, reaction is urgent, particularly in the United States, because of Washington's primary role in accelerating the race to destruction by extending its historically unique military dominance. "The chances of an accidental, mistaken or unauthorized nuclear attack might be increasing," warns former senator Sam Nunn, who has played a leading role in efforts to reduce the threat of nuclear war. "We are running an unnecessary risk of an Armageddon of our own making," Nunn observes, as a result of policy choices that leave "America's survival" dependent on "the accuracy of Russia's warning systems and its command and control." Nunn is referring to the sharp expansion of US military programs, which tilt the strategic balance in ways that make "Russia more likely to launch upon warning of an attack, without waiting to see if the warning is accurate." The threat is enhanced by the fact that "the Russian early warning system is in serious disrepair and more likely to give a false warning of incoming missiles." US reliance on "the high-alert, hair-trigger nuclear posture . . . allows missiles to be launched within minutes," forcing "our leaders to decide almost instantly whether to launch nuclear weapons once they have warning of an attack, robbing them of the time they may need to gather data, exchange information, gain perspective, discover an error and avoid a catastrophic mistake." The risk extends beyond

Russia—and also China if it pursues the same course. Strategic analyst Bruce Blair observes that "the early warning and control problems plaguing Pakistan, India and other nuclear proliferators are even more acute."[28]

Another serious concern, discussed in technical literature well before 9/11, is that nuclear weapons may sooner or later fall into the hands of terrorist groups, who might use these and other weapons of mass destruction with lethal effect. Those prospects are being advanced by Bush administration planners, who do not consider terrorism a high priority, as they regularly demonstrate. Their aggressive militarism has not only led Russia to expand significantly its offensive capacities, including more lethal nuclear weapons and delivery systems, but is also inducing the Russian military to transfer nuclear weapons constantly across Russia's vast territory to counter mounting US threats. Washington planners are surely aware that Chechen rebels, who had already stolen radioactive materials from nuclear waste plants and power stations, have been casing "the railway system and special trains designed for shipping nuclear weapons across Russia."[29]

Blair warns that "this perpetual motion [within Russia] creates a serious vulnerability, because transportation is the Achilles' heel of nuclear weapons security," ranking in danger right alongside maintaining strategic nuclear forces on hair-trigger alert. He estimates that every day "many hundreds of Russian nuclear weapons are moving around the countryside." Theft of one nuclear bomb "could spell eventual disaster for an American city, [but this] is not the worst-case scenario stemming from this nuclear gamesmanship." More ominously, "the seizure of a ready-to-fire strategic long range nuclear missile or a group of missiles capable of delivering bombs to targets thousands of miles away could be apocalyptic for entire nations." Another major threat is that terrorist hackers might break into military communication networks and transmit launch orders for missiles armed with hundreds of nuclear warheads—no fantasy, as the Pentagon learned a few years ago when serious defects were discovered in its safeguards, requiring new instructions for Trident submarine launch crews. Systems in other countries are much less reliable. All of this constitutes "an accident waiting to happen," Blair writes; an accident that could be apocalyptic.[30]

The dangers of nuclear warfare are consciously being escalated by the threat and use of violence, which, as long predicted, is also stimulating jihadi terrorism. Such terrorism traces back to Reagan administration programs to organize, arm, and train radical Islamists—not for defense of Afghanistan, as proclaimed, but for the usual and ugly reasons of state, with grim consequences for the tormented people of Afghanistan. The Reagan administration also cheerfully tolerated Pakistan's slide toward radical Islamist extremism under the rule of Muhammad Zia ul-Huq, one of the many brutal dictators supported by the current incumbents in Washington and their mentors. Reagan and associates also looked away politely while their Pakistani ally was developing nuclear weapons, annually endorsing the pretense that Pakistan was not doing so. They and the Clinton administration paid little attention while Pakistan's leading proliferator, now tapped on the wrist, was carrying out the world's most extraordinary nuclear smuggling enterprise: Abdul Qadeer Khan, who "did more damage in 10 years than any country did in the first 50 years of the nuclear age," according to James Walsh, executive director of Harvard's Managing the Atom project.[31]

Washington's aggressive militarism is not the only factor driving the race to "apocalypse soon," but it is surely a significant one. The plans and policies fall within a much broader context, with roots going back to the Clinton years and beyond. All of this is at the fringe of public discourse, and does not enter even marginally into electoral choices, another illustration of the decline of functioning democracy and its portent.

The only threat remotely comparable to use of nuclear weapons is the serious danger of environmental catastrophe. In preparation for the July 2005 Group of Eight summit in Gleneagles, Scotland, the scientific academies of all G8 nations, including the US National Academy of Sciences, joined those of China, India, and Brazil to call on the leaders of the rich countries to take urgent action to head off this potential disaster. "The scientific understanding of climate change is now sufficiently clear to justify prompt action," their statement said: "It is vital that all nations identify cost-effective steps that they can take now, to contribute to substantial and long-term reduction in net global greenhouse gas emissions." In its lead editorial, the *Financial Times* endorsed this "clarion call," while deploring the fact that "there is, however, one hold-out, and unfortunately it is to be found in the White House where—in spite of the unprecedented statement by the G8 scientists ahead of next month's Gleneagles summit—George W. Bush, the US president, insists we still do not know enough about this literally world-changing phenomenon." Washington then "succeeded in removing language calling for prompt action to control global warming" and eliminating such inflammatory statements as "Our world is warming," because "Mr. Bush has said global warming is too uncertain a matter to justify anything more than voluntary measures." The end result, the *Financial Times* editors comment, is that little remained beyond "pious waffle."[32]

Dismissal of scientific evidence on matters of survival, in keeping with Bush's scientific judgment, is routine. At the 2005 annual meeting of the American Association for the Advancement of Science, "leading US climate researchers . . . released 'the most compelling evidence yet' that human activities are responsible for global warming." The group predicted major climatic effects, including severe reduction in water supplies in regions that rely on rivers fed by melting snow and glaciers. Other prominent researchers at the same session reported evidence that the melting of Arctic and Greenland ice sheets is causing changes in the sea's salinity balance that threaten "to shut down the Ocean Conveyor Belt, which transfers heat from the tropics towards the polar regions through currents such as the Gulf Stream." One possible consequence is significant temperature reduction in Europe. Not long after, climate experts reported further shrinking of the polar ice cap, and warned that the long-predicted "feedbacks in the system are starting to take hold" as the enlarged expanses of open water absorb solar energy instead of reflecting it back to space, hence accelerating the severe threat of global warming. The release of "the most compelling evidence yet," like the G8 warnings, received scant notice in the United States, despite the attention given in the same days to the implementation of the Kyoto protocols regulating greenhouse emissions, with the most important government refusing to take part.[33]

It is important to stress *government*. The standard observation that the United States stood almost alone in rejecting the Kyoto protocols is correct only if the phrase "United States" excludes its population, which strongly favors the Kyoto pact. A majority of Bush backers not only support the protocol, but mistakenly believe that the president does so as well. In general, voters in the 2004 election were seriously deluded about the positions of the political parties, not because of lack of interest or mental capacity, but because elections are carefully designed to yield that result, a topic to which we will return.[34]

IRAQ AND THE "WAR ON TERROR"

US and UK planners were well aware that the invasion of Iraq was likely to increase terror and WMD proliferation, as many analysts and intelligence agencies warned. CIA director George Tenet informed Congress in October 2002 that invading Iraq might lead Saddam Hussein to assist "Islamist terrorists in conducting a WMD attack against the United States." The National Intelligence Council "predicted that an American-led invasion of Iraq would increase support for political Islam and would result in a deeply divided Iraqi society prone to violent internal conflict," hence engendering terror within Iraq and worldwide. The NIC confirmed these expectations in December 2004, reporting that "Iraq and other possible conflicts in the future could provide recruitment, training grounds, technical skills and language proficiency for a new class of terrorists who are 'professionalized' and for whom political violence becomes an end in itself." The NIC also predicted that, as a result of the invasion, this new globalized network of "diffuse Islamic extremist groups" would spread its operations elsewhere to defend Muslim lands from attack by "infidel invaders," with Iraq replacing Afghanistan as a training ground. A CIA report of May 2005 confirmed that "Iraq has become a magnet for Islamic militants similar to Soviet-occupied Afghanistan two decades ago and Bosnia in the 1990s." The CIA concluded that "Iraq may prove to be an even more effective training ground for Islamic extremists than

Afghanistan was in Al Qaeda's early days, because it is serving as a real-world laboratory for urban combat." Two years after the invasion, a high-level government review of the "war on terror" affirmed the same conclusion. Focusing "on how to deal with the rise of a new generation of terrorists, schooled in Iraq over the past couple years," the review noted: "Top government officials are increasingly turning their attention to anticipate what one called 'the bleed out' of hundreds or thousands of Iraq-trained jihadists back to their home countries throughout the Middle East and Western Europe. 'It's a new piece of a new equation,' a former senior Bush administration official said. 'If you don't know who they are in Iraq, how are you going to locate them in Istanbul or London?' "[35]

There is little doubt that the invasion of Iraq had the effect of "greatly strengthening the popular appeal of anti-democratic radicals such as those of al-Qaeda and other *jihadi* salafis" throughout the Muslim world. A crucial illustration is Indonesia, the state with the world's largest Muslim population and a likely source of jihadi terror. In 2000, 75 percent of Indonesians viewed Americans favorably. This number fell to 61 percent by 2002 and plummeted to 15 percent after the invasion of Iraq, with 80 percent of Indonesians saying they feared an attack by the United States. Scott Atran, a specialist on terror and Indonesia, reports that "these sentiments correlate with readiness by over 80 percent of Indonesians to have Islam play an increasing role in personal and national life, but are also associated with tolerance for a broader spectrum of co-religionists, including militant radicals, and readiness to amplify any slight against an Islamic leader or nation into a perceived attack upon the whole Muslim world."[36]

The threat is not abstract. Shortly after the deadly bomb attacks on London's public transportation system in July 2005, Britain's Royal Institute of International Affairs (Chatham House) released a study reiterating the standard conclusions of intelligence agencies and independent analysts: "There is 'no doubt' that the invasion of Iraq has 'given a boost to the al-Qaida network' [in] propaganda, recruitment and fundraising,' while providing an ideal training area for terrorists." The study found that "the UK is at particular risk because it is the closest ally of the United States, has deployed armed forces in the military campaigns to topple the Taleban regime in Afghanistan and in Iraq . . . [and is] a pillion passenger" of American policy, the passenger who rides behind the driver of a motorcycle. In its review of the London bombings, Britain's MI5 internal security service concluded that "though they have a range of aspirations and 'causes,' Iraq is a dominant issue for a range of extremist groups and individuals in the UK and Europe," while some who have traveled to Iraq to fight "may later return to the UK and consider mounting attacks here."[37]

The Blair government angrily denied the obvious, though it was soon reaffirmed when one of the suspects in the follow-up failed bombing, captured in Rome, "claimed the bomb plot was directly inspired by Britain's involvement in the Iraq war" and described "how the suspects watched hours of TV footage showing grief-stricken Iraqi widows and children alongside images of civilians killed in the conflict. He is alleged to have told prosecutors that after watching the footage: 'There was a feeling of hatred and a conviction that it was necessary to give a signal—to do something.' "[38]

Reports by an Israeli think tank and Saudi intelligence concluded that "the vast majority" of foreign fighters in Iraq "are not former terrorists" but "became radicalized by the war itself," stimulated by the invasion to respond "to calls to defend their fellow Muslims from 'crusaders' and 'infidels' " who are mounting "an attack on the Muslim religion and Arab culture." A study by the Center for Strategic and International Studies (CSIS) found that "85 percent of Saudi militants who went to Iraq were not on any government watch list, al-Qaeda members, or terrorist sympathizers" but were "radicalized almost exclusively by the Coalition invasion." Since the invasion, the report confirms, Iraq has become one of the global centers for recruitment and training of extremist ("neo-Salafi") Islamist terrorists; large numbers are likely to return to their countries of origin, carrying terrorism skills and radicalized worldviews, gaining "publicity and credibility among the angry and alienated in the Islamic world," and spreading "terrorism and violence." French intelligence, which has unique experience over many years, concludes that "what the war in Iraq has done is radicalize these people and make some of them prepared to support terrorism. Iraq is a great recruiting sergeant," contributing a new and "enormous jihad zone to train people to fight in their country of origin," as intelligence had previously found "in Afghanistan, in Bosnia, in Kosovo." US officials report that Abu Musab al-Zarqawi, Al Qaeda's top operative in Iraq, "is bringing more and more Iraqi fighters into his fold," displacing foreign fighters, who account "for less than 10 percent of the insurgents in Iraq," perhaps as few as 4 percent, CSIS believes.[39]

According to terrorism specialist Peter Bergen, President Bush "is right that Iraq is a main front in the war on terrorism, but this is a front we created." As "the Iraq war has expanded the terrorists' ranks," he reports, "the year 2003 saw the highest incidence of significant terrorist attacks in two decades, and then, in 2004, astonishingly, that number tripled." In response to Donald Rumsfeld's search for "metrics to know if we are winning or losing the war on terror," Bergen suggests that "an exponentially rising number of terrorist attacks is one metric that seems relevant."[40]

Studies of suicide bombers also reveal that "Iraq appears to be playing a central role—in shifting views and as ground zero in a new wave of suicide attacks." Between 1980 and 2003, there were 315 suicide attacks worldwide, initially for the most part by the secular Tamil Tigers. Since the US invasion, estimates of suicide bombings in Iraq (where such attacks were virtually unknown before) range as high as 400. Terrorism specialists report that "stories of the bravery and heroism of suicide bombers in Iraq" are stimulating imitators among Muslim youth who adopt the jihadi doctrine that the Muslim world is under attack and they must rise to its defense. Former NSC staffers and counterterrorism specialists Daniel Benjamin and Steven Simon conclude that Bush has "created a new haven for terrorism in Iraq that escalates the potential for Islamic violence against Europe and the United States," a policy that is "disastrous": "We may be attacked by terrorists who received their training in Iraq, or attacked by terrorists who were inspired, organized and trained by people who were in Iraq. . . . [Bush] has given them an excellent American target in Iraq but in the process has energized the jihad and given militants the kind of urban warfare experience that will raise the future threat to the United States exponentially."[41]

Robert Pape, who has done the most extensive studies of suicide bombers, writes that "Al Qaeda is today less a product of Islamic fundamentalism than of a simple strategic goal: to compel the United States and its Western allies to withdraw combat forces from the Arabian Peninsula and other Muslim countries," as Osama bin Laden repeatedly declares. Serious analysts have pointed out that bin Laden's words and deeds correlate closely. The jihadis organized by the Reagan administration and its allies ended their Afghan-based terrorism inside Russia after the Russians withdrew from Afghanistan, though they continued it from occupied Muslim Chechnya, the scene of shocking Russian crimes dating back to the nineteenth century. Tolstoy's novella *Hadji Murád* is all too timely today. Bin Laden turned against the United States in 1991 because he took it to be occupying the holiest Arab land (a fact later cited by the Pentagon as a reason for shifting US bases from Saudi Arabia) and because Washington blocked his efforts to join the attack against the secular enemy Saddam Hussein. The jihadis also joined the Muslim side in the Balkan wars, with US tolerance and assistance, at the very same time that they were trying to blow up the World Trade Center in 1993. An Indian strategic analyst and former government official alleges further that the London bombers received training in Bosnia.[42]

In the most extensive scholarly inquiry into Islamic militancy, Fawaz Gerges concludes that after 9/11, "the dominant response to Al Qaeda in the Muslim world was very hostile," specifically among jihadis, who regarded it as a dangerous extremist fringe. Instead of recognizing that opposition to Al Qaeda offered Washington "the most effective way to drive a nail into its coffin" by finding "intelligent means to nourish and support the internal forces that were opposed to militant ideologies like the bin Laden network," the Bush administration did exactly what bin Laden hoped it would do: resort to violence. The invasion of Iraq created strong support for the fatwa issued by Al-Azhar in Cairo, "the oldest institution of religious higher learning in the world of Islam." The fatwa advised "all Muslims in the world to make jihad against invading American forces." Sheikh Tantawi of Al-Azhar, "one of the first Muslim scholars to condemn Al Qaeda [and] often criticized by ultraconservative clerics as a pro-Western reformer . . . ruled that efforts to stop the American invasion are a 'binding Islamic duty.' " The achievements of Bush administration planners in inspiring Islamic radicalism and terror are impressive.[43]

The senior CIA analyst responsible for tracking Osama bin Laden from 1996, Michael Scheuer, writes that "bin Laden has been precise in telling America the reasons he is waging war on us. None of the reasons have anything to do with our freedom, liberty, and democracy, but have everything to do with US policies and actions in the Muslim world." Scheuer notes that "US forces and policies are completing the radicalization of the Islamic world, something Osama bin Laden has been trying to do with substantial but incomplete success since the early 1990s. As a result . . . it is fair to conclude that the United States of America remains bin Laden's only indispensable ally." From his detailed study of Al Qaeda, Jason Burke draws a similar conclusion. "Every use of force is another small victory for bin Laden," he writes, creating "a whole new cadre of terrorists" for a "cosmic struggle between good and evil," the vision shared by bin Laden and Bush.[44]

The pattern is common. To mention another recent case, the US-Israeli assassination of the revered quadriplegic cleric Sheikh Ahmed Yassin (along with half a dozen bystanders) outside a Gaza mosque in March 2004 led to the brutal murder of four US security contractors in Falluja in immediate retaliation, which in turn provoked the marine invasion that killed hundreds of people and set off conflagrations throughout Iraq. There is no mystery here. Unless enemies can be completely crushed, violence tends to engender violence in response. A violent and destructive response to terrorism helps the "terrorist vanguard" mobilize support among the far larger constituency that rejects their methods but shares much of their resentment and concern, a dynamic as familiar to Western policy makers in the post–World War II era as it was to their imperial predecessors.

Paying attention to the world leads to conclusions that some would prefer to ignore. Far better to strike heroic poses about "Islamo-fascism" and denounce the "excuse makers" who seek to understand the roots of terror and to act to reduce the threat, people who are—in the words of *New York Times* columnist Thomas Friedman—"just one notch less despicable than the terrorists and also deserve to be exposed." The category of such despicable characters is rather large, including the most respected specialists on the topic and US and other intelligence agencies. The stance, not unfamiliar, is another gift to bin Laden.[45]

The logic that some prefer to ignore is straightforward, outlined even in the serious journals that tend to support Bush-style aggressive nationalism: if adversaries "fear the unbridled use of America's power, they may perceive overwhelming incentives to wield weapons of terror and mass destruction to deter America's offensive tactics of self-defense. Indeed, the history of the myths of empire suggests that a general strategy of preventive war is likely to bring about precisely the outcome that Bush and Rice wish to avert."[46] That is particularly likely when the strategy is joined with a radical "transformation of the military" and doctrines calling for first use of nuclear weapons and the right to "unilateral use of military power," sharply expanded since the Clinton years.

IRAQ AND FREE WORLD DEMOCRACY

If we hope to understand the world, it is important that we not allow the recent past to be dispatched to oblivion. The United States and United Kingdom proclaimed the right to invade Iraq because it was developing weapons of mass destruction. That was the "single question" that justified invading Iraq, the president declared in a March 2003 press conference, a position stressed repeatedly by Blair, Bush, and their associates. Eliminating the threat of Iraq's WMDs was also the sole basis on which Bush received congressional authorization to resort to force. The answer to the "single question" was given shortly after the invasion, as Washington reluctantly conceded. Scarcely missing a beat, the doctrinal system concocted new pretexts and justifications, which quickly became virtual dogma: the war was inspired by President Bush's noble visions of democracy, shared by his British colleague.[47]

Long after the official concession that the original pretexts for invading Iraq were without merit, key politicians continued to reiterate them in high places. In January 2005, Senate majority leader Bill Frist justified the invasion of Iraq on the grounds that "dangerous weapons proliferation must be stopped. Terrorist organizations must be destroyed." It is apparently irrelevant that the pretexts have been officially abandoned and that the invasion has increased terrorist threats and accelerated the proliferation of dangerous weapons.[48]

Frist's performance followed an earlier script. In the most careful review of the documentary record, national security and intelligence analyst John Prados describes the Bush "scheme to convince America and the world that war with Iraq was necessary and urgent" as "a case study in government dishonesty . . . that required patently untrue public statements and egregious manipulation of intelligence." The planners knew that Iraqi WMD programs "were either nascent, moribund, or non-existent—exactly the opposite of the President's repeated message to Americans." To carry out the deception, "actual intelligence was consistently distorted, manipulated, and ignored . . . in service of a particular enterprise under false pretenses—a story with tremendous implications for America in the twenty-first century"—and for the world. "Americans have not only been hoodwinked" by "George Bush's game of three-card monte," Prados concludes, "they have been shamed. . . . Americans do not like to think of themselves as aggressors, but raw aggression is what took place in Iraq."[49]

Evidence of deceit continued to accumulate. In May 2005, a series of documents known as the Downing Street Memos were leaked to the *Times* of London. One memo revealed that two weeks before the war was launched, Attorney General Lord Goldsmith, Blair's chief legal adviser, counseled that "regime change cannot be the objective of military action." Even if Britain were to limit itself to the announced objective of ending WMD programs, he wrote, "it is for the [UN Security] Council to assess whether any such breach of those obligations has occurred," not individual states. Lord Goldsmith then added that the United States had "a rather different view: they maintain that the fact of whether Iraq is in breach is a matter of objective fact which may therefore be assessed by individual member states [but] I am not aware of any other state which supports this view." He did not have to add that the phrase "individual member states" referred to Washington alone. The basic content of Lord Goldsmith's polite wording was that Britain should at least make some gesture toward recognizing international law, unlike the United States, which is a rogue state that exempts itself from such formalities. The reaction to the leaked memos in the two countries is instructive: the revelations provoked a substantial uproar in England, but received little notice in the United States.[50]

Shortly after Lord Goldsmith's comments were made public, the London *Sunday Times* published an official memo of a secret meeting between Blair and his top advisers in July 2002. The document showed that the Bush administration had already decided to attack Iraq, well before Congress was "hoodwinked" into authorizing force in October 2002 and also before the UN was invited either to endorse Washington's plan to use violence or to become "irrelevant." British Middle East scholar Toby Dodge observed that "the documents show . . . that the case of weapons of mass destruction was based on thin intelligence and was used to inflate the evidence to the level of mendacity." Again, there was considerable reaction in England to these revelations, but the story was "a dud" in the United States, the press observed. Weeks later, when popular pressures led to coverage, much commentary shifted to the opposite mode in a familiar pattern: Why this hysteria from conspiracy theorists about what we always knew and had told the public loud and clear?[51]

In his memo to Blair, Lord Goldsmith also advised that, given the patent criminality of "regime change" by invasion, it would be "necessary to create the conditions in which we could legally support military action." Seeking to provoke Iraq into some action that could be portrayed as a casus belli, London and Washington renewed their bombing of Iraqi targets in May 2002, with a sharp increase in September 2002. In the nine months leading up to the official start of the war in March 2003, US and UK planes flew almost 22,000 sorties, hitting 391 "carefully selected targets," noted Lieutenant General Michael Moseley, commander of the joint operations. These flights, he

explained, "laid the foundations" for the military conquest by eliminating the need for protracted bombardment of Iraqi positions. Iraq
vigorously protested the bombings to the UN, but did not react as
London and Washington had hoped. When no casus belli could be
concocted, the two countries invaded Iraq anyway, proclaiming the
"single question."[52]

The most important raid of the prewar war against Iraq was apparently on September 5, 2002, when US and British planes "flattened
Saddam's airbase, called H-3, in Iraq's western desert," British journalist Ed Harriman reports. "The raid had destroyed military communications and anti-aircraft defences as well as Iraqi planes," he notes,
thus clearing the way for the planned invasion. Two days later, Tony
Blair arrived in Washington to visit Bush. At their joint press conference, Blair described the "catalogue of attempts by Iraq to conceal its
weapons of mass destruction, not to tell the truth about it over not
just a period of months but over a period of years." Blair, while sin-
cerely advising the driver of the motorcycle to follow the diplomatic
route, knew full well that the war was already under way. All the
while, the two leaders were making sure that state violence would be
protected from scrutiny by Parliament, Congress, and the public in
both countries.[53]

The plan for "spikes of activity" against Iraq to try to concoct a
pretext for an invasion—described in a July 23, 2002, memo from
foreign policy aide Matthew Rycroft to the British ambassador to the
United States, David Manning—was the most important revelation of
the Downing Street Memos. The tactic is a venerable one. Psychological warfare specialists in the Eisenhower administration advised that
the United States should "covertly stimulate acts and attitudes of [defi-
ance] short of mass rebellion aimed at . . . provoking open Soviet intervention in both the GDR [East Germany] and the other satellites,"
advice that was secretly accepted by the US government immediately
after Soviet tanks crushed mass worker protests in East Berlin. Another example of this tactic is Israel's attacks on Lebanon in early
1982, seeking to provoke a response by the Palestine Liberation Organization (PLO) that could be used as a pretext for a planned invasion.
Despite failure to elicit a credible pretext, in June 1982 Israel

launched the invasion, for the purpose of blocking PLO diplomatic efforts and ensuring Israeli control over the West Bank, while imposing a client regime in Lebanon. In yet another example, CIA-backed Kosovo Liberation Army guerrillas attacked civilian targets in Kosovo in early 1999, openly announcing that they hoped the violence would provoke a harsh Serbian response that could then be used to arouse popular Western support for an attack on Serbia. It is possible that current US military actions across Syria's borders are likewise designed to provoke some pretext for attack on the one Arab state that is currently defying Washington's orders.[54]

THE RANKING OF PRIORITIES:
TERROR AND REAL INTERESTS

The conventional task of doctrinal managers is to protect power and those who wield it from scrutiny and, most important, to deflect analysis from their rational planning in pursuit of the real interests they serve. Discussion must be diverted instead to noble intent and self-defense, perhaps misguided: in the Iraq case, liberation of the suffering people of Iraq and defense of the United States against terror. It is therefore necessary to protect the doctrine that Iraq would have been selected for invasion even if the world's energy resources happened to be in Central Africa. As if that challenge were not difficult enough, others awaited, among them, concealing the Western role in the dismal prewar fate of Iraq as well as the consequences of the US-UK invasion both in Iraq and worldwide, which are grim.

There are further problems. To begin with, though it was anticipated that the invasion would probably enhance the threat of terror and proliferation, it may have done so even in unanticipated ways. It is common to say that claims about WMDs in Iraq were quickly undermined when, after an exhaustive search, no traces were found. That is not quite accurate, however. There were stores of equipment for developing WMDs in Iraq after the invasion: those produced in the 1980s, thanks to aid provided by the United States and Britain, among others, aid that continued well after Saddam's worst atrocities and the end of the war with

Iran. The aid included means for developing missiles and nuclear weapons as well as virulent strains of anthrax and other biotoxins, the latter in apparent violation of the Biological and Toxin Weapons Convention (BTWC), a serious breach of international law. The threat posed by these installations had been put forth as one reason for invading Iraq.[55]

These sites had been secured by UN inspectors, but the invaders dismissed them, leaving the sites unguarded. The immediate consequence was sophisticated and massive looting of these installations. The UN inspectors continued to carry out their work, relying on satellite imagery. By June 2005, they had discovered 109 sites that had been looted. Most looting was from production sites for solid- and liquid-propellant missiles, where about 85 percent of equipment had been removed, along with biotoxins and other materials usable for chemical and biological weapons, and high-precision equipment capable of making parts for nuclear and chemical weapons and missiles. A Jordanian journalist was informed by officials in charge of the Jordanian-Iraqi border after US and UK forces took over that radioactive materials were detected in one of every eight trucks crossing into Jordan, destination unknown.[56]

"Stuff happens," in Rumsfeld's words.

The ironies are almost inexpressible. The official justification for the invasion was to prevent the use of WMDs that did not exist. The invasion provided the terrorists who had been mobilized by the United States and its allies with the means to develop WMDs—namely, equipment that the United States and others had provided to Saddam Hussein, caring nothing about the terrible crimes they later invoked to whip up support for an invasion to overthrow him. It is as if Iran were now making nuclear weapons using fissionable materials provided by the United States to Iran under the shah—which may indeed be happening, as Graham Allison points out.[57]

The Pentagon civilians in charge did make sure that certain other sites were protected, however: the oil and security ministries. Elsewhere, looting and destruction, including of irreplaceable treasures of civilization, proceeded unconstrained. Two years after the invasion, the president of the American Academic Research Institute in Iraq, Macguire Gibson, sadly confirmed that "Iraq is losing its culture and its wealth." By then, more than half the nation's archeological sites, including most major Sumerian ones, had been destroyed. "The Americans are not doing anything," Gibson added, though he acknowledged there was a little help from the Italian and Dutch contingents. The losses at these sites dwarfed even the massive looting of the National Museum shortly after US troops arrived, in which at least 15,000 of the 20,000 looted pieces disappeared, probably forever. Rumsfeld, Wolfowitz and Co. may even have succeeded in causing "irreversible damage" to Iraq's oil fields. To support the invasion, the fields "are being driven to pump more than they should," which might lead to "permanent decline in production." Recall the confident predictions that the liberation greeted with flowers would be self-financed by booming oil production.[58]

The invasion of Iraq is perhaps the most glaring example of the low priority assigned by Washington planners to the threat of terror, but there are numerous others. A case in point is Washington's imposition of new sanctions on Syria under the Syria Accountability Act, passed almost unanimously by Congress and signed into law by President Bush in late 2003. Syria is on the official list of states sponsoring terrorism, despite Washington's acknowledgment that Damascus has not been implicated in terrorist acts for many years. The true nature of Washington's concern over Syria's links to terror was revealed by President Clinton's offer to remove Syria from the list of states sponsoring terror if Damascus agreed to US-Israeli peace terms. When Syria insisted on recovering territory seized by Israel, the Clinton State Department kept the country on the terrorism list. Nonetheless, Syria had been highly cooperative in providing important intelligence to Washington on Al Qaeda and other radical Islamist groups. Implementation of the Syria Accountability Act deprived the United States of an important source of information about radical Islamist terrorism. Obtaining such information, however, is clearly subordinate to the goal of establishing a regime in Syria that would accept US-Israeli demands. Had Syria been removed from the list of states supporting terror, it would have been the first since 1982, when the Reagan administration removed Saddam so that they could provide him with substantial aid, joined by Britain and many others.

That again tells us something about the attitude toward terror and state crimes.[59]

A core demand of the Syria Accountability Act refers to UN Security Council Resolution 520, which calls for respect for the sovereignty and territorial integrity of Lebanon. Syria had definitely violated the UN resolution by keeping its forces in Lebanon—forces that the United States and Israel had readily accepted in 1976, when their task was to massacre Palestinians, and again in 1990, when the United States was building a coalition to support the coming war in Iraq. This passed in silence, and Congress and the media also neglected to point out that the original Security Council resolution, passed in 1982, was directed against Israel, the only country named in the resolution. There was no call for sanctions against Israel, or for reduction in the huge unconditional military and economic aid it receives, when Israel violated this and other Security Council resolutions regarding Lebanon for twenty-two years. The principle is very clear, Middle East scholar Stephen Zunes writes: "Lebanese sovereignty must be defended only if the occupying army is from a country the United States opposes, but is dispensable if the country is a US ally." Another illustration of the single standard, not restricted to US policy makers, of course. A side observation: by a 2–1 margin, the US population favors an Israel Accountability Act, holding Israel accountable for development of WMDs and human rights abuses in the occupied territories. That is consistent with other studies of public opinion, scarcely reported though plainly of considerable importance in a democratic society.[60]

Outside the Middle East, too, there are numerous illustrations of the low priority assigned to the "war on terror." One is the Bush administration's attitude toward the 9/11 Commission Congress established to recommend means to prevent new terrorist atrocities. "Over its lifespan," Philip Shenon reported, "the Sept. 11 commission repeatedly clashed with the Bush administration, which had originally opposed its creation, especially over the panel's access to important White House documents and to witnesses." A year after its final report was presented, commission members formed a bipartisan 9/11 Public Discourse Project to pressure the government to implement its recommendations to prevent terrorist attacks. The recommendations were largely ignored.

Particularly worrisome, argued Thomas Kean, who chaired the official 9/11 Commission, was the failure to make any serious effort to secure nuclear matériel, the central element of a program to prevent the nuclear terror that intelligence analysts regard as otherwise inevitable. The project's report, issued four years after 9/11, "found that the Bush administration and Congress had made 'minimal' or 'unsatisfactory' progress" on eight of fourteen recommendations by the 9/11 Commission "for overhauling the government to deal with terrorist threats."[61]

Shortly before the London train and bus bombings of July 2005, the US Senate sharply cut funding for rail and mass transit security. The 9/11 Commission had called for a national transportation security strategy, but that remained "among the 50 percent of the 9/11 Commission's specific recommendations a year ago that Congress and Bush have yet to act upon," *Boston Globe* columnist Thomas Oliphant wrote, part of "the unholy alliances between industry and government to avoid taking measures to protect against potentially catastrophic terrorism that is not difficult to imagine." Tax cuts for the rich rank far higher as a priority than protection of the population from terror. A still more ominous example of the negligence in security matters, Oliphant continues, is the success of the chemical industry and its "White House contacts to block stiff rules requiring security upgrades at some 100 [chemical] plants around the country." Congressional efforts "have encountered nothing but industry and administration obstacles in their attempts to force a sensible approach to guarding against disasters that might make 9/11 pale by comparison." Senator Joseph Biden "cited a study by the Naval Research Laboratory that estimated that as many as 100,000 people in a densely populated area could die within 30 minutes if a single, 90-ton freight car carrying chlorine were punctured," Oliphant reported, concluding that "conniving between the Bush administration and its corporate buddies" has blocked any action. The administration is even trying to overturn a court decision supporting a local ban on "shipments of the most dangerous chemicals from certain zones around the nation's capital." All of this illustrates how low the priority of preventing terror is in comparison with corporate welfare.[62]

To select an illustration from another domain, the Treasury Department's Office of Foreign Assets Control (OFAC) is tasked with investigating suspicious financial transfers, a central component of the "war on terror." In April 2004, OFAC informed Congress that of its 120 employees, four were tracking the finances of Osama bin Laden and Saddam Hussein, while almost two dozen were enforcing the illegal embargo against Cuba. From 1990 to 2003, OFAC conducted ninety-three terrorism-related investigations that led to $9,000 in fines, and 11,000 Cuba-related investigations that led to $8 million in fines. The revelations received the silent treatment in the United States, though there was a mention in the national press that "at a time when the United States faces very real terrorist threats in the Middle East and elsewhere, the administration's absurd and increasingly bizarre obsession with Cuba is more than just a shame, it's a dangerous diversion from reality." (Sentor Max Baucus, deploring the "misuse of taxpayer money" to punish Cuba.)[63]

The Bush administration's real priorities are further illustrated by its handling of the leak of the name of CIA agent Valerie Plame after her husband, Joseph Wilson, published an unwelcome report undermining administration charges about Iraq's alleged purchases of "yellowcake" from Niger for its WMD program. Retired CIA agents informed Congress that US intelligence gathering was damaged not only by the leak but even more by the administration cover-up, which caused "irreversible damage [to] the credibility of our case officers when they try to convince an overseas contact that their safety is of primary importance to us," said Jim Marcinkowski, a former CIA case officer. "Each time the political machine made up of prime-time patriots and partisan ninnies display their ignorance by deriding Valerie Plame as a mere paper-pusher, or belittling the varying degrees of cover used to protect our officers, or continuing to play partisan politics with our national security, it's a disservice to this country," he added, harming efforts to prevent terrorist attacks.[64]

As the example illustrates, protecting the country is also a far lower priority than maintaining tight top-down control, as in tyrannical corporate structures. The Cheney-Rumsfeld team for which Bush is the front man has shown repeatedly that it is obsessed with authority and discipline. The ruling clique appears to have been infuriated with the

CIA's competence and unwillingness to provide the "information" they required to implement their plans, particularly in Iraq. One study based on extensive interviews with senior intelligence and ex-intelligence officials describes the undistinguished Porter Goss as a "wrecking ball" who was appointed as director of the CIA to bring the agency in line with executive demands, whatever the facts. Goss's primary qualification seems to have been his unswerving loyalty to Bush. Dozens of senior officials are reported to have quit the CIA in disgust, leaving the demoralized agency with severely diminished competence, particularly with respect to the Middle East. This peculiar mixture of supreme arrogance, utter incompetence, and passion for obedience has had catastrophic consequences, quite possibly laying the groundwork for much worse to come.[65]

Bush and Co. are even willing to sacrifice the "war on terror" to their obsession with torture. In order to kidnap a terror suspect in Italy and send him to Egypt for probable torture, the Bush administration disrupted a major inquiry into the suspect's role in "trying to build a terror recruitment network" and "build a jihadist recruitment network with tentacles spreading throughout Europe." Italian courts indicted thirteen CIA operatives, and Italians are furious. Other European countries have similar complaints about the Bush administration undermining antiterror operations. The sole conviction of a person connected to 9/11, Mounir el-Motassadeq, was overturned because Bush administration officials refused to provide German officials with crucial evidence. Similarly, the Bush administration "has refused to allow the Spanish authorities to interview Ramzi bin al-Shibh, a central Qaeda suspect, to bolster their case against two men on trial in Madrid on charges of helping to plan the 2001 attack" on 9/11.[66]

Though the support of its allies is indispensable in the war on terror, Washington "triggered tensions with allies" once again, the *Wall Street Journal* reported, when a Spanish court issued international arrest warrants and extradition orders for American soldiers accused of killing a Spanish reporter in Iraq, along with a Ukrainian cameraman. The Spanish court acted "after two requests to US authorities for permission to question the soldiers went unanswered, court officials said." The Pentagon had no comment.[67]

The CIA kidnapping and rendition to Egypt led to commentary in the press about the "cultural difference" between the United States and Europe in the "war on terror," adopting Robert Kagan's dismissive reference to Europeans as being "from Venus," while "Americans are from Mars." The soft Europeans believe in old-fashioned notions like criminal justice and law. The tough Americans just go ahead and get the job done, as in cowboy movies. As commentators knew, but skillfully evaded, it is true that the tough Americans pay little attention to criminal justice and law when dealing with terrorists. Rather, leading terrorists are given presidential pardons over the strong objections of the Justice Department, which wants them deported on grounds of national security (Orlando Bosch), or dispatched to more extreme terrorist activities (Luis Posada Carriles), or protected from repeated extradition requests that are simply ignored (Haitian mass murderer Emmanuel Constant), or dismissed by the courts (Posada), to mention just a few of those engaged in "worthy terrorism."[68]

There is, to be sure, another conceivable category: US terrorists, a possibility excluded by doctrinal fiat. The significance of Western state terrorism in Western culture is illustrated by the appointment of John Negroponte to the new position of director of intelligence, in charge of counterterrorism. In the Reagan-Bush administration, he was ambassador to Honduras, running the world's largest CIA station, not because of the grand role of Honduras in world affairs, but because Honduras was the primary US base for the international terrorist war for which Washington was condemned by the International Court of Justice and UN Security Council (absent the US veto). There was virtually no reaction to the appointment of a leading international terrorist to the top counterterrorism position in the world. Nor to the fact that at the very same time, Dora María Téllez, the heroine of the popular struggle that overthrew the vicious Somoza regime in Nicaragua, was denied a visa to teach at the Harvard Divinity School. She was deemed a terrorist because she had helped overthrow a US-backed tyrant and mass murderer.[69]

Orwell would not have known whether to laugh or weep.

By 2005, Michael Lind grandly proclaimed, "The debate about the legitimacy of terrorism is over." The formal end to the debate was UN secretary-general Kofi Annan's declaration in March that "any action constitutes terrorism if it is intended to cause death or serious bodily harm to civilians or non-combatants with the purpose of intimidating a population or compelling a government or an international organisation to do or abstain from doing any act." With this declaration, Lind concluded, "Terrorism against civilians, whether committed by stateless groups or states, should be treated unambiguously as a war crime by every country in the world." Fortunately, Western commentators are saved from the unambiguous conclusion, thanks to our self-exemption from the most elementary of moral principles, the principle of universality.[70]

The willingness of top planners to risk an increase in terrorism, possibly with awesome consequences, does not of course indicate that they welcome such outcomes. Preventing terrorist attacks is simply not a high priority in comparison with serious geopolitical and strategic objectives—specifically, controlling the world's major energy resources, recognized since the 1940s to be "a stupendous source of strategic power" and "one of the greatest material prizes in world history." The British understood that well in their day in the sun. At the dawn of the oil age in 1921, the first lord of the Admiralty informed petroleum technologists that "if we secure the supplies of oil now available in the world we can do what we like." Understanding the point, the United States moved to expel the British from Venezuela, which by 1928 had become the world's leading oil exporter, and put US companies in charge. To achieve that goal, Washington "actively supported the vicious and venal regime of Juan Vicente Gómez," pressuring the government to bar British concessions (while continuing to demand—and secure—US oil rights in the Middle East, where the British and French were in the lead).[71]

Shortly after the invasion of Iraq, one of the more astute of the senior planners and analysts, Zbigniew Brzezinski, pointed out that America's control over Middle East oil producers "gives it indirect but politically critical leverage on the European and Asian economies that are also dependent on energy exports from the region." He was reiterating the conclusions of leading post–World War II planners, George Kennan in this case, who recognized that control of the resources of

the Gulf region would give the United States "veto power" over its industrial rivals. It is a rational calculation, on the assumption that human survival is not particularly significant in comparison with
short-term power and wealth. And that is nothing new. These themes
resonate through history. The difference today is only that the stakes
are enormously higher.[72]

If the United States can maintain its control over Iraq—which has
the world's second largest known oil reserves and is located at the
heart of the world's major energy supplies—it will enhance significantly Washington's "strategic power" and "critical leverage" over its
major rivals in the tripolar world that has been taking shape for the
past thirty years (with US-dominated North America serving as one
pole and Europe and northeast Asia, which is linked to south and
southeast Asia economies, as the other two). These concerns have always been central to post–World War II planning, considerably more
so today than before as substantial alliances are taking shape to
counter American dominance, accelerated, as was predicted, by Bush's
aggressive militarism.[73]

Examples abound of shortsightedness in the interest of power and
profit. To turn to another area, in April 2005 Congress enacted the
Energy Policy of 2005, which, if implemented, will permit drilling in
the Arctic National Wildlife Refuge, thus depleting domestic supplies
and increasing long-term dependence on oil imports. Echoing Washington rhetoric that its lobbyists probably wrote in the first place, the
industry hailed the congressional decision as a step to "Create Jobs
and Reduce Dependence on Foreign Oil." In fact, long-term dependence is increased, and "jobs" is the familiar technical term used to
avoid the vulgar seven-letter word "profits." Emptying the stores of
oil in the Strategic Petroleum Reserve would appear to be a more reasonable way to deplete domestic oil supplies: unlike ANWR drilling, it
would not have harmful effects on the environment and indigenous
people. But that would not yield industry profit, and the plan could
never be sold to the public in those terms.[74]

The bill passed shortly after ExxonMobil released its report *The
Outlook for Energy: A 2030 View*, forecasting that non-OPEC world
oil production would peak by 2010. Previously, the corporation had

taken a conservative stance on peak oil speculations. Looking ahead, the report dismissed alternatives such as Canadian oil sands as unviable, and could foresee no alternative to vastly increased OPEC production, primarily in the Middle East. If the predictions are accurate, depleting domestic oil supplies entails even greater reliance on Middle East oil than had been anticipated, hence further military intervention, instigation of terror, and continued undermining of the initiatives toward democracy and sovereignty that the United States has been blocking for decades, and will have to continue to block in the future.[75]

Middle East oil production means primarily Saudi Arabia and (potentially) Iraq, the latter a particularly valuable prize not only because of its enormous resources, but because it is the only remaining place on earth with huge untapped reserves that are, furthermore, very cheap to extract, hence promising a bonanza to the energy corporations that will have privileged access: primarily American and British, if the invasion succeeds in imposing Washington's effective rule. The crucial issue throughout the post–World War II period, however, has been control, more so than access or profit. And that concern for "critical leverage" in world affairs will presumably remain true for the foreseeable future.

AMONG THE MOST salient properties of failed states is that they do not protect their citizens from violence—and perhaps even destruction—or that decision makers regard such concerns as lower in priority than the short-term power and wealth of the state's dominant sectors. Another characteristic of failed states is that they are "outlaw states," whose leaderships dismiss international law and treaties with contempt. Such instruments may be binding on others but not on the outlaw state. We turn in the next chapter to this principle of self-exemption from the laws of war and other international norms.

Chapter 2

Outlaw States

In one of his last works, John Rawls, America's leading late-twentieth-century political and moral philosopher, outlined his ideas on a morally acceptable international society. He proposed a "Law of Peoples," which, he argued, should be appropriate for "the society of liberal democratic peoples" and "the society of decent peoples," the latter not liberal democracies but with characteristics that render them admissible to a just international community. Outside the realm of these "well-ordered peoples," Rawls says, are "outlaw states" that refuse to comply with the Law of Peoples. The Law of Peoples includes the commitments "to observe treaties and undertakings," to recognize that all are "equal and parties to the agreements that bind them," to reject the use of force "for reasons other than self-defense," and "to honor human rights," and other principles that should be readily accepted—though not by outlaw states and their acolytes.[1]

The idea that all states are "equal and parties to the agreements that bind them" has long been codified in international norms such as the Geneva Conventions—first enacted in 1864 to protect the wounded in times of war and since expanded through a number of additional protocols, most notably in 1949 and 1977—and the principles of the Nuremberg Tribunal, established to prosecute Nazi war crimes during World War II and adopted by the International Law

Commission of the United Nations in 1950. Article III of the Nuremberg principles states clearly: "The fact that a person who committed an act which constitutes a crime under international law acted as Head of State or responsible Government official does not relieve him from responsibility under international law." So, for example, the German foreign minister was hanged for such crimes as his role in the preemptive attack on Norway.[2]

Furthermore, grave breaches of the Geneva Conventions are universal and extraditable offenses within the jurisdiction of any party to the conventions, and these states are obliged to "enact any legislation necessary to provide effective penal sanctions for persons committing, or ordering to be committed" any such breaches. The threat of adherence to the rule of law is serious indeed. Or it would be, if anyone dared to defy the "single, ruthless superpower, whose leadership intends to shape the world according to its own forceful world view."[3]

TORTURE SCANDALS

In 2002, White House counsel Alberto Gonzales passed on to Bush a memorandum on torture by the Justice Department's Office of Legal Counsel. As noted by constitutional scholar Sanford Levinson: "According to the OLC, 'acts must be of an extreme nature to rise to the level of torture. . . . Physical pain amounting to torture must be equivalent in intensity to the pain accompanying serious physical injury, such as organ failure, impairment of bodily function, or even death.'" Levinson goes on to say that in the view of Jay Bybee, then head of the OLC, "The infliction of anything less intense than such extreme pain would not, technically speaking, be torture at all. It would merely be inhuman and degrading treatment, a subject of little apparent concern to the Bush administration's lawyers."[4]

Gonzales further advised President Bush to effectively rescind the Geneva Conventions, which, despite being "the supreme law of the land" and the foundation of contemporary international law, contained provisions Gonzales determined to be "quaint" and "obsolete." Rescinding the conventions, he informed Bush, "substantially reduces the threat of domestic criminal prosecution under the War Crimes Act." Passed in 1996, the act carries severe penalties for "grave breaches" of the conventions: the death penalty, "if death results to the victim" of the breach. Gonzales was later appointed to be attorney general and would probably have been a Supreme Court nominee if Bush's constituency did not regard him as "too liberal."[5]

The Justice Department rulings met with widespread condemnation. Sanford Levinson charged President Bush's legal advisers with "the articulation, on behalf of the Bush administration, of a view of presidential authority that is all too close to the power that [Carl] Schmitt was willing to accord his own Führer," referring to "the leading German philosopher of law during the Nazi period" and "the true éminence grise of the [Bush] administration." Or perhaps the true éminence grise is Robespierre, who instructed the French Convention that the Jacobins should "subdue liberty's enemies by terror." As Levinson points out, however, there was some basis for the rulings. The US Senate, when ratifying in 1994 the UN Convention Against Torture and Other Cruel, Inhuman, or Degrading Treatment or Punishment, provided what Levinson calls a more " 'interrogator-friendly' definition of torture than that adopted by the UN negotiators." This definition has been used by the president's legal advisers to justify the torture of detainees in Guantánamo, Iraq, and Afghanistan, and elsewhere as well, it appears. The United States, "in conjunction with key allies"—presumably the United Kingdom—"is running an 'invisible' network of prisons and detention centres into which thousands of suspects have disappeared without trace since the 'war on terror' began," writes British journalist and terrorism specialist Jason Burke, including a Soviet-era compound in eastern Europe (Dana Priest). Their fate is unknown but not hard to guess. In addition, unknown numbers of suspects have been sent by "rendition" to countries where torture is virtually guaranteed.[6]

In a scathing comprehensive review of the doctrines created by Bush's Justice Department, international law professor Jordan Paust writes: "Not since the Nazi era have so many lawyers been so clearly involved in international crimes concerning the treatment and interrogation of persons detained during war." The lawyers were executing a plan that "emerged within the Bush Administration in 2002 . . . to violate customary and treaty-based international law concerning the treatment and interrogation of so-called 'terrorist' and enemy combatant detainees and their supporters." Paust notes that "the common plan and authorizations have criminal implications," including "violations of the laws of war, which are war crimes," and possible high-level conspiracy to commit such crimes. The Gonzales memo of 2002, according to Paust, "is evidence of an unprincipled plan to evade the reach of law and to take actions in violation of Geneva law while seeking to avoid criminal sanctions." Similarly a memo issued by Bush on February 7, 2002, "necessarily authorized and ordered violations of the Geneva Conventions, which are war crimes." Reviewing subsequent presidential decisions, Paust finds violations of the Geneva Conventions and the Charter of the Nuremberg Tribunal, all war crimes, as well as flagrant violations of the US Constitution. Paust is derisive of the efforts of judicial advisers, among them highly respected professors of law and other legal authorities, who "engaged in complete fabrication [and] clear falsehood," distorting long-standing legal principles and Supreme Court judgments in the "plans to permit war crimes." He can recall no precedent in US history for such crimes "by lawyers and at the highest levels of our government," including the president and Defense Secretary Donald Rumsfeld, who ordered practices "patently violative of the laws of war."[7]

The two major international human rights organizations, Human Rights Watch and Amnesty International, have vigorously affirmed the Nuremberg principle of highest-level responsibility for crimes against peace and crimes against humanity. Referring to the scandal of Guantánamo and resort to torture directly or through the shameful practice of "rendition," Human Rights Watch called for criminal investigations of Donald Rumsfeld and former CIA director George Tenet, along with Generals Ricardo Sanchez (the former top US military commander in Iraq) and Geoffrey Miller (the former commander of the Guantánamo prison camp). Amnesty International called on all governments of the world to carry out criminal investigations of "senior US officials involved in the torture scandal," and, if the investigations support prosecution, to "arrest any official who enters their territory [and] begin legal proceedings against that official," following the precedent of the prosecution of Chilean dictator Augusto Pinochet, in conformity with the directives of international humanitarian law. The common reaction in US elite circles was predictable, given their reflexive rejection of the most elementary moral truisms and the accompanying doctrine of self-exemption from international law and treaties.[8]

Even without detailed information about the criminal practices of Bush and associates in Guantánamo, few could have been in any doubt that it is the site of major atrocities. Condoleezza Rice's solemn assurances to European diplomats about torture and rendition can hardly be taken seriously. Why select Egypt for rendition, not Sweden? Why detain people in Guantánamo rather than in a prison in New York? The pretext that dangerous terrorists might have escaped in New York is without merit. Evidently, the Bush administration selected Guantánamo because legalistic chicanery could portray it as exempt from domestic or international law. The US base in eastern Cuba was seized by force at the end of the nineteenth century and then given to the United States under an imposed "treaty" that permits it to be used as a coaling or naval station. It has since been converted to other purposes, in violation of even that forced concession by occupied Cuba: among them, the detention of Haitian refugees in violation of Article 9 of the Universal Declaration of Human Rights, and now torture and other violations of international law. Maintaining the US base is also a transparent effort to undermine the Cuban economy by denying the country its major port and possibilities for development in the hinterland.

In unintended confirmation of the assessment of Bush administration doctrine by Levinson, Paust, and the human rights organizations, two legal authorities have sought to dismiss another convention of international humanitarian law, the designation of the International Committee of the Red Cross (ICRC) as the sole authority to determine the status of prisoners of war. This convention is ludicrous, we learn from international lawyers Lee Casey and David Rivkin, who served in the Justice Department under Reagan and Bush I. One reason is that "each state is entitled to interpret [international law] itself—this is the essence of sovereignty and self-government." The phrase "each state" refers, of course, to the United States—or its clients, if Washington chooses to delegate the rights to them. Casey and Rivkin do not conclude, for example, that Saddam Hussein was entitled to interpret the law so as to authorize his conquest of Kuwait, or that a future democratic government in Iraq would be entitled to bomb Israel to put an end to its violation of innumerable Security Council orders as well as of the Geneva Conventions. A second reason the ICRC is disqualified is that it disagrees with Washington and has thereby abdicated its role as an "impartial humanitarian body." QED.[9]

Casey and Rivkin could have added others to their list of disqualified authorities, among them, the Organization of American States (OAS) and "the spear carrier for the *pax americana*," as the Blair government is described with scorn in Britain's leading journal of international affairs. The Inter-American Commission on Human Rights of the OAS requested in March 2002 that the United States "take the urgent measures necessary to have the legal status of the detainees at Guantánamo Bay determined by a competent Tribunal," meaning the ICRC. Washington dismissed the request on grounds that it has no binding commitment to accept the commission's decisions. Perhaps with this in mind, a year later, the OAS for the first time voted to exclude the United States from membership in the Inter-American Commission, "a symbolic rebuff—to show our disapproval of US policies," a Latin American diplomat in Washington observed. As for Britain, the Blair government refused to take a stand when a British court of appeal ruled unanimously that Feroz Abassi, a British citizen held without charge at Guantánamo, was being detained arbitrarily in a "legal black hole," invoking rights that trace back to quaint provisions of the Magna Carta. These provisions were, at last, partially recognized by the US Supreme Court in its *Rasul et al. v Bush* decision of June 2004, perhaps also disqualifying the Supreme Court, by Casey and Rivkin's standards—though not Congress, which nullified the ruling in fall 2005.[10]

Among other institutions disqualified from judging US actions are the World Court, ever since it ruled against the United States in the case brought by Nicaragua in 1986, and the UN Security Council, which affirmed the World Court's judgment. But the World Court's in-iquity extends beyond its transgression on Nicaragua. In July 2004, the court issued an advisory ruling that Israel's "Separation Wall" di-viding the West Bank violates international law, and that it is an "ob-ligation for all States not to recognize the illegal situation resulting from construction of the wall and not to render aid or assistance in maintaining the situation created by such construction." US justice Buergenthal alone dissented, but on very narrow grounds. He agreed that "international humanitarian law, including the Fourth Geneva Convention, and international human rights law are applicable to the Occupied Palestinian Territory and must there [sic] be faithfully com-plied with by Israel." Since all Israeli settlements in the occupied terri-tories are in violation of the convention, "the segments of the wall being built by Israel to protect the settlements are *ipso facto* in viola-tion of international humanitarian law"—that is, most of the wall. So presumably he is disqualified as well, though Israel's own High Court still passes muster. A year later, it ruled that any route of the Separa-tion Wall "must take into account the need to provide security for the Israeli residents of Alfei Menashe" in the West Bank, and indeed for all "Israelis living in Israeli communities in the Judea and Samaria area" (the West Bank), including their property rights.[11]

The US political parties agree. The World Court's decision was bit-terly condemned by overwhelming majorities of both parties in con-gressional resolutions. The 2004 Democratic presidential candidate, John Kerry, took a particularly strong stand condemning the court. The reaction, Stephen Zunes commented, reflects "the growing bipar-tisan hostility to any legal restraints on the conduct of the United States and its allies beyond their borders, particularly in the Middle East," and the consensus that "any effort to raise legal questions re-garding the actions of occupying powers must be forcefully challenged"—when the occupying powers are the United States or its clients, that is. Other evidence strongly confirms his judgment.[12]

There should be no need to waste time on the claim that the Sepa-ration Wall is motivated by security concerns. Were that the case, the wall would be built on the Green Line, the international border recog-nized by the entire world, with the exception of Israel and the United

States (which had also recognized the border until it sharply shifted policy in the 1970s to support Israel's rejection of a political settlement in favor of further expansion into the occupied territories). If Israel were to build a wall for self-defense, it could be made utterly impregnable and there would be no international objections for Washington to veto or ignore. But there is a downside. A self-defense wall would not be a major step toward integrating within Israel valuable Palestinian land and crucial resources, primarily water.[13] And it would inconvenience Israelis, including illegal settlers, not Palestinians. Therefore it is excluded as an option—"security" having its usual significance in state practice and public rhetoric.

CRIMES OF WAR AND CRIMES AGAINST HUMANITY

Gonzales's legal advice about protecting Bush from the threat of prosecution under the War Crimes Act was proven sound not long after he gave it, in a case far more severe even than the torture scandals. In November 2004, US occupation forces launched their second major attack on the city of Falluja. The press reported major war crimes instantly, with approval. The attack began with a bombing campaign intended to drive out all but the adult male population; men ages fifteen to forty-five who attempted to flee Falluja were turned back. The plans resembled the preliminary stage of the Srebrenica massacre, though the Serb attackers trucked women and children out of the city instead of bombing them out. While the preliminary bombing was under way, Iraqi journalist Nermeen al-Mufti reported from "the city of minarets [which] once echoed the Euphrates in its beauty and calm [with its] plentiful water and lush greenery . . . a summer resort for Iraqis [where people went] for leisure, for a swim at the nearby Habbaniya lake, for a kebab meal." She described the fate of victims of these bombing attacks in which sometimes whole families, including pregnant women and babies, unable to flee, along with many others, were killed because the attackers who ordered their flight had cordoned off the city, closing the exit roads.[14]

Al-Mufti asked residents whether there were foreign fighters in Falluja. One man said that "he had heard that there were Arab fighters in the city, but he never saw any of them." Then he heard that they had left. "Regardless of the motives of those fighters, they have provided a pretext for the city to be slaughtered," he continued, and "it is our right to resist." Another said that "some Arab brothers were among us, but when the shelling intensified, we asked them to leave and they did," and then asked a question of his own: "Why has America given itself the right to call on UK and Australian and other armies for help and we don't have the same right?"[15]

It would be interesting to ask how often that question has been raised in Western commentary and reporting. Or how often the analogous question was raised in the Soviet press in the 1980s, about Afghanistan. How often was a term like "foreign fighters" used to refer to the invading armies? How often did reporting and commentary stray from the assumption that the only conceivable question is how well "our side" is doing, and what the prospects are for "our success"? It is hardly necessary to investigate. The assumptions are cast in iron. Even to entertain a question about them would be unthinkable, proof of "support for terror" or "blaming all the problems of the world on America/Russia," or some other familiar refrain.

After several weeks of bombing, the United States began its ground attack in Falluja. It opened with the conquest of the Falluja General Hospital. The front-page story in the *New York Times* reported that "patients and hospital employees were rushed out of rooms by armed soldiers and ordered to sit or lie on the floor while troops tied their hands behind their backs." An accompanying photograph depicted the scene. It was presented as a meritorious achievement. "The offensive also shut down what officers said was a propaganda weapon for the militants: Falluja General Hospital, with its stream of reports of civilian casualties." Plainly such a propaganda weapon is a legitimate target, particularly when "inflated civilian casualty figures"—inflated because our leader so declared—had "inflamed opinion throughout the country, driving up the political costs of the conflict." The word "conflict" is a common euphemism for US aggression, as when we read on the same pages that "now, the Americans are rushing in engineers who will begin rebuilding what the conflict has just destroyed"—just "the conflict," with no agent, like a hurricane.[16]

Some relevant documents passed unmentioned, perhaps because they too are considered quaint and obsolete: for example, the provision of the Geneva Conventions stating that "fixed establishments and mobile medical units of the Medical Service may in no circumstances be attacked, but shall at all times be respected and protected by the Parties to the conflict." Thus the front page of the world's leading newspaper was cheerfully depicting war crimes for which the political leadership could be sentenced to severe penalties under US law, the death penalty if patients ripped from their beds and manacled on the floor happened to die as a result. The questions did not merit detectable inquiry or reflection. The same mainstream sources told us that the US military "achieved nearly all their objectives well ahead of schedule," as "much of the city lay in smoking ruins." But it was not a complete success. There was little evidence of dead "packrats" in their "warrens" or on the streets, "an enduring mystery." US forces did discover "the body of a woman on a street in Falluja, but it was unclear whether she was an Iraqi or a foreigner." The crucial question, apparently.[17]

Another front-page story quotes a senior marine commander who says that the attack on Falluja "ought to go down in the history books." Perhaps it should. If so, we know on just what page of history it will find its place. Perhaps Falluja will appear right alongside Grozny, a city of about the same size, with a picture of Bush and Putin gazing into each other's souls. Those who praise or for that matter even tolerate all of this can select their own favorite pages of history.[18]

The media accounts of the assault were not uniform. Qatar-based Al-Jazeera, the most important news channel in the Arab world, was harshly criticized by high US officials for having "emphasized civilian casualties" during the destruction of Falluja. The problem of independent media was later resolved when the channel was kicked out of Iraq in preparation for free elections.[19]

Turning beyond the US mainstream, we discover also that "Dr. Sami al-Jumaili described how US warplanes bombed the Central Health Centre in which he was working," killing thirty-five patients and twenty-four staff. His report was confirmed by an Iraqi reporter for Reuters and the BBC, and by Dr. Eiman al-Ani of Falluja General Hospital, who said that the entire health center, which he reached shortly after the attack, had collapsed on the patients. The attacking forces said that the report was "unsubstantiated." In another gross violation of international humanitarian law, even minimal decency, the US military denied the Iraqi Red Crescent access to Falluja. Sir Nigel Young, the chief executive of the British Red Cross, condemned the action as "hugely significant." It sets "a dangerous precedent," he said: "The Red Crescent had a mandate to meet the needs of the local population facing a huge crisis." Perhaps this additional crime was a reaction to a very unusual public statement by the International Committee of the Red Cross, condemning all sides in the war in Iraq for their "utter contempt for humanity."[20]

In what appears to be the first report of a visitor to Falluja after the operation was completed, Iraqi doctor Ali Fadhil said he found it "completely devastated." The modern city now "looked like a city of ghosts." Fadhil saw few dead bodies of Iraqi fighters in the streets; they had been ordered to abandon the city before the assault began. Doctors reported that the entire medical staff had been locked into the main hospital when the US attack began, "tied up" under US orders: "Nobody could get to the hospital and people were bleeding to death in the city." The attitudes of the invaders were summarized by a message written in lipstick on the mirror of a ruined home: "Fuck Iraq and every Iraqi in it." Some of the worst atrocities were committed by members of the Iraqi National Guard used by the invaders to search houses, mostly "poor Shias from the south . . . jobless and desperate," probably "fan[ning] the seeds of a civil war." Embedded reporters arriving a few weeks later found some people "trickling back to Falluja," where they "enter a desolate world of skeletal buildings, tank-blasted homes, weeping power lines and severed palm trees." The ruined city of 250,000 was now "devoid of electricity, running water, schools or commerce," under a strict curfew, and "conspicuously occupied" by the invaders who had just demolished it and the local forces they had assembled. The few refugees who dared to return under tight military surveillance found "lakes of sewage in the streets.

The smell of corpses inside charred buildings. No water or electricity. Long waits and thorough searches by US troops at checkpoints. Warnings to watch out for land mines and booby traps. Occasional gunfire between troops and insurgents."[21]

Half a year later came perhaps the first visit by an international observer, Joe Carr of the Christian Peacemakers Team in Baghdad, whose previous experience had been in the Israeli-occupied Palestinian territories. Arriving on May 28, he found painful similarities: many hours of waiting at the few entry points, more for harassment than for security; regular destruction of produce in the devastated remains of the city where "food prices have dramatically increased because of the checkpoints"; blocking of ambulances transporting people for medical treatment; and other forms of random brutality familiar from the Israeli press. The ruins of Falluja, he wrote, are even worse than Rafah in the Gaza Strip, virtually destroyed by US-backed Israeli terror. The United States "has leveled entire neighborhoods, and about every third building is destroyed or damaged." Only one hospital with inpatient care survived the attack, but access was impeded by the occupying army, leading to many deaths in Falluja and rural areas. Sometimes dozens of people were packed into a "burned out shell." Only about a quarter of families whose homes were destroyed received some compensation, usually less than half of the cost for materials needed to rebuild them.[22]

The UN Special Rapporteur on the Right to Food, Jean Ziegler, accused US and British troops in Iraq of "breaching international law by depriving civilians of food and water in besieged cities as they try to flush out militants" in Falluja and other cities attacked in subsequent months. US-led forces "cut off or restricted food and water to encourage residents to flee before assaults," he informed the international press, "using hunger and deprivation of water as a weapon of war against the civilian population, [in] flagrant violation" of the Geneva Conventions. The US public was largely spared the news.[23]

Even apart from such major war crimes as the assault on Falluja, there is more than enough evidence to support the conclusion of a professor of strategic studies at the Naval War College that the year 2004 "was a truly horrible and brutal one for hapless Iraq." Hatred of the United States, he continued, is now rampant in a country subjected to years of sanctions that had already led to "the destruction of the Iraqi middle class, the collapse of the secular educational system, and the growth of illiteracy, despair, and anomie [that] promoted an Iraqi religious revival [among] large numbers of Iraqis seeking succor in religion." Basic services deteriorated even more than they had under the sanctions. "Hospitals regularly run out of the most basic medicines, . . . the facilities are in horrid shape, [and] scores of specialists and experienced physicians are leaving the country because they fear they are targets of violence or because they are fed up with the substandard working conditions." Meanwhile, "religion's role in Iraqi political life has ratcheted steadily higher since US-led forces overthrew Mr. Hussein in 2003," the *Wall Street Journal* reports. Since the invasion, "not a single political decision" has been made without Grand Ayatollah Ali al-Sistani's "tacit or explicit approval, say government officials," while the "formerly little-known young rebel cleric" Muqtada al-Sadr has "fashioned a political and military movement that has drawn tens of thousands of followers in the south and in Baghdad's poorest slums." Similar developments have taken place in Sunni areas. The vote on Iraq's draft constitution in fall 2005 turned into "a battle of the mosques," with voters largely following religious edicts. Few Iraqis had even seen the document because the government had scarcely distributed any copies. The new constitution, the *Wall Street Journal* notes, has "far deeper Islamic underpinnings than Iraq's last one, a half century ago, which was based on [secular] French civil law," and had granted women "nearly equal rights" with men. All of this has now been reversed under the US occupation.[24]

The consequences of years of Western violence and strangulation are endlessly frustrating to civilized intellectuals, who are amazed to discover that, in the words of Edward Luttwak, "the vast majority of Iraqis, assiduous mosque-goers and semi-literate at best," are simply unable to "believe what for them is entirely incomprehensible: that foreigners have been unselfishly expending their own blood and treasure to help them." By definition, no evidence necessary.[25]

Commentators have lamented that the United States has changed "from a country that condemned torture and forbade its use to one that practices torture routinely." The actual history is far less benign.

But torture, however horrifying, scarcely weighs in the balance in comparison with the war crimes at Falluja and elsewhere in Iraq, or the general effects of the US and UK invasion. One illustration, noted in passing and quickly dismissed in the United States, is the careful study by prominent US and Iraqi specialists published in the world's leading medical journal, the *Lancet*, in October 2004. The conclusions of the study, carried out on rather conservative assumptions, are that "the death toll associated with the invasion and occupation of Iraq is probably about 100,000 people, and may be much higher." The figures include nearly 40,000 Iraqis killed as a direct result of combat or armed violence, according to a later Swiss review of the study's data. A subsequent study by Iraq Body Count found 25,000 noncombatants reported killed in the first two years of the occupation—in Baghdad, one in 500 citizens; in Falluja, one in 136. US-led forces killed 37 percent, criminals 36 percent, "anti-occupation forces" 9 percent. Killings doubled in the second year of the occupation. Most deaths were caused by explosive devices; two-thirds of these by air strikes. The estimates of Iraq Body Count are based on media reports, and are therefore surely well below the actual numbers, though shocking enough.[26]

Reviewing these reports along with the UNDP "Iraq Living Conditions Survey" (April 2005), British analyst Milan Rai concludes that the results are largely consistent, the apparent variation in numbers resulting primarily from differences in the specific topics investigated and the time periods covered. These conclusions gain some support from a Pentagon study that estimated 26,000 Iraqi civilians and security forces killed and wounded *by insurgents* since January 2004. The *New York Times* report of the Pentagon study also mentions several others, but omits the most important one, in the *Lancet*. It notes in passing that "no figures were provided for the number of Iraqis killed by American-led forces." The *Times* story appeared immediately after the day that had been set aside by international activists for commemoration of all Iraqi deaths, on the first anniversary of the release of the *Lancet* report.[27]

The scale of the catastrophe in Iraq is so extreme that it can barely be reported. Journalists are largely confined to the heavily fortified

Green Zone in Baghdad, or else travel under heavy guard. There are a few regular exceptions in the mainstream press, such as Robert Fisk and Patrick Cockburn, who face extreme hazards, and there are occasional indications of Iraqi opinion. One is a report on a nostalgic gathering of educated westernized Baghdad elites, where discussion turned to the sacking of Baghdad by Hulagu Khan and his vicious atrocities. A philosophy professor commented that "Hulagu was humane compared with the Americans," drawing some laughter, but "most of the guests seemed eager to avoid the subject of politics and violence, which dominate everyday life here." Instead they turned to past efforts to create an Iraqi national culture that would overcome the old ethnic-religious divisions to which Iraq is now "regressing" under the occupation, and discussed the destruction of the treasures of Iraqi and world civilization, a tragedy not experienced since the Mongol invasions.[28]

Additional effects of the invasion include the decline of the median income of Iraqis, from $255 in 2003 to about $144 in 2004, as well as "significant countrywide shortages of rice, sugar, milk, and infant formula," according to the UN World Food Program, which had warned in advance of the invasion that it would not be able to duplicate the efficient rationing system that had been in place under Saddam Hussein. Iraqi newspapers report that new rations contain metal filings, one consequence of the vast corruption under the US-UK occupation. Acute malnutrition doubled within sixteen months of the occupation of Iraq, to the level of Burundi, well above Haiti or Uganda, a figure that "translates to roughly 400,000 Iraqi children suffering from 'wasting,' a condition characterized by chronic diarrhea and dangerous deficiencies of protein." This is a country in which hundreds of thousands of children had already died as a consequence of the US- and UK-led sanctions. In May 2005, UN rapporteur Jean Ziegler released a report of the Norwegian Institute for Applied Social Science confirming these figures. The relatively high nutritional levels of Iraqis in the 1970s and 1980s, even through the war with Iran, began to decline severely during the decade of the sanctions, with a further disastrous decline after the 2003 invasion.[29]

Meanwhile, violence against civilians extended beyond the occupiers and the insurgency. Anthony Shadid and Steve Fainaru reported that "Shiite and Kurdish militias, often operating as part of Iraqi government security forces, have carried out a wave of abductions, assassinations and other acts of intimidation, consolidating their control over territory across northern and southern Iraq and deepening the country's divide along ethnic and sectarian lines." One indicator of the scale of the catastrophe is the huge flood of refugees "fleeing violence and economic troubles," a million to Syria and Jordan alone since the US invasion, most of them "professionals and secular moderates who could help with the practical task of getting the country to run well."[30]

The *Lancet* study estimating 100,000 probable deaths by October 2004 elicited enough comment in England so that the government had to issue an embarrassing denial, but in the United States virtual silence prevailed. The occasional oblique reference usually describes it as the "controversial" report that "as many as 100,000" Iraqis died as a result of the invasion. The figure of 100,000 was the most probable estimate, on conservative assumptions; it would be at least as accurate to describe it as the report that "as few as 100,000" died. Though the report was released at the height of the US presidential campaign, it appears that neither of the leading candidates was ever publicly questioned about it.[31]

The reaction follows the general pattern when massive atrocities are perpetrated by the wrong agent. A striking example is the Indochina wars. In the only poll (to my knowledge) in which people were asked to estimate the number of Vietnamese deaths, the mean estimate was 100,000, about 5 percent of the official figure; the actual toll is unknown, and of no more interest than the also unknown toll of casualties of US chemical warfare. The authors of the study comment that it is as if college students in Germany estimated Holocaust deaths at 300,000, in which case we might conclude that there are some problems in Germany—and if Germany ruled the world, some rather more serious problems.[32]

Washington's decision to exempt itself from international law even beyond the ample precedents has gained the partial support of people regarded as leading advocates of human rights, such as Michael Ignatieff, chair of the human rights program at Harvard, who supports violations of the Geneva Conventions, and indeed of US law, on "lesser evil" grounds that are justified by his personal sentiments. Such grounds are commonly understood to suffice in "just war theory." Thus in his highly praised recent reflections on just war, Michael Walzer describes Afghanistan as a "triumph of just war theory," standing alongside Kosovo as a "just war," no argument or evidence necessary—which is just as well, since one will search his "arguments about war" in vain for any nontrivial conclusion that follows from propositions of just war theory, or from anything else, unless we add such ubiquitous phrases as "I think" or "seems to me entirely justified." Campus opponents of what Walzer designates as just US wars are "pacifists," he informs us, but "pacifism" is a "bad argument" because he thinks violence is sometimes legitimate. We may well agree (I do), but "I think" is hardly an overwhelming argument in the real world cases that he discusses. His adversaries "on the left" are unidentified, apart from Edward Said "and (more intelligent and circumspect) Richard Falk," who give "excuses" for terror; what the "excuses" are we are not told. Walzer's "arguments about war" are primarily directed against "many people on the left," "some critics of the war," "a lot of talk," "leftists," "great simplifiers," and so on, all unidentifiable; and, routinely, Arabs. It is an interesting comment on the prevailing moral-intellectual culture that unsupported slander of opponents who are unidentified is considered legitimate practice, particularly among those who modestly describe themselves as "the decent left"—indeed highly meritorious, as long as the conclusions come out the right way.[33]

"THIEF, THIEF!"

The expectations of Pentagon planners that they would quickly conquer Iraq and establish a stable client regime were not entirely unrealistic. Had it not been for the extraordinary incompetence of the Pentagon civilians in charge, this should have been one of the easiest military conquests in history, even without the preliminary "spikes of activity" and other measures to ensure that Iraqi military forces could not or would not resist. The country had been devastated by war and sanctions, and was known to have very limited military capacities and expenditures even by comparison to the countries nearby. The invasion brought to an end two brutal regimes, and the United States had enormous resources to rebuild the wreckage. Furthermore, any resistance that developed would have only insignificant outside support. Nevertheless, the Pentagon civilians succeeded in creating a substantial armed resistance and massive popular nonviolent resistance, tearing the country to shreds in the process. It is a remarkable fact that Washington planners have had more trouble controlling Iraq than Russia had in its satellites or Germany in occupied Europe, where the countries were run by domestic governments and security forces for the most part, with the ruling power in the background to sustain the client regimes. There were courageous anti-Nazi partisans, but they could hardly have survived without outside support, and Germany was, of course, at war. Despite all of their unusual advantages, the Pentagon civilians brought about "one of the most extraordinary failures in history," veteran Middle East correspondent Patrick Cockburn observed from the scene, quite plausibly.[34]

Of the two murderous regimes brought to an end by the invasion of Iraq, only one is allowed to enter discussion: Saddam's tyranny, and even that enters only through a highly selective filter. Saddam was no longer the US favorite he had been up to August 1990, and became again in March 1991, when Bush I authorized the tyrant to crush the Shiite rebellion that might have overthrown him. The outcome of this new phase of Bush-Saddam complicity was tens of thousands of additional corpses.[35]

The second murderous regime was the US-UK sanctions (for doctrinal reasons, called "UN sanctions," though it is common knowledge that the UN administered them under US pressure). But these are off the agenda because they may have caused more deaths than "all so-called weapons of mass destruction throughout history," two hawkish military specialists estimate, surely hundreds of thousands. Summarizing a rich body of evidence, one of the best-informed American correspondents writes that after "the terrible years of the U.N. sanctions . . . incomes had dropped to one-fifth of pre-war [1990] levels, infant mortality had doubled, and only a minority of Iraqis had access to clean water." Furthermore, half of all sewage treatment tanks were still inoperable after having been destroyed along with power supplies by the US and UK bombing in 1991, which "unleashed epidemics of typhoid and cholera." Education and literacy collapsed, and growing numbers of Iraqis were reduced to "a semi-starvation diet," showing symptoms "usually seen only in famines," leading to a tripling of the death rate by 2003, according to UNICEF.[36]

The sanctions devastated civilian society, strengthened the tyrant, and compelled the population to rely on him for survival, quite possibly saving him from the fate of other murderous dictators who were supported by the United States and UK up to the last moments of their bloody rule: Nicolae Ceauşescu, Suharto, Ferdinand Marcos, Jean-Claude "Baby Doc" Duvalier, Chun Doo-hwan, and quite a rogues' gallery of others, to which new names are being regularly added. For such reasons, the sanctions were bitterly condemned by leading Iraqi opposition figures. Kamil Mahdi wrote that the United States was "in effect acting to stain and paralyse all opposition to the present regime" and had "given a discredited and moribund regime a new lease of life." The sanctions, he wrote, "treat Iraq as a massive refugee camp to be provided with emergency relief. What Iraqis need is to be able to regenerate their economy and resume reconstruction and development. This means that essential services and the infrastructure have to be given a high priority, and the import programme has to be geared to raising domestic production," precisely what the US-imposed sanctions regime prevented.[37]

That Iraqis might have taken care of their own problems had it not been for the murderous sanctions regime was suggested by the Westerners who knew Iraq best, the respected international diplomats Denis Halliday and Hans von Sponeck, who administered the UN oil-for-food program in Iraq and had hundreds of investigators reporting from around the country. Halliday resigned in protest in 1998, condemning the sanctions as "genocidal." Von Sponeck resigned two years later, for similar reasons. The speculation that Saddam Hussein's tyranny was sustained by the sanctions was strengthened by postwar US government investigations, which revealed that the government was being held together virtually by Scotch tape. Subjective judgments about the matter, however, are of little interest. Unless people are at least given the opportunity to overthrow a tyrannical regime, no outside power has the right to carry out the task—inevitably for its own purposes, and in this case, with horrifying results. Von Sponeck alleged further that the United States was blocking his reports to the Security Council. No such means were needed to safeguard the American population from the opinions of the best-informed Western observers. They were barred from the press by their unwanted conclusions and unusual qualifications.[38]

Silence is apparently regarded as insufficient to ensure that the effects of the sanctions will be hidden from view. The government-media complex has therefore resorted to the familiar "Thief, thief!" technique: when you are caught with your hands in someone's pocket, shout "Thief, thief!" and point vigorously somewhere else, in the hope that attention will be shifted while you flee. In this case, the device was to initiate intensive inquiry into alleged UN corruption in administering the oil-for-food program, with much bombast about a missing $20 billion that may have been pocketed by the Iraqis. It is important to bear in mind that if it is later conceded that the charges were discredited, they will nevertheless have served their purpose: to eliminate any prospect, however unlikely, that the truly monstrous scandal—the sanctions themselves and their consequences—might escape from oblivion.

Though the issue is secondary, the course of the "Thief, thief!" technique is nonetheless of some interest. It was quickly shown that though there doubtless was UN corruption, most of the missing $20 billion consisted of illegal US-approved sales of oil to its allies Turkey and Jordan. The bulk of illegal transactions, according to the report of Charles A. Duelfer, the top US inspector in Iraq, consisted of "government to government agreements" between Iraq and other countries, primarily Jordan ("the key to Iraq's financial survival," according to the report) and Turkey. All of these transactions took place outside the UN's oil-for-food program, and all were authorized by the UN Security Council, that is, by Washington. The other transactions passed through the US-run sanctions committee, and hence faced an instant US veto, which was never exercised for illegal kickbacks, though assiduously applied to block humanitarian contracts, US researcher Joy Gordon reports. Any significant smuggling by sea would have been with the tacit cooperation of the US Navy, which virtually constituted the UN Multinational Interception Force (MIF) in the Gulf. In the only serious inquiry into the oil-for-food program, Paul Volcker, chair of a UN-authorized inquiry into possible abuse, came to the preliminary conclusion that questionable kickbacks were "close to the $1.7 billion that Charles Duelfer . . . arrived at," a small fraction of the Turkey-Jordan oil sales under the US aegis. The only nontrivial number cited in one of the many excited reports about the "major scandal at the United Nations" is overcompensation of the Kuwaiti military by $419 million, about one-quarter of Volcker's estimated total of $1.7 billion. The next largest figure reported—$200 million of illegal profits, of which $50 million went to Saddam's associates—was uncovered in an inquiry by the international business press, which also found that "the largest and boldest smuggling operation in the oil-for-food programme was conducted with the knowledge of the US government." Both US and UK authorities were notified, but ignored warnings, sometimes conveyed by the MIF.[39]

Investigations by the *Financial Times* found that "the Clinton and Bush administrations not only knew but told the US Congress that Iraq was smuggling oil to Turkey and Jordan," and that they recommended "turning a blind eye to it." The reason was that the illegal sales were "in the 'national interest,' " since Jordan is an important US client state, and support for Turkey, long a major US base for regional control, promotes "security, prosperity and other vital interests."[40]

Whatever the scale of the preinvasion kickback schemes may have been, it is doubtful that they will even approximate the sums that have disappeared under US management during the occupation of Iraq. As the Coalition Provisional Authority (CPA) ended its rule, the fate of the estimated $20 billion of Iraqi funds that passed into its control—including unspent funds from the oil-for-food program and more than $11 billion in Iraqi oil revenues—remained a mystery. The "lack of transparency is fuelling questions" about corrupt CPA practices, the *Financial Times* reported, providing many illustrations, among them studies concluding that three-fourths of contracts worth more than $5 million were handed out without competitive bidding. That included a "$1.4 [billion] project to rebuild Iraq's oil infrastructure, granted to

Halliburton, the US oil services company formerly headed by Dick Cheney, the US vice president, without competitive tender, [which] made Halliburton the largest single recipient of Iraqi funds." Further inquiries revealed schemes by Texas corporations and "legendary oil men" to subvert "the restrictions imposed by the United Nations' oil-for-food programme," with some indictments under way. What has appeared suggests a morass of corruption by US businesses, among others.[41]

In the most extensive media review of CPA practices, relying primarily on official US audits, Ed Harriman observes that Rumsfeld and Paul Bremer "made sure that the reconstruction of Iraq is paid for by the 'liberated' country." Bremer's CPA "spent up to $20 billion of Iraqi money, compared to $300 million of US funds." No record could be found for "$8.8 billion that passed through the new Iraqi government ministries" under Bremer's control. Payoffs to Texas-based Halliburton and its subsidiaries have been particularly outlandish, but the record of corruption under CPA authority extends far beyond. "The schools, hospitals, water supplies and electricity, all of which were supposed to benefit from [CPA-administered] money, are in ruins. The inescapable conclusion is that foreign contractors grabbed large bundles of cash for themselves and made sweet deals with their Iraqi contacts." Under Saddam's rule, Harriman observes, both he "and the US profited handsomely." In those years, "most of Iraq's oil went to Californian refineries, [which] grew rich. Today the system is much the same: the oil goes to California, and the new Iraqi government spends the country's money with impunity." Stuart Bowen, special inspector general for Iraq reconstruction, found that little was left for reconstruction, in part because an estimated $30 billion of Iraqi funds seized by the occupying army, along with funds from Iraqi oil revenues, had been subject to mismanagement and "potential fraud" by CPA personnel.[42]

Much more exciting than the facts about corruption are fevered tales about possible Russian chicanery, or an unexplained $160,000 in the hands of UN official Benon Sevan, or reports that Kofi Annan might (or might not) have spoken at some gathering to an official of a company that employed his son. Whatever the actual facts, the conclusion is that the UN is in dire need of US-guided reform. Therefore the

Bush administration has "focused on the UN-administered oil-for-food program—which became a pool of corruption while allowing Saddam Hussein to divert millions in oil revenues—viewing it as an example of the deep reforms the UN needs if it is to be effective." Undertaking that task is the "next hurdle" facing newly appointed UN ambassador John Bolton.[43]

The final report of the Volcker commission on corruption at UN headquarters found two instances, Warren Hoge reported: Sevan was accused "of banking at least $147,000 in kickbacks and a procurement officer, Aleksandr V. Yakovlev of Russia, was found to have solicited a bribe, unsuccessfully, from a program contractor," actions that might qualify them for junior management positions at Halliburton. "The report also blamed the Security Council and its sanctions committee"—which means primarily Washington—"for tolerating smuggling that went on outside the oil-for-food program and that benefited countries like Turkey, Jordan and Syria." The scale of corruption is illustrated by the final estimates: "[Saddam] Hussein skimmed $1.8 billion in kickbacks and surcharges from the United Nations–run program." The surcharges were almost all skimmed with Washington's authorization; the kickbacks substantially involved US corporations. The commission chose not to investigate an estimated $9 billion in oil-for-food surpluses handed over to the US occupation authorities, which apparently disappeared.[44]

The end result of the Volcker inquiry is, therefore, barely detectable. But by doctrinal fiat, its revelations are "the largest fraud ever recorded in history," the *Wall Street Journal* editors declared with mock outrage. They also joined the impassioned call for radical reform of the UN to deal with its waste, mismanagement, and corruption—doubtless real, and presumably the responsibility of the UN undersecretary-generals for management, who are regularly Washington political appointees.[45]

In its final compilation on business corruption, the Volcker commission identified thousands of companies engaged in illegal surcharges and kickbacks along with a number of individuals, including fugitive financier Marc Rich, granted a presidential pardon by Clinton as he left office. It also faulted the Security Council (that is, the United States) for failure to monitor the corruption. "Even though we are looking at it from the outside, it kind of screams out at you," Volcker said: "'Why didn't somebody blow a whistle?' The central point is that it all adds up to the same story. You need some pretty thorough-going reforms at the U.N." One of Volcker's investigators answered his question about whistle-blowers: allowing billions of dollars of oil to flow illegally "to the benefit of the economies of American allies, including Jordan and Turkey," he said, "had a compromising effect on the Security Council's willingness to step in and stop the practice." After these vast illegal flows, he asked, "you're going to be very strict about this smaller volume of oil? Unlikely." To put it less obliquely, the United States, which monitored the program with a hawk's eye, was "compromised" by its crucial role in illegal support for Saddam and was not in a position to "blow a whistle" about far smaller sums, which implicated many US companies. Doubtless "pretty thoroughgoing reforms" are needed in many places, but "the central point" is that the UN, with all its faults, does not rank very high among them.[46]

Most of the energy corporations involved in "illicit oil surcharges" covered their tracks by resort to intermediaries, the Volcker report concluded, but not all: "one major oil company was shamed by the 623-page report: Texaco, part of Chevron." There is some poetic justice, perhaps, in Texaco's unique role, not just because of the Texas connection. In the late 1930s, Texaco, then run by an open pro-Nazi, diverted oil shipments from the Spanish republic to Franco—in violation of contract, as well as of official US government orders—while the State Department pretended "not to see" that the fascist forces invading Spain were receiving from the United States the one critical commodity that Nazi Germany and Fascist Italy could not provide. The left-wing press was able to discover it, and later it was officially conceded. Similarly, when Clinton was undermining the embargo against Haiti's vicious terrorist junta, it was Texaco that was authorized to violate the presidential directive against shipping oil, the crucial commodity needed to maintain the terror. So the circle hasn't turned too far.[47]

While Sevan's $150,000 was a major story for months, one would be hard-pressed to find a report of his July 1999 appeal to the Security Council, warning that "the improvement of the nutritional and health status of the Iraqi people through [a] multi-sectoral approach . . . is being seriously affected as a result of [the] excessive number of holds placed on supplies and equipment for water, sanitation and electricity." Most were blocked by US objections, including switches, sockets, window frames, ceramic tiles and paint, heart and lung machines, and many other items of "paramount importance to the welfare of the Iraqi people," Kofi Annan reported, while urging the Security Council to relax interventions that were "seriously impairing the effective implementation of the programme" to provide desperately needed humanitarian assistance.[48]

Unilateral US sanctions, even apart from those under a UN cover as in Iraq, overwhelm all others in scale. When powerful states are opposed to international sanctions, they simply evade them by one or another device: US evasion of UN sanctions against South Africa during the Reagan years and of OAS sanctions against the terrorist military junta in Haiti under Bush I and Clinton, to mention two examples. Those who have attended to the history of sanctions will not be surprised to learn that US sanctions on Iran are perceived by Iranian reformers as harmful to their cause. One of Iran's most influential intellectuals, Saeed Hajjarian, warns that "America is looking for any excuse—the nuclear issue, terrorism, human rights, the Middle East peace process" to impose pressures on Iran, which often "make the situation here more militarised, and in such an atmosphere democracy is killed." Known as "the brain of the reformists," Hajjarian was shot in the face by a Muslim militant in 2000, and though slowly recovering, he "is a reminder of the price some Iranians have paid for reform." He remains an opponent of sanctions, which "hurt the people," he says, and undermine democracy and reform, rejecting the comparison to South Africa, where the sanctions evaded by the Reaganites were welcomed by the black majority despite the harm caused them. That criterion, regularly ignored, should be a primary factor in judging the propriety of sanctions.[49]

There is no great secret about why Washington has been "looking for any excuse" to impose sanctions ever since Iranians dared to overthrow the brutal tyrant imposed by the US-UK coup that destroyed the Iranian parliamentary system in 1953. There is little need to tarry over the pretexts, which should shame and embarrass any honest observer.

SELF-EXCLUSION

In one of the many outraged comments on the justifications of torture provided by Justice Department lawyers, Dean Harold Koh of Yale Law School—who as an assistant secretary of state had presented Washington's denunciation of all forms of torture to the international community—said that "the notion that the president has the constitutional power to permit torture is like saying he has the constitutional power to commit genocide." The same legal advisers should have little difficulty arguing that the president does indeed have that right, so recent practice suggests.[50]

The torture convention is unusual in that it was ratified, though amended by the Senate. Few international conventions on human rights are even ratified, and those few are commonly accompanied by reservations rendering them inapplicable to the United States. They are deemed to be "non-self-executing," or subject to RUDs ("reservations, understandings, and declarations"). This includes the Genocide Convention, which the United States finally ratified forty years after it was drafted, but with the usual reservations. The matter reached the World Court in the context of NATO bombing of Serbia in 1999. When an international tribunal was established to try war crimes in the Balkan wars, a group of international lawyers requested the tribunal to investigate NATO crimes during the Serbian bombing campaign, presenting documentary evidence recorded by the major international human rights organizations, along with revealing admissions by the NATO command. The prosecutors rejected the request without investigation, in violation of the statutes of the tribunal, stating that they accepted NATO assurances of good faith. Yugoslavia then brought charges to the World Court, invoking the Genocide Convention. The US government excused itself, on grounds of its self-exclusion from charges of genocide. The court, keeping to its statutes, accepted this argument.[51]

There are other examples of self-exemption from core principles of international law, also of crucial contemporary relevance. One arose in the case brought to the World Court by Nicaragua against the United States. Part of Nicaragua's case, presented by Harvard University law professor and former legal adviser to the State Department Abram Chayes, was rejected by the court on the grounds that in accepting World Court jurisdiction in 1946, the United States had entered a reservation excluding itself from prosecution under multilateral treaties, including the UN Charter and the OAS Charter. The court therefore restricted its deliberations to customary international law and a bilateral US-Nicaragua treaty. Even on these very narrow grounds, the court charged Washington with "unlawful use of force"—in lay language, international terrorism—and ordered it to terminate the crimes and pay substantial reparations, which would go far beyond paying off the huge debt that is strangling Nicaragua. We return to the bitter aftermath. The relevant point here is that the court correctly recognized that the United States is self-exempted from the fundamental principles of world order that it played the primary role in formulating and enacting.[52]

It would seem to follow that Washington is entitled to commit aggression as well as genocide. Aggression, in the wording of the Nuremberg Tribunal, is "the supreme international crime differing only from other war crimes in that it contains within itself the accumulated evil of the whole"—all the evil in the tortured land of Iraq that flowed from the US and UK invasion, for example. That includes Abu Ghraib, Falluja, and everything else that happened in the "truly horrible and brutal [years] for hapless Iraq" since the invasion. And if, as seems reasonable, we take the "accumulated evil" to include effects outside Iraq itself, the accounting is still more grim, leading right to the "inescapable question."

The concept of aggression was defined clearly enough by Justice Robert Jackson, chief of counsel for the United States at Nuremberg, and was restated in an authoritative General Assembly resolution. An "aggressor," Jackson proposed to the tribunal in his opening statement, is a state that is the first to commit such actions as "Invasion of its armed forces, with or without a declaration of war, of the territory of another State," or "Provision of support to armed bands formed in the territory of another State, or refusal, notwithstanding the request of the invaded State, to take in its own territory, all the measures in its power to deprive those bands of all assistance or protection." The second provision clearly applies to the US war against Nicaragua, though giving the Reaganites the benefit of the doubt, one might consider them to be guilty only of the lesser crime of international terrorism on a scale without precedent. The first applies to the US and UK invasion of Iraq, unless we avail ourselves of the more imaginative devices of defense attorneys, for example, the proposal by one respected legal scholar that the United States and UK were acting in accord with the UN Charter under a "communitarian interpretation" of its provisions: they were carrying out the will of the international community, in a mission implicitly delegated to them because they alone had the power to carry it out. It is irrelevant that the international community vociferously objected—even more strongly if people are included within the international community.[53]

Also irrelevant are Justice Jackson's eloquent words at Nuremberg on the principle of universality: "If certain acts of violation of treaties are crimes, they are crimes whether the United States does them or whether Germany does them, and we are not prepared to lay down a rule of criminal conduct against others which we would not be willing to have invoked against us." And elsewhere: "We must never forget that the record on which we judge these defendants is the record on which history will judge us tomorrow. To pass these defendants a poisoned chalice is to put it to our own lips as well." Telford Taylor, Jackson's chief counsel for war crimes, writes that "those were beautiful words, but did the results match the aspiration?" Hardly, which I take it was Taylor's point. In the early phases of preparation for the tribunal, Taylor had already voiced his skepticism with regard to the core principle of Nuremberg, the crime of launching aggressive war. "This phase of the case," Taylor wrote, "is based on the assumption that it is, or will be declared, a punishable offense to plan and launch (and lose?) an aggressive war." It was indeed so declared at Nuremberg. But the principle of universality was quickly rescinded, and Taylor's concerns proved all too valid.[54]

The official explanation for Washington's self-exemption from the rule of law in the Nicaragua case, presented by State Department legal adviser Abram Sofaer, might also have received a nod of approval from Carl Schmitt. The World Court was disqualified for the same reasons as was the ICRC: it disagreed with Washington. Accordingly, it was a "hostile forum," as the *New York Times* editors concluded in approving Washington's rejection of court orders—which has left the United States in splendid isolation in defiance of World Court rulings, no longer in the exalted company of Muammar Qaddafi and Enver Hoxha, now that Libya and Albania have complied with the final judgments. The bias of the World Court in fact extends to the world generally, Sofaer explained. The world majority "often opposes the United States on important international questions," so that we must "reserve to ourselves the power to determine" which matters fall "essentially within the domestic jurisdiction of the United States, as determined by the United States"—in this case, international terrorism that practically destroyed the targeted country.[55]

The basic principles taught to the world by Sofaer were spelled out to Mexicans by Condoleezza Rice when she visited in March 2005 to ensure that they would live up to their obligations under a 1944 treaty to deliver water to the United States. That compliance was the only formal outcome of the seven-hour visit, the Mexican press reported, though Rice did comment on another matter of interest to Mexicans: Washington's abrupt withdrawal from the Vienna Convention on Consular Relations after the World Court ruled against the United States in the cases of fifty-one Mexicans who had been sentenced to death after the United States had violated their right to consult with officials from a Mexican consulate. "We will continue to believe in the importance of consular notification," Rice explained, but international court jurisdiction has "proven inappropriate for the United States." In short, the Mexican press concluded, "Rice was telling the Mexicans . . . that while they had a water treaty to live up to, the United States could simply withdraw from a signed agreement that it found 'inappropriate.' Confirming the enforceability of those different options was surely one of the things Rice's visit was all about."[56]

More generally, it is what international law is all about when those with the power to set the rules are permitted to do so by their own citizens. Neither Nicaraguans, nor Mexicans, nor many others need the instructions provided to them once again. A long history suffices.

The Vienna Convention was proposed by the United States in 1963 and ratified in 1969. The United States was the first country to invoke it before the World Court, successfully, in its suit against Iran after the 1979 hostage taking. International law and court judgments are fine, but only when they come out the right way. Anything else is "inappropriate for the United States."[57]

The basic problem with the World Court and the world, so we learn from UN ambassador John Bolton, is that they misinterpret international law. One of the administration's legal specialists, Bolton writes that "in the rest of the world, international law and its 'binding' obligations are taken for granted." But no such binding obligation can apply to the United States. That follows from the fact that the "accumulating force" of international law interferes with Washington's freedom to act as it chooses and "will even more dramatically impede us in the future." Treaties are not "legal" obligations for the United States, but at most "political" commitments. Therefore, contrary to what others mistakenly believe, it was quite appropriate for Washington to refuse to pay its UN dues from the Reagan years until 2001, when Washington changed course because it then needed international support. True, at Washington's initiative, the World Court ruled in 1962 that payment of UN dues is obligatory for members. But that ruling was applied to official enemies, and it was delivered before the World Court was disqualified by disagreeing with Washington. Nor does it matter that the US share of UN dues has always been below a rate that would accurately reflect US economic strength.[58]

The reasoning throughout is straightforward, and is in full accord with what Bush calls "new thinking in the law of war," which takes international law and treaties to be "private contractual rules" that the more powerful party "is free to apply or disregard as it sees fit": sternly enforced to ensure a safer world for investors, but quaint and obsolete when they constrain Washington's resort to aggression and other crimes.[59]

It would only be fair to add that in these respects the Bush administration is within the approved spectrum, which is quite narrow. The "new thinking" had been clearly formulated at the opposite extreme of the spectrum by the most prominent among the liberal "wise men" who are honored for having created the modern order, senior statesman and Kennedy adviser Dean Acheson. In January 1963, just after the Cuban missile crisis, Acheson instructed the American Society of International Law that no "legal issue" arises when the United States responds to a challenge to its "power, position, and prestige," as in Cuba. Acheson was surely aware that the international terrorist war that was a significant factor in driving the world to the brink of disaster had been quickly resumed by Kennedy when the missile crisis was resolved. It would not be easy to conjure up a more straightforward enunciation of the "new thinking"—which, throughout history, has been among the prerogatives of overwhelming power.[60]

THE FABRIC OF LAW ON WHICH SURVIVAL RESTS

Returning to the "inescapable question" posed by Russell and Einstein, another prominent strategic analyst who joins in the warnings of nuclear catastrophe is Michael MccGwire. He writes that under current policies, largely driven by Washington, "a nuclear exchange is ultimately inevitable," following the "dreadful logic" that should be familiar to anyone concerned with the fate of the species. "If present trends persist," he argues, "we are virtually certain to see a return to nuclear arms racing, involving intercontinental ballistic systems and space-based assets (offensive and defensive), reactivating the danger of inadvertent nuclear war," with a probability that "will be extremely high." As a step toward reducing the danger, he urges Britain to abandon its useless nuclear weapons, by now merely "the lace curtains of our political poverty." But the crucial choices, as everyone knows, are made in Washington. Comparing the two crises that literally threaten survival, MccGwire has this to say: "By comparison with global warming, the cost of eliminating nuclear weapons would be small. But the catastrophic results of global nuclear war would greatly exceed those of progressive climate change, because the effects would be instantaneous and could not be mitigated. The irony of the situation is that it is in our power to *eliminate* the threat of global nuclear war, but climate change cannot be evaded." The phrase "our power," again, refers primarily to the United States.[61]

MccGwire's immediate concern was the NPT and the regular five-year-review conference scheduled for May 2005, but more generally the threat to survival resulting from the dismantling of the rule of law. Reflecting on the Iraq invasion, he writes:

> There were many reasons—political, military, legal, ethical and economic—for concluding *before* the event that the decision to wage war on Iraq was fundamentally flawed. But in the longer term, by far the most important was that such an operation (and the reasoning that led to the decision to undertake it) threatened to undermine the very fabric of international relations. That decision repudiated a century of slow, intermittent and often painful progress towards an international system based on cooperative security, multilateral decision-making, collective action, agreed norms of behaviour and a steadily growing fabric of law

—which is being torn to shreds by the world's most powerful state, now a self-declared "outlaw state," taking perilous steps toward "ultimate doom."

The success of the effort "to *eliminate* the threat of global nuclear war" depends significantly on the effectiveness of the NPT. As MccGwire writes, the NPT "used to be seen as an unexpectedly successful example of international cooperation," but by now "it is more like a wisdom tooth that is rotten at its root, and the abscess is poisoning the international body politic." The NPT was based on two central agreements: "In return for renouncing the option of acquiring nuclear weapons for themselves, 'non-nuclear-weapon states' were promised, first, unimpeded access to nuclear energy for nonmilitary use, and second, progress on nuclear disarmament" by the five acknowledged nuclear-weapons states (the United States, United Kingdom, Russia, France, and China). At the May 2005 review conference, Washington's goal was to rescind both promises. That stand naturally reinforces the "cynical view," MccGwire writes, "that, whatever the original intentions, the NPT is now a convenient instrument of US foreign policy."[62]

A good case can be made for Washington's call for restricting Article IV of the NPT, which grants non-nuclear states the right to produce uranium fuel for reactors, bringing them, with contemporary technology, to just a step away from nuclear weapons. But to be more than mere cynicism, any such agreement would have to ensure "unimpeded access" for nonmilitary use, in accord with the initial bargain between declared nuclear powers and the non-nuclear states under the NPT. One reasonable proposal to this end was put forth by Nobel Peace Prize laureate Mohamed ElBaradei, head of the International Atomic Energy Agency (IAEA). ElBaradei suggested that all production and processing of weapon-usable material be restricted "exclusively to facilities under multinational control" and should be accompanied "above all, by an assurance that legitimate would-be users could get their supplies." That should be the first step, he argued, toward fully implementing the 1993 UN resolution calling for a Fissile Material Cutoff Treaty (FMCT, FISSBAN), which "could cap and make public all inventories of fissile material still available, and serve as a starting point for future arms reductions." This call for "a halt to the production of fissile materials for weapons," writes the distinguished Princeton arms control specialist Frank N. von Hippel, is "the most fundamental nuclear arms control proposal," putting a ceiling on the number of nuclear weapons that can be made. A second, crucial step would be the fulfillment of the pledge of the nuclear states to eliminate nuclear weapons.[63]

ElBaradei's proposal, regrettably, was dead in the water. The US political leadership, surely in its current stance, would never agree to the first step, thereby abrogating its unique exemption from international law and treaty obligations. And the more general framework remains mere words, as we see directly, and is likely to remain so unless the democratic deficit can be overcome in the reigning superpower. Washington's call for restricting Article IV is therefore regarded by much of the world, quite rationally, as the cynical intention to convert the NPT to what MccGwire calls "a convenient instrument of US foreign policy."

US specialists have presented other proposals, but all require faith in Washington's benign intentions. Graham Allison cites ElBaradei's proposal, keeping just to its first step, which he regards as "not practical . . . or feasible," a polite way of saying that Washington would not accept it. Instead, he advocates a system based on trust in the nuclear states (meaning the United States) to provide "unimpeded access" to nuclear

facilities. A more elaborate proposal for an Assured Nuclear Fuel Services Initiative (ANFSI) also suggests a "more pragmatic approach"
than ElBaradei's, recognizing that his proposal would be blocked by "di-
vergent national interests"—another oblique reference to likely US rejection. ANFSI calls for an array of "national and commercial assurances,"
reinforced by "a firm multilateral guarantee" and supervised by the
IAEA and the UN Security Council—hence all under the control of the
outlaw state that rejects their authority and regards "assurances" as subject to its will. Like Allison's, the ANFSI study does not explain why others should trust the United States to refrain from acting unilaterally to
terminate supplies when it so chooses, or to withdraw its first-use option
against non-nuclear states, thus at least reducing the need for a deterrent,
though not eliminating it until the nuclear states accept their part of the
NPT bargain.[64]

The scant media coverage of the May 2005 NPT five-year review
conference kept pretty much to Washington's agenda. As the conference opened, the *New York Times* reported that it "was meant to offer hope of closing huge loopholes in the treaty, which the United
States says Iran and North Korea have exploited to pursue nuclear
weapons." An accompanying map highlighted Tehran and Pyongyang, with the caption "Talk in Tehran and Pyongyang is dampening
nonproliferation hopes"—that is, Washington's agenda, not shared by
the world, nor by prominent strategic analysts. The report did note in
passing that Washington intends "to work around the United Nations,
and avoid subjecting the United States to a broad debate about
whether it is in compliance with its own obligations under the treaty,"
and that the Bush administration now unilaterally rejects some of the
thirteen steps toward nuclear disarmament that all parties at the 2000
NPT review conference had unanimously approved—a considerable
understatement. But such matters do not bear on the hopes that the
conference was "meant to" realize. The *New York Times* report on
the opening sessions focused almost entirely on Washington's demand
"that Iran dismantle all the 'equipment and facilities' it has built over
the past two decades to manufacture nuclear material." The *Times*
added, "Both American officials and officials of the International
Atomic Energy Agency said they were concerned that as Iran's June

elections draw nearer, a politically popular drive to restart the nuclear program may accelerate."[65]

The wording is of interest, including the casual recognition of the Bush administration's fear of democracy—hence the urgency to nullify expression of public opinion in an election. Also instructive is the phrase "the past two decades." The selected time span avoids the uncomfortable fact that the policies Washington now condemns, and the "huge loopholes in the treaty" that the conference was "meant to" close, are the very same policies and loopholes that the United States supported when Iran was under the rule of the shah, from 1953 to 1979. Today, the standard claim is that Iran has no need for nuclear power, so it must be pursuing a secret weapons program: "For an oil producer such as Iran, nuclear energy is a wasteful use of resources," Henry Kissinger explains. When the shah was in charge, Kissinger, as secretary of state, held that "introduction of nuclear power will both provide for the growing needs of Iran's economy and free remaining oil reserves for export or conversion to petrochemicals." Washington acted to assist these efforts, with Cheney, Wolfowitz, and Rumsfeld also playing significant roles. US universities (my own, MIT, for one, despite overwhelming student opposition) were arranging to train Iranian nuclear engineers, doubtless with Washington's approval, if not initiative. Asked about his reversal, Kissinger responded with his usual engaging frankness: "They were an allied country" before 1979, so therefore they had a genuine need for nuclear energy.[66]

Washington's charges about an Iranian nuclear weapons program may, for once, be accurate. As many analysts have observed, it would be remarkable if they were not. Reiterating the conclusion that the invasion of Iraq, as widely predicted, increased the threat of nuclear proliferation, Israeli military historian Martin van Creveld writes that "the world has witnessed how the United States attacked Iraq for, as it turned out, no reason at all. Had the Iranians not tried to build nuclear weapons, they would be crazy." Washington has gone out of its way to instruct Iran on the need for a powerful deterrent, not only by invading Iraq, but also by strengthening the offensive forces of its Israeli client, which already has hundreds of nuclear weapons as well as air and armored forces larger and more advanced than any NATO power other than the United States.

Since early 2004, the United States has sent Israel the biggest shipment of advanced jet bombers in its history. The planes, very publicly advertised as capable of bombing Iran, are equipped with unspecified "special weaponry" and deep-penetration bombs.[67]

It is likely that Washington's saber rattling is not a sign of impending war. It would not make much sense to signal an attack years in advance. The purpose may be to provoke the Iranian leadership to adopt more repressive policies. Such policies could foment internal disorder, perhaps weakening Iran enough so that the United States might hazard military action. They would also contribute to Washington's efforts to pressure allies to join in isolating Iran. The latter effect has been achieved. Such major European firms as Thyssen-Krupp and the British oil giant BP have withdrawn major investments in Iran, fearing US government sanctions or other consequences of actions "offensive to the US." In addition, US pressures are reported to have induced Japan to back away from plans to develop an enormous oil field in Iran.[68] But Iran is not devoid of options, which may find their place in much broader tendencies in world affairs, to which we will return in the afterword.

MccGwire reviews the reasons why Iran can be expected to develop a nuclear deterrent, in the light of Washington's hostile actions and threats and Iran's virtual encirclement by the global superpower and its powerful client, along with other nuclear-armed states. If logic and moral truisms mattered, the US and British governments and supporters of their doctrine of "anticipatory self-defense" should be calling on Iran to develop a nuclear deterrent. That Iran would initiate nuclear war is hardly plausible, unless it is intent on instant suicide. Surely Iran faces threats from the United States and Israel that are far more serious, imminent, and publicly advertised than any Washington or London could conjure up. Of course, every sane person hopes that ways will be found to prevent Iran from developing a nuclear weapons program. A sensible way to proceed, if this were the goal, would be to take ElBaradei's proposals seriously and to reduce, rather than escalate, the threats that, by US and UK standards, fully entitle Iran to develop a nuclear deterrent—in fact, to go far beyond. As is often noted, similar observations hold for North Korea. According to South Korean president Roh Moo-hyun, "North Korea professes that nuclear capabilities are a deterrent for defending itself from external aggression. In this particular case it is true and undeniable that there is a considerable element of rationality in North Korea's claim."[69]

Other US actions have had similar effects. Political scientist John Mearsheimer observes that India's determination to develop a nuclear deterrent was "hardened" by the Persian Gulf war of 1991 and the bombing of Serbia in 1999. "Had either foe possessed nuclear weapons, the United States might not have gone to war," a lesson that "was not lost on India"—and there were, in both cases, reasons to believe that peaceful options existed, particularly in 1999. Bush's endorsement of India's nuclear weapons program contributed further to erosion of the NPT. National security analyst Lawrence Korb points out that "India was not even compelled to stop producing fissile material for further weapons" in return for Bush's endorsement of its rejection of the NPT. The move was very dangerous, he adds, though not surprising, since "the Bush administration has demonstrated over the past five years that it does not believe the [NPT] to be worth preserving," even expressing "its disdain by dispatching a low-level State Department official to the important NPT Review Conference."[70]

Despite the focus on Iran and North Korea, the primary reason the NPT now faces collapse is the failure of the nuclear states to live up to their obligation under Article VI to pursue "good faith" efforts to eliminate nuclear weapons. That requirement was further underscored by a unanimous 1996 World Court judgment that the nuclear powers are legally obligated "to bring to a conclusion negotiations leading to nuclear disarmament in all its aspects under strict and effective international control." As long as they refuse, it is unlikely that the bargain will be sustained. ElBaradei merely reiterates the obvious when he emphasizes that "reluctance by one party to fulfil its obligations breeds reluctance in others." The United States has led the way in refusal to abide by the Article VI obligations and, under Bush, is alone in flatly rejecting the unanimous agreement at the 2000 conference on "an unequivocal undertaking by the nuclear-weapon states to accomplish the total elimination of their nuclear arsenals," along with the thirteen steps enumerated to carry this forward. While none of the nuclear states has met its obligations, the Bush administration has by far the worst record and stands alone in having explicitly renounced Article VI. At the 2005 NPT review conference, the Bush administration stated that "the United States balances its obligations under Article VI with our obligations to maintain our own security and the security of those who depend on us." At the close of the conference, the spokesperson for the US mission to the UN, Richard Grenell, went so far as to say "that the treaty requires reductions . . . but not the elimination of weapons," a transparent falsehood.[71]

More important than declarations are actions, such as plans to develop new nuclear weapons and a formal policy based on the "core assumption of indefinite US reliance on nuclear forces." That policy, if maintained, effectively terminates the NPT, which will wither away unless the United States recognizes that "a viable nonproliferation regime depends crucially on the implementation of the obligation to disarm nuclear weapons as well as the obligation not to acquire them." As MccGwire, McNamara, and others emphasize, another central part of the NPT compact was the commitment of the nuclear powers to enact and implement additional treaties: the Comprehensive Test Ban Treaty, rejected by the Senate in 1999 and declared off the agenda by Bush; the Anti-Ballistic Missile Treaty, which Bush rescinded; and, perhaps most important, a verifiable FISSBAN, which, according to Thomas Graham, Clinton's special representative for arms control, would prohibit the addition of "more nuclear bomb material to the vast amount" already in the world. In July 2004, Washington had announced its opposition to a verifiable FISSBAN on the grounds that effective verification "would require an inspection regime so extensive that it could compromise key signatories' core national security interests." Nevertheless, in November, the UN Committee on Disarmament voted in favor of a verifiable FISSBAN. The vote was 147 to 1, with two abstentions: Israel, which reflexively sides with the US position, and Britain, which explained its abstention on the grounds that the resolution "had divided the international community at a time when progress should be a prime objective"—divided it 147 to 1.[72]

A few days later, the General Assembly again reaffirmed "the importance and urgency of preventing an arms race in outer space and the readiness of all States to contribute to that common objective," and called upon "all States, in particular those with major space capabilities, to contribute actively to the objective of the peaceful use of outer space and of the prevention of an arms race in outer space and to refrain from actions contrary to that objective." The resolution passed 178 to 0, with four abstentions: the United States, Israel, Haiti, and Palau.[73]

Not surprisingly, the 2005 NPT review conference ended in complete failure. The main culprits were held to be Iran and Egypt. Iran was blamed for insisting on its right under the NPT to pursue the programs that Washington had supported when it was ruled by the shah; Egypt, for insisting that the conference discuss Israel's nuclear weapons, though it was aware that Washington would bar any reference to its leading client state. The unmentioned background is that Egypt was calling for adherence to the agreement at the 1995 NPT review conference that, in return for accepting unlimited extension of the NPT, Egypt and other Arab states would be assured that "attention be drawn to Israel's anomalous status as a de facto [nuclear weapons state] that had not signed the NPT and was not subject to IAEA safeguards." That agreement was one of the terms of the "'resolution on the Middle East' that was an integral part of the final 'package' of decisions—the 'bargain' adopted at [Review Conference] 95." However, "within a couple of years the United States was insisting that the resolution was relevant only to the discussions in 1995 and refusing to address its implementation, . . . a blatant example of bad faith" on Washington's part. Therefore, it was considered irresponsible for Egypt to bring the matter up, just as it is Egypt's fault, not Washington's, that Egypt continues to draw attention to Security Council Resolution 487, which *Calls upon* Israel urgently to place its nuclear facilities under the safeguards of the International Atomic Energy Agency."[74]

Though coverage of the failed 2005 NPT review generally kept to the US agenda, the diligent reader could learn more. The Associated Press reported that "the United States fought every reference to its 1995 and 2000 commitments," angering many delegates, among them the head of Canada's delegation, Paul Martin, whose speech at the conference stressed that "if governments simply ignore or discard commitments whenever they prove inconvenient, we will never be able to build an edifice of international cooperation and confidence in the security realm." Martin's remarks were "a thinly veiled criticism of Washington," the *Boston Globe* observed. After the review conference, former president Jimmy Carter also blasted the United States as

> the major culprit in this erosion of the NPT. While claiming to be protecting the world from proliferation threats in Iraq, Libya, Iran and North Korea, American leaders not only have abandoned existing treaty restraints but also have asserted plans to test and develop new weapons, including antiballistic missiles, the earth-penetrating "bunker buster" and perhaps some new "small" bombs. They also have abandoned past pledges and now threaten first use of nuclear weapons against non-nuclear states.[75]

Similarly, Robin Cook, who resigned as Tony Blair's foreign secretary to protest the decision to invade Iraq, wrote that Britain had maintained a fairly good record of compliance with the 2000 NPT review conference commitments, but its voice had been "obscured by our close identification with the Bush administration and our willingness in the review conference to lobby for understanding of their position" that "obligations under the non-proliferation treaty are mandatory on other nations and voluntary on the US." The usual standard. Accordingly, Washington felt quite free, "while the review conference was sitting," to proceed with plans to research new nuclear weapons "designed not to deter but to wage war," in contradiction to commitments "the US gave to the last review conference."[76]

On the eve of the May 2005 conference, Thomas Graham, Clinton's special representative for arms control, warned that "the NPT has never seemed weaker or the future less certain." If the treaty should fail, he suggested, a "nuclear nightmare world" may become reality. Like other analysts, Graham recognized that, while the other nuclear states share responsibility, the primary threat to the NPT is US government policy. The NPT may not have breathed its last, but the May 2005 conference was a serious blow.[77]

So we march on, following our leaders, toward an "Armageddon of our own making."

Chapter 3

Illegal but Legitimate

The hideous crimes of the twentieth century led to dedicated efforts to save humans from the curse of war. The word *save* is no exaggeration. It has been clear since 1945 that the likelihood of "ultimate doom" is much higher than any rational person should be willing to tolerate. These efforts to end war led to a broad consensus on the principles that should guide state action, formulated in the United Nations Charter, which in the United States is "the supreme law of the land." The charter opens by expressing the determination of the signatories "to save succeeding generations from the scourge of war, which twice in our lifetime has brought untold sorrow to mankind." The "scourge of war" had threatened not just "untold sorrow" but total destruction, as all the participants knew but refrained from mentioning. The words *atomic* and *nuclear* do not appear in the charter.

The postwar consensus on the use of force was reiterated in a December 2004 report by the UN High-level Panel on Threats, Challenges and Change, which included many prominent figures, among them Brent Scowcroft, who was the national security adviser for Bush I and has a long record in the military and security apparatus. The panel firmly endorsed the principles of the charter: force can be lawfully deployed only when authorized by the Security Council, or under Article 51 of the charter, which permits the "right of individual or collective self-defence if an armed attack occurs against a Member of the United Nations, until the Security Council has taken measures necessary to maintain international peace and security." Article 51 is commonly interpreted with sufficient latitude to allow the use of force when the "necessity of self-defense" is "instant, overwhelming, leaving no choice of means, no moment for deliberation," in Daniel Webster's classic phrase. Any other resort to force is a war crime, in fact the "supreme international crime," in the words of the Nuremberg Tribunal. The High-level Panel concluded that "Article 51 needs neither extension nor restriction of its long-understood scope" and "should be neither rewritten nor reinterpreted."[1]

The UN World Summit in September 2005 reaffirmed that "the relevant provisions of the Charter are sufficient to address the full range of threats to international peace and security," specifically, "the authority of the Security Council to mandate coercive action to maintain and restore international peace and security . . . acting in accordance with the purposes and principles of the Charter," and the role of the General Assembly in this regard "in accordance with the relevant provisions of the Charter." The summit further endorsed "the responsibility to commit ourselves, as necessary and appropriate, to helping States build capacity to protect their populations from genocide, war crimes, ethnic cleansing and crimes against humanity and to assisting those which are under stress before crises and conflicts break out." The summit granted no new "right of intervention" to individual states or regional alliances, whether under humanitarian or other professed grounds.[2]

The report of the December 2004 UN High-level Panel went on to say that "for those impatient with [their conclusion about Article 51], the answer must be that, in a world full of perceived potential threats, the risk to the global order and the norm of nonintervention on which it continues to be based is simply too great for the legality of unilateral preventive action, as distinct from collectively endorsed action, to be accepted. Allowing one to so act is to allow all."[3]

UNIVERSALITY

The panel is presupposing the principle of universality, perhaps the most elementary of moral truisms. The principle, however, is flatly rejected in the elite intellectual, moral, and political culture of the most powerful states, again raising the prospect of terminal catastrophe of which prominent analysts warn.

Formally, the postwar consensus on the principles governing the use of force remains in effect. It is, however, revealing—and disturbing—to see how the spectrum of opinion has shifted in Western elite sectors. While the consensus is not usually rejected explicitly (though sometimes it is), it is more likely to be ignored, taken to be too extreme to consider, and drifting to the margins of public discussion and electoral politics.

This departure from the postwar consensus was forcefully articulated in the last years of the millennium, when acclaim resonated across a broad political spectrum for Clinton's foreign policy, which had entered a "noble phase" with a "saintly glow," creating a "deep ideological divide between an idealistic New World bent on ending inhumanity and an Old World equally fatalistic about unending conflict." For the first time in history, a state—the "idealistic New World"—was observing "principles and values," acting from "altruism" and "moral fervor," while leading the "enlightened states." It was therefore free to resort to force for what its leaders determine to be right. These quotes are a small sample of an extraordinary deluge, drawn only from respected liberal voices. After several years of such flights of self-adulation, probably without historical precedent, a few events were brought forth as evidence for the pronouncements, foremost among them the 1999 NATO bombing of Serbia. It was with regard to that action that the phrase "illegal but legitimate" was coined.[4]

The discussion of Article 51 by the High-level Panel appears to have been both a response to the enthusiastic support by Western intellectuals for resort to violence that they determine to be legitimate, as well as a direct retort to the Bush doctrine of "anticipatory self-defense," articulated in the National Security Strategy of September 2002. The High-level Panel's discussion therefore takes on unusual significance, even apart from the fact that it reaffirms the stand of the world outside what the West calls "the international community," namely itself. Consider, for example, the Declaration of the South Summit in 2000, the highest-level meeting ever held by the former nonaligned movement, accounting for 80 percent of the world's population. Surely with the recent NATO bombing of Serbia in mind, the declaration firmly rejected "the so-called 'right' of humanitarian intervention." The declaration, which also provided a detailed and sophisticated analysis of neoliberal globalization, was ignored apart from scattered derision, a standard reaction to the bleatings of the *unpeople* of the world, to borrow the phrase of diplomatic historian Mark Curtis in the latest volume of his (predictably ignored) chronicle of Britain's postwar crimes.[5]

The Bush doctrine of "anticipatory self-defense" was outlined by a "senior American official," reported to be Condoleezza Rice, who explained that the phrase refers to "the right of the United States to attack a country that *it thinks* could attack it first." The formulation is not surprising, given her conclusion that international court jurisdiction has "proven inappropriate for the United States," and that the United States is not subject to "international law and norms" generally. Such views reflect a broad range of elite perceptions, but not those of the general public. A large majority of the American public continue to take the position that states are entitled to use force only if there is "strong evidence that the country is in imminent danger of being attacked." Thus this same large majority rejects the bipartisan consensus on "anticipatory self-defense" (sometimes mislabeled "preemptive war") and agrees with the much-maligned South Summit and the UN High-level Panel. The legitimacy of use of force is not the only issue on which public opinion in the United States diverges sharply from elite political culture. Another case, already mentioned, is the Kyoto protocols. And there are many others, matters bearing directly on the state of American democracy, to which we return in chapter six.[6]

The provisions of the UN Charter were spelled out further at the Nuremberg Tribunal. The accompanying Tokyo judgments were far more severe. Though the principles they enunciated were significant, both tribunals were deeply flawed; they were founded on rejection of the principle of universality. To bring the defeated war criminals to justice, it was necessary to devise definitions of "war crime" and "crime against humanity." How this was done was explained by Telford Taylor, chief counsel for war crimes prosecution and a distinguished international lawyer and historian:

> Since both sides had played the terrible game of urban destruction—the Allies far more successfully—there was no basis for criminal charges against Germans or Japanese, and in fact no such charges were brought. . . . Aerial bombardment had been used so extensively and ruthlessly on the Allied side as well as the Axis side that neither at Nuremberg nor Tokyo was the issue made a part of the trials.

The operative definition of "crime" is: Crime that you carried out but we did not. To underscore the fact, Nazi war criminals were absolved if the defense could show that their US and UK counterparts carried out the same crimes. Thus the tribunal excused Admiral Karl Dönitz from "breaches of the international law of submarine warfare" on grounds of testimony from the British Admiralty and US admiral Nimitz that the United States and UK had carried out the same crimes from the first days of the war.[7]

As Taylor explains, "to punish the foe—especially the vanquished foe—for conduct in which the enforcing nation has engaged, would be so grossly inequitable as to discredit the laws themselves." That is correct, but the operative definition of "crime" also discredits the laws themselves. Subsequent tribunals are discredited by the same moral flaw: the Yugoslavia Tribunal is an example already discussed, along with far more serious illustrations of Washington's self-exemption from international law and the fundamental principle of universality.

The consistency of practice and doctrine is understandable. Just consider the consequences if the privileged and powerful were willing to entertain for a moment the principle of universality. If the United States has the right of "anticipatory self-defense" against terror, or against those it *thinks* might attack it first, then, a fortiori, Cuba, Nicaragua, and a host of others have long been entitled to carry out terrorist acts within the United States because of its involvement in very serious terrorist attacks against them, often uncontroversial. Surely Iran would also be entitled to do so in the face of serious threats that are openly advertised. Such conclusions are, of course, utterly outrageous, and advocated by no one.

Outrageous conclusions would also follow about past crimes. An inquiry by several highly regarded British journalists shortly after 9/11 found that "Osama bin Laden and the Taliban received threats of possible American military strikes against them two months before the terrorist assaults on New York and Washington," which "raises the possibility that Bin Laden, far from launching the attacks on the World Trade Center in New York and the Pentagon out of the blue, was launching a pre-emptive strike in response to what he saw as US threats." By US and UK standards, that should be legitimate anticipatory self-defense. Again, the idea is unthinkable, of course.[8]

Similarly, no one would argue that Japan exercised the legitimate right of anticipatory self-defense when it bombed military bases in the virtual US colonies of Hawaii and the Philippines, even though the Japanese knew that B-17 Flying Fortresses were coming off the Boeing production lines and could read in the American press that the planes were capable of burning down Tokyo, a "city of rice-paper and wood houses." A November 1940 plan to "bomb Tokyo and other big cities" was enthusiastically received by Secretary of State Cordell Hull. FDR was "simply delighted" at the idea—described graphically by its mastermind, air force general Claire Lee Chennault: to "burn out the industrial heart of the Empire with fire-bomb attacks on the teeming bamboo ant heaps of Honshu and Kyushu." By July 1941, the air corps was ferrying B-17s to the Far East for this purpose, moving half of all the big bombers from the Atlantic sea-lanes to this region. If needed, the planes would be used "to set the paper cities of Japan on fire," General George C. Marshall explained in a confidential press briefing on November 15, adding that "there won't be any hesitation about bombing civilians." Four days later, *New York Times* senior correspondent Arthur Krock, presumably basing himself on Marshall's briefing, reported US plans to bomb Japan from Siberian and Philippine bases, to which the air force was rushing incendiary bombs intended for civilian targets. Washington knew from decoded messages that Japan was aware of the dispatch of B-17s.[9]

All of this provides far more powerful justification for anticipatory self-defense than anything conjured up by Bush, Blair, and their associates. There is no need to spell out what would plainly be implied, if elementary moral principles could be entertained.

Domestic and international law are not formal axiom systems. There is scope for interpretation, but their general meaning and implications are clear enough. As international law specialists Howard Friel and Richard Falk point out, "international law presents clear and authoritative standards with respect to the use of force and recourse to war that should be followed by *all* states," and if "under *exceptional* circumstances" any departure is allowed, "a heavy burden of persuasion is on the state claiming the exception." That should be the conventional understanding in a decent society. And so it appears to be among the general American population, though, in sharp contrast, the idea receives little expression within elite opinion. Friel and Falk add to the ample documentation of that conclusion with a detailed analysis of the "persistent refusal [of the *New York Times*] to consider international law arguments" that oppose the recourse to war and the conduct of war by American political leaders for the forty years they survey. The *Times*, they show, is "vigorous in its denunciation of global adversaries of the United States who contemplate aggressive wars or engage in hostile acts against American citizens" in violation of international law, but ignores such matters in the case of US actions. As one illustration, they point out that the words "UN Charter" or "international law" never appeared in its seventy editorials leading up to the invasion of Iraq, and they find that absence to be virtually uniform in opinion columns and other articles. They select the *Times* only because of its unusual importance but, as many other studies show, it is typical in these respects.[10]

The articulation of Washington's unilateral right to resort to force in the Bush administration's National Security Strategy broke little new ground. Writing in *Foreign Affairs* before the 2000 election, Condoleezza Rice, for example, had condemned the "reflexive appeal . . . to notions of international law and norms, and the belief that the support of many states—or even better, of institutions like the United

Nations—is essential to the legitimate exercise of power." The US government need not conform to "illusory 'norms' of international behavior," she explained, or "adhere to every international convention and agreement that someone thinks to propose." Clients and allies apart, all states of course must rigorously obey those norms, as the United States interprets them. Or else.[11]

This stand has long been conventional, even at the liberal end of the narrow US political spectrum: from the "wise men present at the creation" to the Clinton doctrine that the United States is entitled to resort to "unilateral use of military power" to ensure "uninhibited access to key markets, energy supplies, and strategic resources." Taken literally, the Clinton doctrine was more expansive than Bush's 2002 National Security Strategy, which aroused fear and concern around the world and immediately elicited harsh criticism from the heart of the foreign policy establishment. A response to the NSS in *Foreign Affairs*, for example, warned that Bush's "new imperial grand strategy" posed great dangers for the United States and the world. The more expansive Clinton doctrine, in contrast, was barely noticed. The reason was given by Clinton's secretary of state Madeleine Albright, who observed that every president has a position much like the Bush doctrine in his back pocket, but it is simply foolish to smash people in the face with it and to implement it in a manner that will infuriate even allies. A little tact is useful. It is not good form to declare: "There is no United Nations. There is an international community that occasionally can be led by the only real power left in the world—that's the United States—when it suits our interests and when we can get others to go along." Or perhaps it is good form. The words are those of UN ambassador John Bolton. While his style is more offensive than most, Bolton was following the precedent of President Bush and Secretary of State Powell, who instructed the UN that it could be "relevant" by endorsing US and UK plans to invade Iraq, or it could be a debating society.[12]

Amplifying the conclusion as she announced the Bolton nomination, Condoleezza Rice informed the world that "through history, some of our best ambassadors have been those with the strongest voices, ambassadors like Jeane Kirkpatrick and Daniel Patrick Moynihan." We need not tarry over Kirkpatrick's role at the UN, but Moynihan's is more interesting, since he gained much acclaim as a lonely and courageous fighter for the sanctity of international law, particularly during his tenure as ambassador to the United Nations, where he forthrightly condemned Idi Amin and defended Israel, acts that took real courage in New York. "Moynihan deserves great credit for his work at the United Nations," Jacob Weisberg writes in a typical encomium, expanding on an earlier tribute to Moynihan's dedication to international law in the same journal.[13]

Unmentioned, here and elsewhere, are Moynihan's most significant contributions to international law as UN ambassador. No others begin to approach the success that he proudly recounts in his memoirs: rendering the UN "utterly ineffective in whatever measures it undertook" to deter Indonesia's invasion of East Timor—which, he observes in passing, killed 60,000 people in the next few months, going on to become perhaps the closest approximation to genocide in the post–World War II period. All of this proceeded thanks to the generous diplomatic, military, and economic support of the United States, joined by the UK as atrocities peaked in 1978, with France and others joining to gain what benefits they could from cooperating with the aggressors. Finally, under great international and domestic pressure, Clinton informed the Indonesian generals in mid-September 1999 that the game was over. They instantly withdrew, revealing with brilliant clarity just where responsibility lies for the crimes of the preceding quarter century, to which Moynihan made a signal contribution, so he informs us.[14]

Rice's choices provide useful insight into what Bolton is expected to bring to the UN.

Henry Kissinger described the Bush doctrine as "revolutionary," undermining the seventeenth-century Westphalian system of international order (among the powerful), and of course subsequent international law. He approved of the doctrine, but with the standard qualifications about style and manner. He also added a crucial proviso. The doctrine, he said, must not be "universalized": the right to use force at will—to be an outlaw state—must be reserved to the United States alone, perhaps delegated to its clients. As often, Kissinger deserves credit for his honesty, and his understanding of intellectual opinion, which indicates no concern over such explicit demand for rights denied to others—rights with lethal impact, in this case.[15]

Kissinger's assessment was confirmed again in 2004, when the press reported the release of tapes of Nixon-Kissinger conversations. Among them were Nixon's instructions to Kissinger to order bombing of Cambodia, as he did, with these words: "A massive bombing campaign in Cambodia. *Anything that flies on anything that moves.*" One would be hard put to find a comparable call for monstrous war crimes, virtual genocide, in the archives of any state. It elicited no comment or reaction, as far as I could determine, even though the terrible consequences of those orders have long been known.[16]

Let us return to the Yugoslavia Tribunal, where Milošević was charged with genocide. The indictment was restricted to crimes in Kosovo. It kept almost entirely to crimes subsequent to the NATO bombing, which, as anticipated by the NATO command and the Clinton administration, elicited serious atrocities in reaction. Presumably because the Kosovo charges were so ambiguous, Bosnia was later added, specifically the charge of genocide at Srebrenica. That too raises a few questions, if only because after these events, Milošević was accepted by the United States and its allies as a partner for diplomatic settlement. A further problem is that the most detailed inquiry into the Srebrenica massacre, by the Dutch government, concluded that Milošević had no connection to it, and that he "was very upset when he learnt about the massacres," the Dutch scholar who headed the team of intelligence specialists reported. The study describes the "incredulity" in the Belgrade government, including Milošević, when they learned of the executions.[17]

Suppose we adopt prevailing Western opinion that such unwelcome facts are irrelevant. Even so, the prosecution has had considerable difficulty in establishing the charge of genocide. Suppose, however, that someone were to unearth a document in which Milošević orders the Serbian air force to reduce Bosnia or Kosovo to rubble, with the words "Anything that flies on anything that moves." The prosecutors would be overjoyed, the trial would be over, and Milošević would be sent off to many successive life sentences for the crime of genocide—a death sentence, if the tribunal followed US conventions. But as always, the principled exemption from moral truisms prevails.

PRECEDENTS

Prevailing elite attitudes on the use of force receive instructive expression in scholarly literature. A leading US historian, John Lewis Gaddis of Yale, published the first book to explore the historical origins of the Bush administration's "preemptive war" doctrine, which he basically supports, with the usual provisos about style, tactical flaws, and possible overreaching. The book was respectfully received in the scholarly literature, and "was so popular in the White House that Gaddis was invited over for a discussion."[18]

Gaddis traces the Bush doctrine to one of his intellectual heroes, the grand strategist John Quincy Adams. In the *New York Times* paraphrase, Gaddis "suggests that Bush's framework for fighting terrorism has its roots in the lofty, idealistic tradition of John Quincy Adams and Woodrow Wilson." Gaddis's scant references to Wilson focus on his interventions in Mexico and the Caribbean in alleged defense against Germany. Whatever one thinks of the validity of the pretexts, Wilson's shocking crimes in the course of those interventions, particularly in Haiti, are a curious—though conventional—illustration of his "lofty" idealism. The Adams example, Gaddis's centerpiece, is much more relevant to his main thesis on the roots of current doctrine—a realistic thesis, I believe, with significant implications for both understanding the past and considering what lies ahead.

As secretary of state under President James Monroe, Adams established "the lofty, idealistic tradition" in his justifications for General Andrew Jackson's conquest of Spanish-held Florida in the first Seminole war of 1818. The war was justified in self-defense, Adams argued. Gaddis concurs that the conquest was driven by legitimate security concerns. In his version, after Britain sacked Washington in 1814, Adams recognized that the country was in danger and adopted the principle that has always defined US strategic thinking: "Expansion, we have assumed, is the path to security." On this invariant American principle, the United States conquered Florida, and the doctrine has now been extended to the whole world by Bush. Gaddis concludes, plausibly, that when Bush warned "that Americans must 'be ready for preemptive action when necessary to defend our liberty and

to defend our lives,' he was echoing an old tradition rather than establishing a new one," reiterating principles that presidents from Adams
to Woodrow Wilson "would all have understood . . . very well." All
of Bush's predecessors, Gaddis explains, recognized that US security
was threatened by "failed states": dangerous power vacuums that the
United States should fill to guarantee its own security, from Florida in
1818 to Iraq in 2003.

Gaddis cites the right scholarly sources, primarily historian
William Earl Weeks, but omits what they say. We learn a lot about
the precedents for current doctrines, and the current consensus, by
examining the omitted information. Weeks describes in lurid detail
what Jackson was doing in the "exhibition of murder and plunder
known as the First Seminole war," which was just another phase in
his project of "removing or eliminating native Americans from the
southeast," under way long before the sacking of Washington in
1814—in a war declared by the United States. Far from inspiring
Adams's grand strategy, the sacking of Washington was apparently of
little concern to him even while he was negotiating the peace treaty
that ended the war.[19]

Florida was a problem both because it had not yet been incorporated into the expanding "American empire," in the terminology of
the Founding Fathers, and because it was a "haven for Indians and
runaway slaves . . . fleeing either the wrath of Jackson or slavery."
There was an Indian attack, which Jackson and Adams used as a pretext. After US forces had driven a band of Seminoles off their lands,
killing several and burning their village to the ground, members of the
tribe retaliated by attacking a supply boat under military command.
Seizing the opportunity, Jackson "embarked on a campaign of terror,
devastation, and intimidation," destroying villages and "sources of
food in a calculated effort to inflict starvation on the tribes." So matters continued, leading to Adams's endorsement of Jackson's attempt
to establish in Florida "the dominion of this republic upon the odious
basis of violence and bloodshed." These words of the Spanish ambassador are a "painfully precise description" of Adams's stand, Weeks
writes. Adams "had consciously distorted, dissembled, and lied about
the goals and conduct of American foreign policy to both Congress

and the public," grossly violating his proclaimed moral principles, "implicitly defending Indian removal, slavery, and the use of military force without congressional approval." The crimes of Jackson and Adams "proved but a prelude to a second war of extermination" against the Seminoles, in which the remnants either fled westward, to suffer the same fate later, "or were killed or forced to take refuge in the dense swamps of Florida." Today, Weeks observes, "the Seminoles survive in the national consciousness as the mascot of Florida State University"—an example that is all too familiar, and a "painfully precise" reflection of how we make use of our freedom, while condemning with derision those who refuse to face up to their own sordid past.

Adams recognized the "absurdity" of his justifications, Weeks explains, but felt that—in Adams's own words—"it was better to err on the side of vigor than on the side of weakness": to speak in ways "clearer than truth," as Dean Acheson was later to express the sentiment. The account Adams gave, Weeks writes, "stands as a monumental distortion of the causes and conduct of Jackson's conquest of Florida, reminding historians not to search for truth in official explanations of events." Sound advice, to the present. Elsewhere Weeks notes that Adams's distortions were publicly revealed in the report of a special Senate committee charged with investigating the Seminole war, which concluded that Jackson had inflicted "a wound on the national character" with the support of Adams, who alone persuaded Monroe to endorse Jackson's crimes. "But few Americans took much notice of these criticisms," Weeks notes. "Adams's bold defense of Jackson had shifted the focus from international law and constitutional scruple to a sacred narrative of American 'right' versus Spanish, Indian, and British 'wrong.' "[20]

Weeks stresses the important point that by endorsing Jackson's crimes, Adams transferred the power to make war from Congress to the executive branch, in violation of the Constitution. He was isolated in taking that stand. The editor of Adams's papers writes that President Monroe and all the members of his cabinet, except Adams, "were of the opinion that Jackson had acted 'not only without, but against, his instructions; that he had committed war upon Spain, which cannot be justified, and which if not disavowed by the Administration, they will

be abandoned by the country' "—a prediction that was quickly refuted.[21]

Near the end of his life, Adams bitterly condemned this usurpation
of the congressional power to make war. In an 1847 letter to another
sharp critic of the Mexican war, he denounced President Polk's war
message as "a direct and notorious violation of the truth," lamenting
that "it is now established as an irreversible precedent that the President
of the United States has but to declare that war exists . . . and the war is
essentially declared." Adams finally recognized "the danger to liberty
and republicanism" implied by his shredding of the Constitution, but
"seems not to have acknowledged his part in establishing the precedent," Weeks comments. The principle remains in force, not troubling
the "originalists" who pride themselves on their strict adherence to the
intentions of the framers. The principle continues to undermine liberty
and democracy, not to speak of the fate of the victims of executive wars.

Weeks points out that Adams also established the "presidential
'rhetoric of empire' designed to marshal public (as well as congressional) support for its policies." The rhetorical framework, "a durable
and essential aspect of American diplomacy inherited and elaborated
by successive generations of American statesmen but fundamentally
unchanged over time," rests on three pillars: "the assumption of the
unique moral virtue of the United States, the assertion of its mission to
redeem the world" by spreading its professed ideals and the "American way of life," and, always, "the faith in the nation's divinely or-
dained destiny." The theological framework reduces policy issues to a
choice between good and evil, thus undercutting reasoned debate and
fending off the threat of democracy.

The issue of defense against Britain, the only credible enemy—
more accurately, deterrent—did not arise. British minister Castlereagh
was so eager to cement Anglo-American relations that he even over-
looked Jackson's murder of two innocent British citizens, which
Adams defended for its "salutary efficacy for terror and example."
Adams was heeding the words of Tacitus, his favorite historian, Weeks
suggests: that "crime once exposed had no refuge but in audacity."

The goal of Adams's diplomacy was not security in any meaningful
sense, but rather territorial expansion. British military power barred the

conquest of Canada and also Cuba, which, Adams predicted, would drop into US hands by the laws of "political gravitation," just as "an apple severed by a tempest from its native tree cannot but choose to fall to the ground," once the United States succeeded in subduing its British rival. By the end of the century, the laws of political gravitation had shifted, as Adams had anticipated. The British deterrent was overcome and the United States was able to intervene in Cuba in 1898. The pretext was to liberate Cuba from Spain. The effect, however, was to block Cuba's liberation and to turn it into a "virtual colony," as it remained until 1959.[22]

Jacksonian Democrats worked hard to shift the laws of political gravitation, matters discussed in another important scholarly work that Gaddis cites, by Thomas Hietala. What Gaddis omits is again informative. Hietala describes the efforts of the Jacksonians to gain a monopoly over cotton, which played roughly the same role in the industrial economies as petroleum does today. "By securing the virtual monopoly of the cotton plant," President Tyler observed after the annexation of Texas in 1845 and the conquest of almost half of Mexico, the United States had acquired "a greater influence over the affairs of the world than would be found in armies however strong, or navies however numerous." He went on to say that the monopoly over cotton "now secured, places all other nations at our feet. . . . An embargo of a single year would produce in Europe a greater amount of suffering than a fifty years' war. I doubt whether Great Britain could avoid convulsions." President Polk's secretary of the Treasury informed Congress that the conquests would guarantee "the command of the trade of the world." The same monopoly power neutralized British opposition to the takeover of the Oregon Territory—title to which had been granted by the will of God, Adams informed Congress, echoing sentiments that had by then become almost a cliché.[23]

It is perhaps of some interest that the logic of the annexation of Texas was essentially that attributed to Saddam Hussein when he conquered Kuwait. There are, of course, many differences. Iraq's claim to Kuwait had deep roots, stemming from the days when Britain established the borders of Iraq to ensure that Britain, not Turkey, would have control of the oil of the north, and that the

British colony of Kuwait would effectively bar Iraq's access to the sea. Furthermore, Saddam Hussein did not mimic Jacksonian Democrats in expressing his fear that slavery in Iraq would be threatened by independent states nearby, and he may not have invoked divine Providence, at least with such eloquence. As far as I know, leading Iraqi intellectuals did not call for "miserable, inefficient Kuwait" to be taken over to carry forward "the great mission of peopling the Middle East with a noble race" of Iraqis, nor declare that "it is very certain that the strong Iraqi race which has now overrun much of the region, must also overrun that trace, and the Arabian peninsula also, and it will in the course of ages be of small import by what particular occasions and methods it was done"—to quote Walt Whitman and Ralph Waldo Emerson speaking of Mexico and the Oregon Territory (with appropriate change of names). And no one alleged that Saddam Hussein in his wildest dreams might have hoped to gain control over the world to anything like the extent of the ambitions of the Jacksonian Democrats—always in self-defense, and pursuant to God's will.

Filling in these and many other instructive omissions, the picture provided by Gaddis's scholarly sources lends considerable support to his judgment about the origins of the Bush doctrine and its implementation, from Adams through "Wilsonian idealism," and on to the present. As for the expansion of the precedents to the entire world, others must judge for themselves. And they have. Fear and often hatred of the United States have risen to unprecedented heights, significantly increasing the threat of terror and the likelihood of "ultimate doom." The current space-age version of the Adams doctrine that "expansion . . . is the path to security" is having the same effect.

THE NORMATIVE REVOLUTION

As illustrated above, there is a spectrum of articulate opinion on the resort to military force. At one extreme is the postwar consensus formally articulated in the UN Charter, reiterated at the South Summit, and recently again by the UN High-level Panel and the UN World Summit a year later. The rest of the spectrum—keeping to its liberal internationalist end—basically adopts the principle that the United States is uniquely exempt from international law and jurisdiction, and is accordingly entitled to resort to any measures it chooses to respond to a challenge to its "power, position, and prestige" and to ensure "uninhibited access to key markets, energy supplies, and strategic resources." I should stress again, however, that the American public appears to keep quite firmly to the postwar consensus that is virtually excluded from the political system and general commentary.

At the margins we do find more nuanced opinions on the resort to force. One of the most important is the study by the International Independent Commission of Inquiry on the Kosovo war, headed by the distinguished South African jurist Richard Goldstone. The commission rendered the harshest criticism anywhere near the mainstream of the NATO bombing of Serbia in 1999, concluding that the bombing was "illegal but legitimate": "It was illegal because it did not receive approval from the UN Security Council, but it was legitimate because all diplomatic avenues had been exhausted and there was no other way to stop the killings and atrocities in Kosovo." Goldstone suggested that the UN Charter might need revision in the light of the report of the commission (the conclusion that was explicitly rejected by the High-level Panel in December 2004). The NATO intervention, he explained, "is too important a precedent" for it to be regarded as "an aberration." Rather, "state sovereignty is being redefined in the face of globalization and the resolve by the majority of the peoples of the world that human rights have become the business of the international community." Goldstone also stressed the need for "objective analysis of human rights abuses."[24]

The last comment is good advice. One question that objective analysis might address is whether indeed "the majority of the peoples of the world" accept the judgment of the United States, the United Kingdom, and some allies on the bombing of Serbia. Review of the world press and official statements reveals little support for that conclusion, to put it mildly. In fact, the bombing of Serbia was bitterly condemned outside the NATO countries, with little notice in the United States. Furthermore, it is hardly likely that the decision of the self-declared "enlightened states" to exempt themselves from the UN Charter and the Nuremberg principles would gain the approval of much of the world's population. Another question that objective analysis might address is whether indeed "all diplomatic options had been exhausted" in Kosovo. This conclusion, too, is not easy to sustain. When NATO decided to bomb, there were two diplomatic options on the table: a NATO proposal and a Serbian proposal (the latter kept from the public in the United States, perhaps the West in general). After seventy-eight days of bombing, a compromise was reached between them (though violated at once by NATO), so it appears that diplomatic options were available, after all. A third question is whether "there was no other way to stop the killings and atrocities in Kosovo," as the independent commission asserts, clearly a crucial matter. Here objective analysis happens to be unusually easy. There is a vast documentary record available from impeccable Western sources, including several compilations by the State Department released in justification of the war, in addition to detailed records of the Organization for Security and Co-operation in Europe (OSCE) and NATO, the international Kosovo Verification Mission (KVM) monitors, the UN, and a lengthy British parliamentary inquiry. They all reach the same conclusion: the killings and atrocities did not precede but followed the bombing, as the indictment of Milošević has also revealed. That could hardly have come as a surprise. The violence was predicted by NATO commander Wesley Clark as soon as the bombing began, quite publicly. Other sources make clear that the Clinton administration also anticipated the crimes that followed the bombing, as Clark confirms in more detail in his memoirs. It is hard to imagine that other NATO authorities were more deluded.[25]

In the extensive literature on the topic, from media to scholarship, this documentation is almost universally ignored and the chronology reversed. I have reviewed the dismal record elsewhere, and will put it aside here, with only a few current examples to illustrate the effect of consistent fabrication in support of state power and the systematic refusal even to look at unwanted fact, however trusted the source.

Former secretary of defense Frank Carlucci writes that NATO bombed after "Milosevic embarked on an ethnic cleansing operation" and other atrocities. The inversion of chronology is typical; it is un-controversial that the atrocities he describes were the anticipated con-sequence of the bombing, not its cause. Historian Niall Ferguson states, without evidence, that "there was a plausible ground for intervention—to avert genocide." David Rieff presents what he calls evidence: "According to both German intelligence officials and Greek diplomats . . . the Belgrade authorities had always intended to deport a large number of Kosovars (the usual figure was 350,000)." Even if Rieff's unidentified sources exist, they would be meaningless. To dis-cover that Belgrade had contingency plans to expel Kosovars, we do not have to adduce unknown "officials and diplomats." It would have been astonishing had they not had such plans, just as other states do, including the "enlightened states." It is an extraordinary comment on Western intellectual culture that people can take seriously someone who adduces such reasons to justify his own state's carrying out ag-gression that, as he himself acknowledges, led to the forcible deporta-tion of some 800,000 Kosovars, among other atrocities. Crossing the Atlantic, Karl-Heinz Kamp, of the Adenauer Foundation, criticizes the December 2004 UN panel because it rejected NATO's right to resort to force in violation of the charter. He cites one example, the usual one: the NATO bombing of Serbia, which was undertaken, he asserts without evidence, because "NATO placed a higher value on the pro-tection of human rights than on obedience to the charter"—namely by bombing with the expectation that so doing would elicit massive human rights violations, as it did.[26]

Some of the examples descend to low comedy. Thus to illustrate the highbrow "anti-Americanism" that reigns beyond our shores, com-mentator James Traub takes as his example the Nobel Prize awarded in 2005 to playwright Harold Pinter, whose "politics are so extreme that they're almost impossible to parody." The proof is Pinter's out-rage over "NATO's 1999 air war in Kosovo," which, according to Traub, he described as "a criminal act . . . designed to consolidate 'American domination of Europe.'" All right-thinking people, Traub explains, know that "the bombing was essentially a last resort in the face of Slobodan Milosevic's savage campaign of ethnic cleansing." While such crazed ideas flourish among European highbrows, Traub continues, within our more sober intellectual culture "it is hard to think of anyone save Noam Chomsky and Gore Vidal who would not choke on Pinter's bile." It is actually not so hard to think of others. One choice could be the only American author (to my knowledge) who has actually taken the position "so extreme that it is impossible to parody": the respected academic military historian Andrew Bacevich, author of a well-known book in which he dismissed the pretense of humanitarian motive for the Kosovo war, or the Bosnia intervention, charging that they were undertaken solely to ensure "the cohesion of NATO and the credibility of American power" and to "sustain American primacy" in Europe. Among others who might not choke are those who have not been content with propaganda so vulgar that it was even refuted by the daily press reports at the time, and who may even have taken the trouble to look at the massive official documentation on the chronology of the bombing and ethnic cleansing, which reveals conclusively that the truth is precisely the opposite of Traub's anguished lament. Though the facts are uncontroversial, they are clearly irrelevant, for reasons that Traub rightly explains: it is impossible to "dissuade implacable ideologues, any more than you can an implacable jihadist."[27]

Justice Goldstone is unusual in that he does recognize the facts. In his words: "The direct result of the bombing was that almost one million people fled Kosovo into neighboring countries and about 500,000 people were displaced within Kosovo itself, a tremendous catastrophe for the people of Kosovo"—compounded by serious crimes under Western military occupation afterward. Reviewing the (anticipated) consequences of the bombing, Justice Goldstone adds that supporters of the war "had to console themselves with the belief that 'Operation Horseshoe,' the Serb plan of ethnic cleansing directed against the Albanians in Kosovo, had been set in motion before the bombing." That is small consolation, however. The rich Western documentary record reveals no significant changes in Serbian practices before the bombing was announced and the monitors withdrawn, and makes it clear that the major atrocities, including expulsion, began later. As for Operation Horseshoe, Wesley Clark reported several weeks after the bombing that he knew nothing about it. Publicized by NATO powers after the shocking effects of the bombing were evident, it was long ago exposed as a probable intelligence fabrication. In fact it is rather odd that it continues to be cited in scholarship and journalism, since there is no need to fabricate. As mentioned, it can hardly be doubted that Serbia had such contingency plans in the event of a NATO attack, just as Israel surely has contingency plans to expel the Palestinian population in some emergency. As for US contingency plans, those we know of are utterly shocking, and one hardly expects others to be particularly gentle.[28]

Kosovo was an ugly place before the NATO bombing—though, regrettably, not by international standards. According to Western sources, about 2,000 people were killed on all sides in the year prior to the invasion, many by Kosovo Liberation Army (KLA) guerrillas attacking Serbs from Albania in an effort, as they openly stated, to elicit a harsh Serbian response that could rally Western opinion to their cause. The British government makes the remarkable claim that up until January 1999, most of the 2,000 were killed by the KLA, and Western sources consistently report that there was no significant change until the NATO war was announced and implemented. One of the few serious scholarly studies even to pay attention to these matters estimates that Serbs were responsible for 500 of the 2,000 killed. This is the careful and judicious study by Nicholas Wheeler, who supports the NATO bombing on the grounds that there would have been worse atrocities if NATO had not bombed. The fact that these are the strongest arguments that can be contrived by serious analysts tells us a good deal about the decision to bomb, particularly when we recall that there were diplomatic options.[29]

It is perhaps worth mentioning an astonishing justification for the bombing contrived by some of its supporters, though not put forth by British and American authorities: that the NATO attack was justified by the crimes at Srebrenica, or Bosnia generally. Suppose we try to take the argument seriously. If we do, it is easy to show that the same humanitarians should have been calling even more stridently for the bombing of Washington and London. To mention just the most obvious reason, as the war drums were beating over Kosovo in early 1999, Indonesia began to escalate its crimes in East Timor. Its record in early 1999 was far more criminal than anything reported from Kosovo, even putting aside the fact that this was illegally occupied territory. Furthermore, the Indonesian military openly announced that much worse would come unless the Timorese agreed to annexation by Indonesia in an August referendum—and they lived up to their word. Their earlier crimes in East Timor go vastly beyond Srebrenica or anything plausibly attributed to Serbia. And, crucially, these crimes, approaching true genocide, were supported throughout by the United States and Britain (also France and others), continuing right through the atrocities of August–September 1999, which finally aroused sufficient protest that Clinton called off the hounds. The conclusion follows at once, and suffices to reveal the shocking immorality of the Srebrenica excuse for bombing.

The actual reasons for the war were not concealed. Putting aside the predictable—hence meaningless—professions of benign intent and the usual chronological fabrications, the primary reasons were stressed clearly throughout by Clinton, Blair, and others, reaffirmed by Secretary of Defense William Cohen, and confirmed by Clark's memoirs: to assure "the credibility of NATO," meaning the United States, the position extended to extremes by Andrew Bacevich. Nevertheless, the bombing of Serbia "has gone down in history as a victory of military might deployed in the service of liberal humanitarianism," the liberal *Boston Globe* reports approvingly, and accurately. When history is crafted in the service of power, evidence and rationality are irrelevant.[30]

Kosovo was one of the two great achievements brought forth to give retrospective proof that for the first time in history, states were observing "principles and values" under the guidance of their "noble" and "altruistic" Anglo-American tutors, and that the UN Charter must be revised to allow the West to carry out "humanitarian intervention." The other was East Timor. The example is truly atrocious. That it can even be brought up without shame is a remarkable comment on Western intellectual culture. The matter is extensively reviewed in print, so I will skip it, along with some other recent examples that merit discussion, which I think lead to the same conclusions. It is worth noting, however, that the Iraq war was also justified as "illegal but legitimate," though some legal scholars who took that stand rescinded it after the collapse of the pretexts, concluding that "the invasion was both illegal and illegitimate" (Anne-Marie Slaughter, dean of the Woodrow Wilson School at Princeton and president of the American Society of International Law).[31]

FEW QUESTIONS ARE more important today than the propriety of the use of force. No doubt one can imagine, perhaps even find, genuine cases of humanitarian intervention. But there is, always, a heavy burden of proof. And the historical record should give us pause. We might recall, for example, the observations of one of the major scholarly studies of humanitarian intervention. The author finds three examples of such intervention between the 1928 Kellogg-Briand pact outlawing war and the UN Charter in 1945: Japan's invasion of Manchuria and northern China, Mussolini's invasion of Ethiopia, and Hitler's takeover of parts of Czechoslovakia. Not, of course, that he regards these as genuine examples, but rather that they were depicted as such, and evidence was provided, which, however grotesque, was regarded with some ambivalence—and sometimes support—by the United States and Britain.[32]

Inquiry might also unearth genuine cases of intervention that are "illegal but legitimate," though the prize example offered leaves this as a dubious doctrine for the times. It also tends to reinforce the measured judgment of the World Court, in 1949, that "the Court can only regard the alleged right of intervention as the manifestation of a policy of force, such as has, in the past, given rise to most serious abuses and such as cannot, whatever be the defects in international organization, find a place in international law . . . ; from the nature of things, [intervention] would be reserved for the most powerful states, and might easily lead to perverting the administration of justice itself."[33]

Inquiry very definitely does reveal that state terror and other forms of threat and use of force have brought vast suffering and destruction, and have sometimes brought the world very close to the edge of disaster. It is shocking to observe how easily such discoveries are ignored in the intellectual culture. Such observations—and they are all too well confirmed—lead us back to the challenge of Russell and Einstein fifty years ago, which we ignore at our peril.

Chapter 4

Democracy Promotion Abroad

"The promotion of democracy is central to the George W. Bush administration's prosecution of both the war on terrorism and its overall grand strategy." So begins the most extensive scholarly article on "the roots of the Bush doctrine." The statement is unsurprising. By 2005, it had reached the level of ritual. In scholarship we routinely read that the conviction that democracy can be imposed from the outside "is the assumption driving America's intervention in Iraq" and has been "posited as a potential new pillar of ambition for US foreign policy elsewhere." The pronouncement is sometimes amplified: "promoting democracy abroad" has been a primary goal of US foreign policy ever since Woodrow Wilson endowed it with a "powerful idealist element"; it gained "particular salience" under Ronald Reagan, and then was taken up with "unprecedented forcefulness" under Bush II. In journalism and commentary, the assumption is taken to be the merest truism.[1]

When an assertion of such obvious importance is adopted with near unanimity, a sensible reaction is to investigate the evidence produced both for and against the thesis. The character of that evidence gives a certain measure of functioning democracy. To go to the extreme, if similar declarations are produced in North Korea, no one troubles to ask about the evidence: it suffices that the Dear Leader has spoken. In a democratic culture, substantial evidence should be required along with serious argument refuting apparent counterevidence. We will return to these questions in the case of the Bush doctrine. But first some reflections on relevant background.

It is no easy task to gain some understanding of human affairs. In some respects, the task is harder than in the natural sciences. Mother Nature doesn't provide the answers on a silver platter, but at least she does not go out of her way to set up barriers to understanding. In human affairs, such barriers are the norm. It is necessary to dismantle the structures of deception erected by doctrinal systems, which adopt a range of devices that flow very naturally from the ways in which power is concentrated.

Sometimes eminent figures are kind enough to provide us with some assistance in the task. In 1981, Samuel Huntington, professor of the science of government at Harvard University, explained the function of the Soviet threat: "you may have to sell" intervention or other military action "in such a way as to create the misimpression that it is the Soviet Union that you are fighting. That is what the United States has done ever since the Truman Doctrine." On the same grounds, he warned a few years later, Mikhail Gorbachev's "public relations can be as much a threat to American interests in Europe as were [Leonid] Brezhnev's tanks."[2]

To facilitate the marketing effort, doctrinal systems commonly portray the current enemy as diabolical by its very nature. The characterization is sometimes accurate, but crimes are rarely the reason for demanding forceful measures against a selected target. One of many sources of evidence for this is the easy transition a state may make from favored friend and ally (who, irrelevantly, commits monstrous crimes) to ultimate evil that has to be destroyed (because of those very same crimes).

A recent illustration is Saddam Hussein. The impassioned denunciations of the awful crimes of Saddam that impelled the United States to punish the people of Iraq managed to avoid the words "committed with our help, because we do not care about atrocities that contribute to our ends." As already noted, discipline remained in force as Saddam was brought to trial for his crimes. The first trial dealt with atrocities he had committed in 1982—the year when the

Reagan administration dropped Iraq from the list of states supporting terrorism so that military and other aid could flow to the murderous tyrant, aid that continued until he committed the first crime that mattered: disobeying (or possibly misunderstanding) US orders in August 1990. The facts are hardly obscure, but fall under the "general tacit agreement that 'it wouldn't do' to mention that particular fact," in Orwell's phrase.[3]

"EXCEPTIONALISM"

Huntington's observation generalizes broadly, but is only part of the story. It is necessary to create misimpressions not only about the current "Great Satans," but also about one's own unique nobility. In particular, aggression and terror must be portrayed as self-defense and dedication to inspiring visions. Japanese emperor Hirohito was merely repeating a broken record when he said in his surrender speech of August 1945, "We declared war on America and Britain out of Our sincere desire to ensure Japan's self-preservation and the stabilization of East Asia, it being far from Our thought either to infringe upon the sovereignty of other nations or to embark upon territorial aggrandizement." There is little reason to doubt the emperor's sincerity; still more uplifting rhetoric accompanied the Japanese invasions of Manchuria and northern China, even in internal state records. The history of international crimes overflows with similar sentiments. Writing in 1935, with the dark clouds of Nazism settling, Martin Heidegger declared that Germany must now forestall "the peril of world darkening" *outside* the borders of Germany, which was defending the "supreme possibility of human being, as fashioned by the Greeks" from the "active onslaught that destroys all rank and every world-creating impulse of the spirit." With its "new spiritual energies" revived under Nazi rule, Germany was at last able "to take on its historic mission" of saving the world from "annihilation" at the hands of the "indifferent mass" elsewhere, primarily in the United States and Russia.[4]

Even individuals of the highest intelligence and moral integrity succumb to the pathology. At the peak of Britain's crimes in India and China, of which he had an intimate knowledge, John Stuart Mill wrote his classic essay on humanitarian intervention, in which he urged Britain to undertake the enterprise vigorously—specifically, to conquer even more of India, thus gaining greater control over the opium production that was needed to force open Chinese markets and pay the costs of empire. Britain should pursue this course, he argued, even though it would be "held up to obloquy" by backward Europeans, unable to comprehend that England was "a novelty in the world," an angelic nation that acted only "in the service of others," desired "no benefit to itself," and was "blameless and laudable" in everything it did. England, Mill explained, selflessly bore the costs of bringing peace and justice to the world, while "the fruits it shares in fraternal equality with the whole human race," including the "barbarians" it conquered and destroyed for their own benefit. There is no need to tarry on France's "civilizing mission" and its many counterparts.[5]

The famed "American exceptionalism" merits some skepticism; the image of righteous exceptionalism appears to be close to universal. Also close to universal is the responsibility of the educated classes to endorse with due solemnity the sincerity of the high-minded principles proclaimed by leaders, on the basis of no evidence apart from their declarations, though it is often conceded that their actions systematically refute their noble visions. We then face a puzzling paradox, which is miraculously resolved in the United States by proclaiming a sudden "change of course"—an event that takes place every few years, effacing inappropriate history as we march on to a glorious future. One of its constant themes is the dedication to bring justice and freedom to a suffering world, recently resurrected as the driving passion for "democracy promotion."

There are always recalcitrants who raise questions about official pronouncements. Some even go as far as Adam Smith, who had little use for England's posture of noble intent. Smith held that "the principal architects" of global policy, "our merchants and manufacturers," have sought to ensure that their own interests have "been most peculiarly attended to," however "grievous" the impact on others, particularly the victims of their "savage injustice" in India and elsewhere, but even the domestic population. Smith therefore falls into the category of "conspiracy theorists," people who attend to the historical and documentary record, and to domestic structures of power and the interests served by state planners. They do not reflexively admire professions of benign intent, such as the dedication to promote democracy, justice, and freedom. Their pernicious influence must be stemmed—in more violent states, by force; in more free societies by other means.[6]

CREATING MISIMPRESSIONS

Throughout the Cold War years, the framework of "defense against Communist aggression" was available to mobilize domestic support for subversion, terror, and mass slaughter. In the 1980s, however, the device was beginning to wear thin. By 1979, according to one careful estimate, "the Soviets were influencing only 6% of the world population and 5% of the world GNP" outside its borders.[7] But details aside, the basic picture was becoming harder to evade. There were also domestic problems, notably the civilizing effects of the activism of the 1960s, which had many consequences, among them less willingness to tolerate the resort to violence, well understood by the political leadership as leaked documents and other sources reveal. The task of "creating the misimpression that it is the Soviet Union that you are fighting" was facing obstacles.

The Reagan administration's public relations system sought to deal with the problem by fevered pronouncements about the "evil empire" and its tentacles everywhere about to strangle us—a simplified version of Kennedy's "monolithic and ruthless conspiracy" to conquer the world. But new devices were needed. The Reaganites declared a worldwide campaign to destroy "the evil scourge of terrorism" (Reagan), particularly state-backed international terrorism, a "plague spread by depraved opponents of civilization itself [in a] return to barbarism in the modern age" (George Shultz). The official list of states sponsoring terrorism, initiated by Congress in 1979, was elevated to a prominent place in policy and propaganda, with delicate choices of the kind already illustrated.

When Gorbachev's public relations became a more serious threat to

American interests, as Huntington warned, and the conventional pretexts eroded, "the 'war on drugs' quickly filled the vacuum" in Latin
America, the traditional domain of US direct or indirect violence—
later transmuted to "narcoterrorism," exploiting opportunities offered by 9/11. By the end of the millennium, "total [US] military and
police assistance in the hemisphere exceeded economic and social
aid." This is a "new phenomenon," the analysts point out: "even at
the height of the Cold War, economic aid far exceeded military aid."[8]

Predictably, the policies "strengthened military forces at the ex-
pense of civilian authorities, . . . exacerbated human rights problems
and generated significant social conflict and even political instability."
From 2002 to 2003, the number of Latin American troops trained by
US programs increased by more than 50 percent. The U.S. military's
Southern Command (Southcom) now has more people working in
Latin America than most key civilian federal agencies combined, focusing now on "radical populism" and street gangs as major threats.
The police are being trained in light infantry tactics. Foreign military
training is being shifted from the State Department to the Pentagon,
freeing it from human rights and democracy conditionality under
congressional supervision.[9]

In September 1989, just as the Berlin Wall was about to crumble,
Bush I redeclared the "war on drugs" with a huge government-media
propaganda campaign. It went into effect right in time to justify the
invasion of Panama to kidnap a thug who was convicted in Florida for
crimes committed mostly when he was on the CIA payroll—and, incidentally, killing unknown numbers of poor people in the bombarded
slums, thousands according to the victims. The "war on drugs" also
had an important domestic component: much like the "war on
crime," it served to frighten the domestic population into obedience as
domestic policies were being implemented to benefit extreme wealth
at the expense of the large majority.

In 1994, Clinton expanded the category of "terrorist states" to include "rogue states."[10] A few years later another concept was added
to the repertoire: "failed states," from which we must protect ourselves, and which we must help, sometimes by devastating them. Later

came the "axis of evil," which we must destroy in self-defense, following the will of the Lord as transmitted to his humble servant—
meanwhile escalating the threat of terror, nuclear proliferation, and
perhaps "apocalypse soon."

The rhetoric has always raised difficulties, however. The basic
problem is that under any reasonable interpretation of the terms—
even official definitions—the categories are unacceptably broad, impli-
cating the United States rather than justifying its actions, as
faithfulness to doctrine requires. It takes discipline not to recognize
the element of truth in historian Arno Mayer's immediate post-9/11
observation that since 1947, "America has been the chief perpetrator
of 'preemptive' state terror" and innumerable other " 'rogue' actions,"
causing immense harm, "always in the name of democracy, liberty,
and justice."[11]

The concept of "rogue states" is no less problematic. By the late Clinton years, it was evident that for much of the world the United States
was "becoming the rogue superpower," considered "the single greatest external threat to their societies," and that "in the eyes of much of
the world, in fact, the prime rogue state today is the United States."
After Bush took over, mainstream scholarship no longer just reported
world opinion, but began to assert as fact that the United States "has
assumed many of the very features of the 'rogue nations' against which
it has . . . done battle." Though kept at bay by the doctrinal institutions,
the difficulties are always lurking in the background.[12]

Problems are also raised by invoking the "war on drugs" to "fill the
vacuum" left by the erosion of traditional pretexts. One is that the most
cost-effective and humane approaches—prevention and treatment—are
consistently neglected in favor of radical increase of incarceration at
home and violence abroad, with little if any effect on drug prices, hence
use. Another is the causal relation between US violence abroad and the
drug trade, well established by scholarship, and even evident from the
daily press, recently again in Afghanistan. It is useful to recall, however,
that no narco-trafficking enterprise begins to approach that of ninteenth-
century Britain, a mainstay of the empire.[13]

Similar problems beset the category "failed state." Like "terrorist
state" and "rogue state," the concept is "frustratingly imprecise," sus-

ceptible to too many interpretations. Again, careful shaping of evidence is required to exclude the United States while including the intended examples. Take Haiti, a prototypical "failed state." The standard version in much scholarship—and, almost invariably, in the media—is that Clinton's intervention in 1994 "to restore democracy" has, regrettably, "not led to democracy but instead to political chaos, renewed repression, and dismal US-Haiti relations." Also standard, as in this case, is avoidance of the relevant facts, specifically those revealing that Clinton's invasion was just another step in Washington's efforts to undermine Haitian democracy, leading to chaos and repression, as was predicted at once.[14]

The category "failed state" was invoked repeatedly in the course of the "normative revolution" proclaimed in the self-designated "enlightened states" in the 1990s, entitling them to resort to force with the alleged goal of protecting the populations of (carefully selected) states in a manner that may be "illegal but legitimate." As the leading themes of political discourse shifted from "humanitarian intervention" to the redeclared "war on terror" after 9/11, the concept "failed state" was given a broader scope to include states like Iraq that allegedly threaten the United States with weapons of mass destruction and international terrorism. In scholarship that (approvingly) traces the historical roots of the Bush doctrine, the concept "failed state" has been extended to include the "power vacuums" that the United States has been forced to fill for its own security, as Americans "concentrated on the task of felling trees and Indians and of rounding out their natural boundaries."[15]

Under this broader usage, "failed states" need not be weak. Iraq was not considered a failed state that threatened US security because it was weak. One legal authority writes that "the aggressive, arbitrary, tyrannical or totalitarian State would equally be regarded as having 'failed'—at least according to the norms and standards of modern-day international law." And that makes good sense. Nazi Germany and Stalinist Russia were hardly weak, but they merit the designation "failed state" as fully as any in history. Even in the narrowest interpretation, "failed states" are identified by the failure to provide security for the population, to guarantee rights at home or abroad, or to maintain functioning (not merely formal) democratic institutions.

The concept must surely also cover "outlaw states" that dismiss with contempt the rules of international order and its institutions, carefully constructed over many years, overwhelmingly under US initiative. The familiar difficulties again arise: the category covers too broad a range to be doctrinally acceptable.[16]

The world dominant power is consciously choosing policies that typify outlaw states, that severely endanger the domestic population and that undermine substantive democracy. In crucial respects, Washington's adoption of the characteristics of failed and outlaw states is proudly proclaimed. There is scarcely any effort to conceal "the tension between a world that still wants a fair and sustainable international legal system, and a single superpower that hardly seems to care [that it] ranks with Burma, China, Iraq and North Korea . . . in terms of its adherence to a seventeenth-century, absolutist conception of sovereignty" for itself, while dismissing as old-fashioned tommyrot the sovereignty of others.[17]

The rich documentary and historical record amply supports Huntington's judgment about creating misimpressions, though it is convenient to plead Cold War paranoia, ignorance, and error. Case by case, we discover from the internal record and other standard sources that there has been rational planning to promote dominant domestic interests. As historian Charles Bergquist concludes in his review of justifications for intervention in Latin America, "to conserve . . . faith in liberal democracy" analysts must "distort . . . evidence, and transform the rational consistency in US policy (the defense of capitalist interests) into irrationality (unfounded fear of Communism)." The same has regularly been true elsewhere as well.[18]

RATIONAL CONSISTENCY

Quite generally, inquiry reveals that the real enemy of the United States has long been independent nationalism, particularly when it threatens to become a "contagious example," to borrow Henry Kissinger's characterization of democratic socialism in Chile, a virus that, he feared, might infect other countries as far away as southern

Europe—a concern he shared with Leonid Brezhnev. The source of contagion therefore had to be extirpated, as it was, on Tuesday, September 11, 1973, a date often called the first 9/11 in Latin America. We can learn a lot about the most important topic—ourselves—by examining the effects of the two 9/11s on the targeted societies and beyond, as well as the reactions to them.[19]

On 9/11 in 1973, after years of US subversion of Chilean democracy, support for terror, and "making the economy scream," General Augusto Pinochet's forces attacked the Chilean presidential palace. Salvador Allende, the elected president, died in the palace, apparently committing suicide because he was unwilling to surrender to the assault that demolished Latin America's oldest and most vibrant democracy and established a regime of torture and repression. Its primary instrument was the secret police organization DINA, which US military intelligence compared to the KGB and the Gestapo. Meanwhile, Washington firmly supported Pinochet's regime of violence and terror and had no slight role in its initial triumph.[20]

The official death toll of the first 9/11 is 3,200. The actual toll is commonly estimated at about double that figure. As a proportion of the population, the corresponding figure for the United States would be between 50,000 and 100,000 killed. An official inquiry thirty years after the coup found evidence of 30,000 cases of torture—some 700,000 in the US equivalent. Pinochet soon moved to integrate other US-backed Latin American military dictatorships into an international state terrorist program called Operation Condor. The program killed and tortured mercilessly within the region and branched out to terrorist operations in Europe and the United States. Throughout these hideous crimes, and long after, Pinochet was greatly honored—by Ronald Reagan and Margaret Thatcher in particular, but far more widely as well. The assassination of the respected Chilean diplomat Orlando Letelier in Washington, D.C., in 1976, however, was going too far. Operation Condor had to be called off. But the venom continued to spread. The worst atrocities in Argentina were yet to come, along with the expansion of state terror to Central America by the current incumbents in Washington and their immediate mentors.[21]

After 9/11 in 2001, it is commonly agreed, the world irrevocably changed. But not after the first 9/11. Those who enjoy wealth, freedom, and privilege might ask how the world would have changed if the oldest democracy in the hemisphere had been destroyed by a military coup, its president killed, more than 50,000 killed and 700,000 tortured, instigating a plague of terror throughout the continent and beyond. We might also ask how one should respond to those who participated in and laud such actions, or to those who dismiss them as eminently forgettable.

The fear of independent nationalism can go to impressive lengths. An illustration is what Senator Baucus called "the administration's absurd and increasingly bizarre obsession with Cuba," which has taken precedence over the threat of terror in the Clinton and Bush II administrations, as we have seen. The obsession may be bizarre, but it is not absurd from the perspective of policy makers. The basic reasons were explained in internal documents from the Kennedy-Johnson years. State Department planners warned that the "very existence" of the Castro regime is "successful defiance" of US policies going back 150 years; the threat is not Russians, but intolerable defiance of the master of the hemisphere, much like Iran's crime of successful defiance in 1979, or Syria's rejection of Clinton's demands. By June 1960, longtime presidential adviser Adolf Berle, a former member of FDR's brain trust, warned that "this is the end of the Monroe Doctrine." The savagery and fanaticism of the assault on Cuba has been, indeed, remarkable, so much so that the US Army War College in 1993 cautioned against the "innate emotional appeal" driving US policy makers who saw Castro as "the embodiment of evil who must be punished for his defiance of the United States as well as for other reprehensible deeds."

The punishment of the people of Cuba intensified when Cuba was in dire straits after the collapse of the Soviet Union, at the initiative of liberal Democrats. The author of the 1992 measures to tighten the blockade proclaimed that "my objective is to wreak havoc in Cuba" (Representative Robert Torricelli of New Jersey, later senator). That punishment of the population was legitimate had been determined as far back as the Eisenhower administration. "The Cuban people [are] responsible for the regime," Undersecretary of State Douglas Dillon explained in March 1960, so the United States has the right to cause them to suffer by economic strangulation. Eisenhower approved economic sanctions in the expectation that "if [the Cuban people] are hungry, they will throw Castro out." Kennedy agreed that the embargo would hasten Fidel Castro's departure as a result of the "rising discomfort among hungry Cubans." Along with expanding the embargo, Kennedy initiated a major terrorist campaign designed to bring the "terrors of the earth" to Cuba, the goal of Robert Kennedy, who was put in charge of the operation, according to his biographer Arthur Schlesinger. The basic thinking was expressed by Deputy Assistant Secretary of State Lester Mallory in April 1960: Castro would be removed "through disenchantment and disaffection based on economic dissatisfaction and hardship [so] every possible means should be undertaken promptly to weaken the economic life of Cuba [in order to] bring about hunger, desperation and [the] overthrow of the government."[22]

US leaders could not tolerate "Cuban refusal to submit to the United States," the reaction of "a people still convinced that they have a right of self-determination and national sovereignty," Latin American scholar Louis Pérez writes, summarizing forty years of terror and economic warfare. The record illustrates principles that are well established, internally rational, and clear enough to the victims, but scarcely perceptible in the intellectual world of the agents.

It was not only Cuba's "successful defiance" that led the Kennedy administration to punish the population of the criminal state. There was also fear that Cuba might be another of those "contagious examples," like Chile and innumerable other targets of subversion, aggression, and international terrorism. Cuban independence would encourage others, who might be infected by the "Castro idea of taking matters into their own hands," Latin American adviser Arthur Schlesinger warned incoming President Kennedy. President Eisenhower had already expressed his concern that Castro had "gained great prestige in Latin America," which meant that "governments elsewhere cannot oppose him too strongly since they are shaky with respect to the potentials of action by the mobs within their own countries to whom Castro's brand of demagoguery appeals." The dangers are particularly grave, Schlesinger elaborated, when "the distribution of land and other forms of national wealth greatly favors the propertied classes . . . and the poor and underprivileged, stimulated by the example of the Cuban revolution, are now demanding opportunities for a decent living." The whole system of domination might unravel if the idea of taking matters into one's own hands spread beyond Cuba's shores.

British intelligence concurred, benefiting from its rich experience with insubordination. In June 1961, the Joint Intelligence Committee warned that "Castroism still retains much of its popular appeal. If, in the longer term, the Cuban revolution succeeds in achieving a stable regime, which appears to meet the aspirations of the depressed classes, there will be a serious risk that it will inspire similar revolutions elsewhere in Latin America." The threats are dire and persistent, a constant frustration to planners dedicated to "democracy promotion," revived again today in Venezuela, in fact much of South America.[23]

Concern over viruses and the infections they may spread has been a persistent theme among great powers. Sober European statesmen feared that the virus of the American revolution might poison the civilized world order. The reaction was far more furious when Haiti became the first free country in the hemisphere in 1804, after a brutal struggle against the combined forces of civilization: England, France, and the United States. Its liberation was particularly frightening for the slave state to its north, which refused even to recognize Haiti until 1862—the year it also recognized Liberia, both considered to be possible places to dispatch freed slaves. In later years, the United States took over from France the primary role of tormenting Haiti, continuing to the present.[24]

Similar concerns were aroused by the most awesome virus of all, when Russia broke free of the West in October 1917. President Wilson and British prime minister David Lloyd George feared that the Bolshevik virus might infect other countries, even the United States and England. These concerns persisted into the 1960s, when the Soviet economy began to stagnate, largely because of the huge military programs undertaken in reaction to Kennedy's military buildup and his refusal to consider the offers of sharp mutual reduction in offensive weapons by Russian premier Nikita Khrushchev, who was hoping to avoid an arms race that would devastate the far weaker Soviet economy. That the Soviet Union was weaker militarily (and of course economically) had been understood on both sides.

The issue at the heart of the Cold War was described accurately by one of the most respected figures of Cold War scholarship, John Lewis Gaddis, who plausibly dates its origins to 1917–18. The immediate Allied intervention in 1918 was virtuous in intent, Gaddis explains: Woodrow Wilson was inspired "above all else" by his fervent desire "to secure self-determination in Russia"—that is, by forceful installation of the rulers we select. In accord with the same righteous vision, the United States was devoted to self-determination for Vietnam and Central America, the Kremlin was dedicated to self-determination in Afghanistan and Eastern Europe, and so on throughout history, as commonly proclaimed by the visionaries in charge.[25]

The 1918 Western invasion was really in self-defense, Gaddis explains, much as in the case of the Jackson-Adams liberation of Florida in self-defense against runaway Negroes and lawless Indians. The West's assault was undertaken "in response to a profound and potentially far-reaching intervention by the new Soviet government in the internal affairs, not just of the West, but of virtually every country in the world," namely, "the Revolution's challenge—which could hardly have been more categorical—to the very survival of the capitalist order." Accordingly, "the security of the United States [was] in danger" already in 1918. Gaddis criticizes Soviet historians who see the Western intervention as "shocking, unnatural, and even a violation of the legal norms that should exist between nations." This is plainly absurd, he responds. "One cannot have it both ways," complaining about a Western invasion while "the most profound revolutionary challenge of the century was mounted against the West"—by changing the social order in Russia and proclaiming revolutionary intentions.

After World War II, Gaddis continues, Russian aggression took a more virulent form, as "the increasing success of communist parties in Western Europe, the Eastern Mediterranean, and China" justifiably

aroused renewed "suspicion about the Soviet Union's behavior," even
though the parties' popularity "grew primarily out of their effectiveness as resistance fighters against the Axis." The appeal of the antifas-
cist resistance required the United States and United Kingdom to move
quickly, and often brutally, to dismantle the resistance and its accom-
plishments, particularly in northern Italy, where workers had taken
over plants and the germs of a free self-governing society were beginning to flourish. The first National Security Council memorandum, in
1947, considered military intervention in Italy if Communists gained
power by legal means, a position reiterated in NSC 5411/2 in 1954.
Subversion of Italian democracy continued actively at least into the
1970s. A more general task in liberated areas was to undermine the labor movement and the left, while restoring much of the traditional political and economic structure, often returning fascist collaborators to
positions of authority. Initiatives to subvert democracy continued for
many years, in southern Europe particularly. Substantial efforts were
also devoted to deterring the threat of genuine democracy in Japan.[26]

In the postwar years, Washington's fears of infection extended far
more broadly, as the United States became the world dominant power,
supplanting Britain. The domino-virus theory was immediately invoked, under the Truman Doctrine, to justify massacres in Greece and
reinstatement of the traditional order, including Nazi collaborators.
For similar reasons, Washington backed the installation of Europe's
first postwar fascist government in Greece in 1967, continuing its support until the dictatorship was overthrown in 1974. The concept was
repeatedly deployed to justify destruction of parliamentary regimes
and imposition of murderous dictatorships throughout much of the
world in order to guarantee "stability" and control of vital resources
(Middle East petroleum, in the case of Greece in the 1940s).

In 1948, George Kennan, head of the State Department Policy
Planning Staff, warned that if Indonesia fell under "Communism," it
could be an "infection [that] would sweep westward" through all of
South Asia. For such reasons, Kennan held, "the problem of Indonesia
[is] the most crucial issue of the moment in our struggle with the
Kremlin"—which had little to do with Indonesia, apart from serving
to create misimpressions. The threat of a "Communist Indonesia" was

sufficiently severe for the Eisenhower administration to support a military rebellion, primarily out of fear of democracy: what scholarship calls a "party of the poor" was gaining too much political support for comfort. The threat of democracy was not overcome until the 1965 Suharto coup and the huge slaughter that immediately followed, establishing one of the most brutal regimes of the late twentieth century. There was no further concern about democracy, or about awesome human rights violations and war crimes. Suharto remained "our kind of guy," as the Clinton administration described him, until he committed his first real crime, in 1998: dragging his feet on IMF orders and losing control over the population. At that point he was instructed by Secretary of State Madeleine Albright that the time had come for "democratic transition," though some, like Suharto's longtime advocate Paul Wolfowitz, continued to find him meritorious.[27]

The Indochina wars fall into the same pattern. The justifications put forth were the usual ones, though "defense against Communist aggression" had to be construed rather broadly. It was necessary to portray France as defending Vietnam from Vietnamese aggression while it sought to reconquer its former colony. Thus Canada's Nobel Peace Prize laureate Lester Pearson identified the outside threat to Vietnam as "Russian colonial authority," although there were no Russians in sight but tens of thousands of US-armed French forces in plain view. The US Joint Chiefs of Staff defined "aggression" in Southeast Asia to include "aggression other than armed, i.e., political warfare, or subversion." Adlai Stevenson and John F. Kennedy railed about "internal aggression" and an "assault from the inside . . . manipulated from the North." By the North, they meant the northern half of Vietnam, divided by the United States after it undermined the 1954 international agreement on unification and elections (which, it recognized, would have come out the wrong way).[28]

In January 1963, after reports of military success, Kennedy informed the country that "the spearpoint of aggression has been blunted in South Vietnam." His close adviser historian Arthur Schlesinger described 1962 as "not a bad year," with "aggression checked in Vietnam"; 1962 was the year when Kennedy sent the US Air Force to bomb South Vietnam, authorized the use of napalm and

chemical warfare to destroy food crops and ground cover for the indigenous resistance, and began the programs to send millions of South
Vietnamese to virtual concentration camps where they could be "protected" from the guerrillas who, admittedly, they were supporting. The
administration's own primary sources reveal that the major provinces
in the South were being taken over by indigenous forces roused to resistance by the brutal repression of the US client state in southern Vietnam, with only reluctant support from the northern part of the divided
country. The public and internal record until Kennedy's assassination
in November 1963 reveals no hint of departure from his insistence
that the United States must stay the course until victory was achieved
over "the assault from the inside." After the war became highly unpopular in the late 1960s, particularly after the 1968 Vietnamese Tet
offensive turned elite sectors against the war, memoirists radically revised their accounts, while they and others produced "recollections"
to support the doctrinally more acceptable view that Kennedy and
others were secret doves. Very secret. There is no credible trace of it in
the record.[29]

Recent efforts to sustain the image of Kennedy as a secret dove
have come up with a few scraps of evidence, which are interesting in
their assumptions: they implicitly define a "dove" as someone who insists on assurance of victory before withdrawal, Kennedy's position
throughout. One of the rare examples of nontrivial new evidence adduced in these efforts is a White House communication instructing
John Kenneth Galbraith, the ambassador to India, to tell Indian foreign secretary M. J. Desai "that if Hanoi takes steps to reduce guer-
rilla activity, we would correspond [sic] accordingly," and if Hanoi
were to "stop the activity entirely, we would withdraw to a normal
basis."[30] In short, if Hanoi will somehow find a way to terminate the
indigenous rebellion against the US-imposed terror state, then the
United States will leave its client in place and be satisfied with victory.
The Kremlin would have been happy to convey a similar offer with
regard to Afghanistan in the 1980s.

The real reasons for the US assault on Indochina are conventional.
Washington feared that an independent Vietnam might be a virus in-
fecting others, perhaps even resource-rich Indonesia, and eventually

leading Japan—the "superdomino," as Asia historian John Dower termed it—to accommodate to an independent Asian mainland, becoming its industrial center. That would in effect have established the New Order that Japan sought to create by conquest in the 1930s. The United States was not prepared to lose the Pacific phase of World War II shortly after its military victory. The pre–World War II diplomatic record indicates that there was no fundamental objection to Japan's New Order as long as the United States maintained free access to it. And with its much broader postwar ambitions, Washington intended to provide Japan with "some sort of empire toward the south," in George Kennan's phrase, something like the New Order but within the US-dominated global system, and therefore acceptable. Other "functions" of the region, as outlined by Kennan's staff, were to ensure that Britain have access to the resources of its former Asian colonies, and to facilitate the "triangular trade" patterns that were to be the basis of the postwar reconstruction of Europe and the creation of markets and investment opportunities for US corporations, then moving to the multinational stage. These plans might have been disrupted by a Vietnamese virus, if it were not contained.[31]

The proper way to deal with a virus is to destroy it, and to inoculate those who might be infected. In this case, the virus was destroyed by demolishing Indochina. The broader region was then inoculated by the establishment of harsh military dictatorships in the countries susceptible to infection. Indonesia was protected by the "staggering mass slaughter" of 1965, a "gleam of light in Asia," the New York Times exulted. The reaction captured the undisguised Western euphoria over the outcome of the massacre of hundreds of thousands of people, mostly landless peasants, and the destruction of the only mass-based political party, the Indonesian Communist Party, as the country was opened up to free Western exploitation by crimes that the CIA compared to those of Hitler, Stalin, and Mao.[32]

The essential logic of the Indochina wars was articulated by Kennedy-Johnson national security adviser McGeorge Bundy. He observed in retrospect that "our effort" in Vietnam was "excessive" after 1965, when Indonesia was safely inoculated.[33] The basic war aims had been achieved. By the late 1960s the US business community had come to realize that it was pointless to extend the war, which by then was harming the US economy, largely because the antiwar movement compelled Washington to follow a costly "guns and butter" policy instead of calling a national mobilization that could have been beneficial for the economy, as during World War II, a popular war. Elite opinion and government policy shifted accordingly.

Across the political spectrum, the outcome is described as an "American defeat," which is true if we keep to maximal aims: the United States did not manage to impose client states in Indochina, and the "credibility" of US power was perhaps marginally harmed. But in terms of its basic war aims, the United States prevailed, as one would expect given the enormous disparity of means of violence.

The public version of the domino theory maintained that Ho Chi Minh would conquer Southeast Asia, Nicaragua would take over Central America and soon after the hordes would be sweeping over Texas, with the Russians only a footstep behind, and so on. The public version is commonly derided as a "naive error" after it has served its function of creating misimpressions at home. The internal version of the domino theory, however, is never abandoned, because it is plausible: successful independent development and steps toward democracy, out of US control, might well have a domino effect, inspiring others who face similar problems to pursue the same course, thus eroding the global system of domination. That is why it was constantly necessary to sell intervention by creating the misimpression that it is the Soviet Union that you are fighting—or China, or the Sino-Soviet axis, or the Huns (Woodrow Wilson's pretext for invading Haiti and the Dominican Republic), or narco-traffickers—or whatever can be conjured up. On these matters, the documentary record is rich, and remarkably consistent.

Such misimpressions commonly provide the framework not only for public discourse but also for the intelligence services. Perhaps the most striking example, considerably more significant than the much-discussed case of Iraq, is revealed in the Pentagon Papers. When Washington decided to support France's reconquest of Vietnam, intelligence was instructed to demonstrate that the Viet Minh resistance was a mere tool of Russia or China (or both). With great effort, intelligence was able to discover only that Hanoi appeared to be the one place in the region lacking such contacts. That was taken to be proof that Ho Chi Minh was such a loyal puppet he had "a special dispensation," with no need for instructions. US intelligence was so deeply indoctrinated that for the two-decade period recorded in the Pentagon Papers, up to 1968, it was scarcely able even to entertain the possibility that North Vietnam might be pursuing national interests rather than serving as a loyal puppet of its masters—hardly in question, whatever one thinks of Hanoi. The South Vietnamese resistance (NLF) was simply dismissed, except on the ground, where it was the commanding presence.[34]

"UNQUESTIONED POWER"

Prior to World War II, the United States, though by far the world's richest economy, had not been a major global actor. Its reach extended to its own region with forays into the Pacific and, by the 1920s, initiatives began to gain a share of the vast energy resources of the Middle East. But even before the United States entered the war, high-level planners and foreign policy advisers recognized that it should be able "to hold unquestioned power" in the new global system, ensuring the "limitation of any exercise of sovereignty" by states that might interfere with its designs. They also developed "an integrated policy to achieve military and economic supremacy for the United States" in the "Grand Area," which was to include at least the Western Hemisphere, the former British empire, and the Far East. As the war progressed, and it became clear that "Soviet military power . . . had crushed Hitler's Reich," Grand Area planning was extended to include as much of Eurasia as possible.[35] Since that time the world has undergone many dramatic changes, but no less striking—and of far-reaching significance for the future—are the fundamental continuities in these policies, with tactical modifications and shifting of justifications adapted to circumstances.

During World War II, Joseph Stalin became an ally, the beloved "Uncle Joe," as Russia first endured and then beat back the Nazi wave. "It cannot be overemphasized," historian Omer Bartov writes, "that however criminal and odious Stalin's regime surely was, without the Red Army and its horrendous blood sacrifice, the Wehrmacht would not have been defeated and Nazism would have remained a fact in Europe for many generations."[36] Roosevelt scholar Warren Kimball concludes that "when military assessments pointed out that only the Red Army could achieve victory over Hitler in a land war, aid to the Soviet Union became a presidential priority" on the assumption that the Russian army would grind Germany down and keep US soldiers out of a land war. Roosevelt's strategy was for the United States to be the reserves, he confided privately. Nevertheless, "Roosevelt treated the aid-to-Russia program more as a matter of 'good faith' than for its value to the Soviet war effort," Kimball adds, estimating its value at about 10 percent of Russian production, making it critical but secondary to Roosevelt's broader plans. His design, unchanged to the end, Gaddis observes, was that US allies should "do most of the fighting" in Europe, so as "to keep [US] casualties to a minimum." "Allies" meant mostly Russians: for every US soldier who died fighting the war, "some 60 Russians were doing so." A corresponding intention, largely achieved, was that in the Pacific the United States would have total domination, with no interference from allies or even participation from "the major victims of Japanese aggression."[37]

In the early stages of the war, Harry Truman's view was simple: "if we see that Germany is winning we ought to help Russia and if Russia is winning we ought to help Germany and that way let them kill as many as possible," what political scientist Timothy Crawford calls a "pivotal strategy [to] prolong war." Truman's generally pragmatic view was tempered, however, by his genuine affection and admiration for "old Joe," whom he regarded as "a decent fellow [who] can't do what he wants to" because, as Truman put it in 1948, he is "a prisoner of the Politburo." Truman stopped expressing such views publicly when his advisers convinced him that doing so was "a damaging blunder." But in private he continued to describe old Joe as "honest" and "straightforward," "as near like Tom Pendergast as any man I know," referring to the Missouri boss who launched his political career. As president, Truman felt that he could get along with the tyrant as long as the United States got its way 85 percent of the time.[38]

War planners took a much dimmer view. The British in particular regarded the Western-Soviet wartime alliance as an "aberration" from the start. From early 1944 Western military intelligence was "marking the Soviets as the next enemy" and withholding crucial information about German forces from the Russians while obtaining "superbly detailed and accurate" information about Russian military forces. Almost all Western-Russian intelligence cooperation ceased by the end of 1944, and British and US intelligence began gathering information for air attacks against Russia. Field Marshal Sir Alan Brooke, the British wartime chief of the Imperial General Staff, had always loathed what he called "this semi-Asiatic race," who were perhaps almost as degraded as the "little yellow dwarf slaves" in Japan who disgusted Sir Alexander Cadogan, the senior official at the Foreign Office. Brooke concluded in 1943 that the USSR "cannot fail to become the main threat" after the war, so that it would be necessary to "foster Germany, gradually build her up and bring her into the Federation of Western Europe," though it was a difficult policy to carry out "under the cloak of a holy alliance between England, Russia and America." Richard Aldrich observes that "like Harry S. Truman in Washington," Brooke and his deputy General Henry Pownall "rejoiced to see [Germany and Russia] going for each other with vigor." By late 1944, the British military was producing war plans, including rearming of Germany, for the planned attack against Russia. British intelligence had also found " 'super-secret' appreciations of the Soviet Union as the next enemy that were circulating in Washington."[39]

In May 1945, as the war against Germany ended, Churchill ordered war plans to be drawn up for "Operation Unthinkable." His "stated objective was 'the elimination of Russia,'" Aldrich writes. The plans, only declassified in 1999, "called for a surprise attack by hundreds of thousands of British and American troops, joined by 100,000 rearmed German soldiers," while the Royal Air Force "would attack Soviet cities from bases in Northern Europe." Nuclear weapons were soon added to the mix. Earlier Cadogan had raged about how the Russians are "dominated by an almost insane suspicion," requiring "infinite patience" as we try to deal with them "as though we thought they were reasonable human beings."[40]

The dilemma is a persistent one in attempts to deal with the *unpeople* of the world. Thirty years after the criminal atrocities he directed, Robert McNamara was still puzzling over the unwillingness of the South Vietnamese resistance to lay down their arms and become part of an "independent, non-Communist South Vietnam," following the path of Indonesia, which had "reversed course" after the killing of "300,000 or more PKI members . . . and now lay in the hands of independent nationalists led by Suharto."[41]

How could the Vietnamese not appreciate the merits of the bright future McNamara was recommending to them? Perhaps the answer is the one Henry Kissinger offered in his musings at the same time about "the deepest problem of the contemporary international order," nothing like starvation or war, but rather the "difference of philosophical perspective" that separates the West, which "is deeply committed to the notion that the real world is external to the observer," from the rest of the world, which still believes "that the real world is almost completely *internal* to the observer." Perhaps that is why the Vietnamese did not react rationally to our efforts to bomb them to the negotiating table where we offered them the fate of the PKI in independent Indonesia. The Russians, Kissinger continued, are poised uneasily astride the great divide of philosophical perspective. And they are particularly difficult to deal with because of their delusion "that 'objective' factors such as the social structure, the economic process, and above all the class struggle are more important than the personal convictions of statesmen." Hence they do not "accept protestations of good will at face value," as we do.[42]

A few years after the end of World War II, British assessments began to change. By 1951, the retiring director of naval intelligence, Vice Admiral Eric Longley-Cook, informed the "innermost circle [that] the stolid Russians were a force for stability in the world system," seeking to further their objectives by "psychological or economic means but 'not a general military offensive.'" He suggested that "the main threat to strategic stability and indeed to the survival of the United Kingdom came from America," which is preparing for "a shooting war with the Soviet Union" from which the United States would be secure, while Britain might be destroyed.[43]

These fears would only have been exacerbated by the rhetoric of NSC 68, had it been known. Formulated in 1950, shortly before the Korean War, NSC 68 is recognized to be a founding document of the contemporary world order, widely cited in scholarship, though much of the contents is generally ignored, including the scattered data revealing Soviet military weakness relative to the West and the remarkable rhetorical framework of the document.[44] NSC 68 was drafted by Paul Nitze under the direction of Dean Acheson, two of the "wise men" who are honored for their sobriety and thoughtfulness in creating the new world order of the day. They contrast the "fundamental design [of the] slave state" with the "fundamental purpose" of the United States. The "implacable purpose" and inherent "compulsion" of the slave state is to gain "absolute authority over the rest of the world," destroying all governments and the "structure of society" everywhere. Its ultimate evil contrasts with our sheer perfection. The "fundamental purpose" of the United States is to assure "the dignity and worth of the individual" everywhere. Its leaders are animated by "generous and constructive impulses, and the absence of covetousness in our international relations," qualities particularly evident in the traditional domains of US influence, which have enjoyed the privilege of "our long continuing endeavors to create and now develop the Inter-American system." Hence the admiration for US power south of the border.

By comparison with the Truman administration wise men who were "present at the creation," the rhetoric about Good and Evil that Bush's speech writers plagiarize from ancient epics and children's fairy tales seems rather subdued.

The basic continuity of policy was illustrated again when the Soviet Union collapsed, offering new opportunities along with the need for new misimpressions. The assault on Cuba was intensified, but reframed: it was no longer defense against the Russians, but rather Washington's sincere dedication to democracy that required strangulation of Cuba and US-based terror. The sudden shift of pretexts elicited little reflection, in fact no detectable notice. (As we see directly, the model was followed closely in 2003 after the collapse of the pretexts for invading Iraq.) Bush's invasion of Panama immediately after the fall of the Berlin Wall in 1989 was in itself hardly more than a footnote to the history of the region. But it, too, revealed changes. One was pointed out by Reaganite State Department official Elliott Abrams, who observed that "Bush probably is going to be increasingly willing to use force" now that there was little fear of its leading to a Russian reaction. In Panama, too, new pretexts were needed: not the Russian menace, but narco-trafficking by Noriega, a longtime CIA asset who was becoming uncooperative (embellished with a few tales about threats to Americans). In August 1990, when Saddam Hussein invaded Kuwait, the United States and United Kingdom felt free to place a huge expeditionary force in the Saudi Arabian desert in their buildup to the January 1991 invasion, no longer deterred by the superpower rival.[45]

With the Cold War no longer available, it was necessary to reframe pretexts not only for intervention but also for militarized state capitalism at home. The Pentagon budget presented to Congress a few months after the fall of the Berlin Wall remained largely unchanged, but was packaged in a new rhetorical framework, presented in the National Security Strategy of March 1990. One priority was to support advanced industry in traditional ways, in sharp violation of the free market doctrines proclaimed and imposed on others. The National Security Strategy called for strengthening "the defense industrial base" (essentially, high-tech industry) with incentives "to invest in new facilities and equipment as well as in research and development." As in the past, the costs and risks of the coming phases of the industrial economy were to be socialized, with eventual profits privatized, a form of state socialism for the rich on which much of the advanced US economy relies, particularly since World War II, but with precedents in the advanced economies back to the early days of the industrial revolution.[46] In the past several decades, Pentagon funding for research and development has declined, while support through the National Institutes of Health and other "health-related" components of the state sector has increased, as the cutting edge of the economy of the future shifts from electronics- to biology-based industry. The longtime chairman of the Federal Reserve Alan Greenspan and other ideologues may hail the wonders of "entrepreneurial initiative," "consumer choice," and "free trade," but those who channel public funds to development of the economy and those who profit from these decisions know better.[47]

It is sometimes argued that concealing development of high-tech industry under the cover of "defense" has been a valuable contribution to society. Those who do not share that contempt for democracy might ask what decisions the population would have made if they had been informed of the real options and allowed to choose among them. Perhaps they might have preferred more social spending for health, education, decent housing, a sustainable environment for future generations, and support for the United Nations, international law, and diplomacy, as polls regularly show. We can only guess, since fear of democracy barred the option of allowing the public into the political arena, or even informing them about what was being done in their name.

The justification for sustaining the dynamic state sector of the economy had to be revised in the light of new contingencies after the end of the Cold War. Since the reason could no longer be the threat of Russian aggression, it became "the growing technological sophistication of Third World conflicts," which "will place serious demands on our forces" and "continue to threaten US interests," even without "the backdrop of superpower competition." The same revision was needed for the second function of the Pentagon: ensuring global "stability," the code word for obedience. In the "new era" after the Cold War, the administration explained, "we foresee that our military power will remain an essential underpinning of the global balance, but less prominently and in different ways. We see that the more likely demands for the use of our military forces may not involve the Soviet Union and may be in the Third World, where new capabilities and approaches may be required"—in fact, very much the old approaches but with new pretexts accompanying the new capabilities. "In the future, we expect that non-Soviet threats to [US] interests will command even greater attention"—in reality, comparable attention but adjusted to circumstances, both in deed and in word. As before, we must have the means "to reinforce our units forward deployed or to project power into areas where we have no permanent presence." This is necessary, particularly in the Middle East, because of "the free world's reliance on energy supplies from this pivotal region," where the "threats to our interests" that require direct military engagement cannot "be laid at the Kremlin's door"—contrary to decades of pretense, now shelved as useless. The sudden revisions elicited no comment. At the time, Saddam Hussein was not among the non-Soviet threats. Rather, he was still a favored friend and ally and recipient of ample aid and support.[48]

Military commanders echoed the political echelon, emphasizing that the end of the Cold War would not change security policies significantly: "In fact, the majority of the crises we have responded to since the end of World War II have not directly involved the Soviet Union," marine general A. M. Gray observed, quite accurately, in May 1990. The problems remain, as before, insurgencies resulting from "the underdeveloped world's growing dissatisfaction over the gap between rich and poor nations," which may "jeopardize regional stability and our access to vital economic and military resources," on which the United States and its allies will become "more and more dependent." We must therefore "maintain within our active force structure a credible military power projection capability with the flexibility to respond to conflict across the spectrum of violence throughout the globe," to ensure "unimpeded access" both to "developing economic markets throughout the world" and "to the resources needed to support our manufacturing requirements."[49]

This basic thinking remained in force a decade later. New millennium intelligence projections expect "globalization" (in the standard doctrinal sense) to continue on course. "Its evolution will be rocky, marked by chronic financial volatility and a widening economic divide." It will bring "deepening economic stagnation, political instability, and cultural alienation," which will "foster ethnic, ideological and religious extremism, along with the violence that often accompanies it," much of that violence directed against the United States. A 2004 intelligence update expects "the perceptions of the contradictions and uncertainties of a globalized world [to] come even more to the fore than is the case today," as "gaps will widen between those countries benefiting from globalization . . . and those underdeveloped nations or pockets within nations that are left behind." The "pockets" happen to be immense, dramatically so in the poster children of "globalization."[50]

The 2004 intelligence assessment also warns that "over the next 15 years the increasing centrality of ethical issues, old and new" has "the potential to divide worldwide publics and challenge US leadership" on such matters as "the environment and climate change, privacy, cloning and biotechnology, human rights, international law regulating conflict, and the role of multilateral institutions." The United States "increasingly will have to battle world public opinion, which has dramatically shifted since the end of the Cold War," a subdued allusion to the fact that the Bush II administration significantly increased fear and often hatred of the United States.[51]

Huntington's observations about the need to create misimpressions to control the domestic population illustrate what should be the merest truism: professions of benign intent by leaders should be dismissed by any rational observer. They are near universal and predictable, and hence carry virtually no information. The worst monsters—Hitler, Stalin, Japanese fascists, Suharto, Saddam Hussein, and many others—have produced moving flights of rhetoric about their nobility of purpose. The same holds for "Peace Institutes" and "Endowments for Democracy." If we are serious, we will ask about their actions, paying little attention to their words, an elementary observation that has inspired a rich literature from Pascal to Zamyatin to Orwell.

"THE DEMOCRATIZATION BANDWAGON"

With all of this in mind, let us turn to Iraq and the revived passion for "democracy promotion" that is held to be central to Bush's "grand strategy."

Welcoming the Iraqi elections in January 2005, the foreign minister of Iran declared that Iran "supports the wishes of Iraqi citizens for a democratic government, living prosperously in a unified nation and expecting peaceful relationships with their neighbors," a fully sovereign Iraq in a stable and peaceful region of democratic states. Rational observers will view Iran's dedication to democracy promotion with due skepticism. And the same should be true when Bush, Blair, Rice, and their associates issue similar pronouncements. Far more so, in fact, for reasons that it takes some effort to ignore. The most glaring is occasionally—though very rarely—articulated. Thus Middle East specialist Augustus Richard Norton writes that "as fantasies about Iraq's weapons of mass destruction were unmasked, the Bush administration increasingly stressed the democratic transformation of Iraq, and scholars jumped on the democratization bandwagon." Before the fantasies were unmasked, there was, of course, occasional invocation of the standard pieties about democratic transformation, but not beyond the usual meaningless norm. In the documents reviewed in the most extensive study of the justifications for the Iraq invasion, by John Prados, such terms as "democracy" are not even indexed.[52]

To put it plainly, while asking us to appreciate the sincerity of their eloquent orations about their sudden conversion to "democratic transformation," US and UK leaders were also informing us that they are brazen liars, since they had driven their countries to war because of a "single question": will Saddam abandon his WMD programs? By August 2003, when the tale was falling to pieces, the press reported that "as the search for illegal weapons in Iraq continues without success, the Bush administration has moved to emphasize a different rationale for the war against Saddam Hussein: using Iraq as the 'linchpin' to transform the Middle East and thereby reduce the terrorist threat to the United States"—more accurately risk *enhancing* the terrorist threat, which happened, as even their own intelligence agencies confirm.[53]

The timing alone suffices to undermine the credibility of the "different rationale," and that is only the bare beginning. Nonetheless, the new rationale quickly became holy writ. The sincerity of our leader passed beyond challenge after the president's address on "Freedom in Iraq and Middle East" at the twentieth anniversary of the National Endowment for Democracy in Washington on November 6, 2003. The "single question" was dispatched to the memory hole, replaced by Bush's "messianic mission" to bring democracy to the Middle East in what "may be the most idealistic war fought in modern times," inspired by "idealist in chief" Paul Wolfowitz.[54]

With considerable effort, I have found only the rarest exceptions to this stance in media and intellectual commentary, though there are indeed critics, who warn that the "noble" and "generous" vision may be beyond our reach. It may be too costly, or the beneficiaries may be too backward to benefit from our solicitude. Some skeptics agree with New York University law professor Noah Feldman, who was assigned the task of teaching Iraqis about democracy and preparing their constitution (against their will), but warned that "if you move too fast"—that is, as fast as Iraqis wanted to—"the wrong people could get elected." More generally, David Brooks explained, as "Noah Feldman . . . observes, people in the Middle East don't always act rationally," despite our patient tutelage and Britain's before us.[55]

Evidence for the Brooks-Feldman assessment of people in the Middle East was provided just as President Bush formally revealed his messianic mission at the National Endowment for Democracy anniversary celebration. A Gallup poll in Baghdad provided the opportunity for respondents to join Western intellectuals in leaping on the "democratization bandwagon," but some failed to do so: 99 percent. Asked why they thought the United States invaded Iraq, 1 percent felt that the goal was to bring democracy and 5 percent that the goal was "to assist the Iraqi people." Most of the rest assumed that the goal was to take control of Iraq's resources and to reorganize the Middle East in US and Israeli interests—the "conspiracy theory" derided by rational Westerners, who understand that Washington and London would have been just as dedicated to the "liberation of Iraq" if its chief exports happened to be lettuce and pickles rather than petroleum.[56]

The irrationality and backwardness of the people of the Middle East has repeatedly been demonstrated, once again in September 2005, when the White House sent public relations specialist Karen Hughes to explain to them that they fail to understand Washington's dedication to their welfare and freedom. But her "I'm a mom" exercise in public diplomacy did not work too well. The problem, the press explained, was that she kept to "concise sound bites rather than sustained arguments. In American campaigns, such messages repeated over and over can have an effect because a presidential candidate dominates the news with every statement he makes, and if that fails to work, money can be poured into saturation advertising. By contrast, in the lively and percussive environment of this region, Ms. Hughes came nowhere near the commanding heights of the media." In brief, sound bites, media amplification, and saturation advertising are not effective among primitive people who think that sustained argument and lively discussion are components of democracy. The lesson is apparently not easy to learn. At a debate at the American University in Beirut a few weeks later, Juliet Wurr, the public affairs officer at the US embassy in Lebanon, explained to the audience that the United States seeks to "reach out to people in order to achieve US policy objectives" by promoting the "4Es": exchange, engagement, education, and empowerment. Apparently, that fell flat in Beirut, where the environment has long been particularly "lively and percussive." The task of "democracy promotion" is plainly a difficult one.[57]

Still, Richard Norton is a bit unfair to scholarship. Some scholars did recognize that it was only *after* the "single question" had been definitively answered the wrong way that "President George W. Bush and Prime Minister Tony Blair began speaking passionately about the importance of bringing 'democracy and freedom' to Iraq and the Middle East" in an "after-the-fact justification of the war," which evidently cannot be taken seriously. But outside of scholarship, and almost invariably within, Norton's observation is depressingly accurate.[58]

Quite apart from the timing, faith in the conversion is a little difficult to sustain in light of the behavior of the missionaries barely moments before. The Bush and Blair exploits in evading the perils of democracy as they proceeded with the invasion of Iraq in 2002 have already been reviewed. This rather significant illustration aside, it is hard to recall any display of contempt for democracy as clear as the distinction between Old Europe and New Europe announced by Donald Rumsfeld during the buildup to the invasion, and eagerly taken up by commentators and the political class. The criteria distinguishing the categories were sharp, clear, and highly instructive. One distinguishing criterion illuminates the operative concept of democracy: Old Europe consists of the countries in which the government took the same stand on the war as the large majority of the population, whereas in New Europe governments overruled even larger majorities and took orders from Crawford, Texas. Therefore Old Europe is to be disparaged and New Europe lauded as the hope for democracy and enlightenment.[59]

The most honored representatives of New Europe were the renowned democratic figures Silvio Berlusconi and José María Aznar. Berlusconi was rewarded by a visit to the White House, in recognition of the fact that 80 percent of the Italian population opposed the war that he endorsed (or perhaps in honor of his reconstruction of the Italian judiciary so as to escape conviction on charges of corruption). Aznar received an even greater reward. He was invited to join Bush and Blair at the Azores summit announcing the invasion of Iraq, shortly after polls in Spain revealed that he was backed in his support for war by 2 percent of the population.[60]

The display of hatred for democracy reached its peak when the government of Turkey, to general surprise, actually followed the will of 95 percent of the population and rejected Washington's commands to allow the US military to open a front from Turkey into Iraq. Turkey was bitterly condemned in the national press for lacking "democratic credentials." Colin Powell announced harsh punishment for this defection from good order. Paul Wolfowitz took the most extreme position. He berated the Turkish military for not compelling the government to follow Washington's orders, and demanded that military leaders apologize and say, "We made a mistake" by overruling virtually unanimous public opinion. "Let's figure out how we can be as helpful as possible to the Americans," they should say, thus demonstrating their understanding of democracy. No wonder he was declared "idealist in chief," whose sole flaw might be that he is "too idealistic—that his passion for the noble goals of the Iraq war might overwhelm the prudence and pragmatism that normally guide war planners."[61]

The evaluation of Wolfowitz in the elite press is instructive. His "passion is the advance of democracy," Sebastian Mallaby declares in the *Washington Post*. In another admiring account, Andrew Balls writes in the *Financial Times* that "promotion of democracy has been one of the most consistent themes of his career." No evidence is cited apart from Wolfowitz's self-image. Praising Wolfowitz's qualifications

to take over as the new head of the World Bank in 2005, Mallaby
writes that his "main exposure to development comes from his time as
ambassador in Indonesia, which combined miraculous poverty reduction with state intervention." And his experience in Indonesia will be
particularly significant because of the "new consensus" in Washington
that "holds that the chief challenge in poor countries is . . . to fight the
corruption that deters private investment and to create the rule of
law."[62]

A look at the actual record is revealing. Jeffrey Winters, an academic specialist on Indonesia, writes that Wolfowitz's main achievement in the economic sphere as ambassador to Indonesia was to help
"set the stage" for the 1997 "collapse of the Indonesian economy under Suharto, a tragedy that plunged tens of millions into abject
poverty." Wolfowitz's most important initiative was to sponsor "one
of the most reckless deregulations of a banking sector ever undertaken," which led to economic collapse and widespread misery.
Suharto, Wolfowitz's favorite, meanwhile earned "the dubious title of
being the most corrupt world leader in recent history," a "clear win-
ner, according to British-based Transparency International," having
amassed a family fortune "estimated at anything between fifteen billion and thirty-five billion US dollars," far outstripping second-place
Ferdinand Marcos of the Philippines and third-place Mobutu Sese
Seko of Congo, also members in good standing in the rogues' gallery
of the administrations in which Wolfowitz served. Wolfowitz has further credentials in development, having been the architect of postwar
reconstruction in Iraq, which, Transparency International warned,
"could become the biggest corruption scandal in history if strict anti-
bribery measures are not adopted rapidly."[63] They were not, and the
prediction is well on its way to verification, as we have seen. Clearly
"Wolfie," as GWB affectionately calls him, has impressive qualifications to carry forward the new consensus on fighting corruption and
promoting economic development.

The idealist in chief's "record from his Indonesia days on human
rights and democracy is even worse," Winters continues. "In a Lexis-
Nexis search of every mention of Wolfowitz in the press during his
years as ambassador, there is not one instance where he is quoted as

speaking up on human rights or democracy in Indonesia. Instead, he is consistently apologetic for the Suharto regime, always turning the focus toward matters of business, investment, and the local and regional stability the iron-fisted Suharto helped promote." Wolfowitz not only intervened to "undercut the Australian journalists who focused attention on a murderous and torturing American ally in Southeast Asia, but he lectured the Australians on how to handle an embarrassing flap . . . —play it down, ignore it." His "cowardly behavior prompted a rare rebuke from the head of the Australian government." Wolfowitz was "specifically singled out for criticism by Australian Prime Minister Bob Hawke for his comments."[64]

Wolfowitz's candidacy for World Bank president immediately "triggered criticism from rights activists in Indonesia." The head of Indonesia's state-sponsored National Human Rights Commission reported that "of all former US ambassadors, he was considered closest to and most influential with Suharto and his family. But he never showed interest in issues regarding democratization or respect of human rights," and never even visited the commission's office. "I also never heard him publicly mention corruption, not once," the commission's head added. Other human rights and anticorruption activists also said that "they do not remember his speaking out against the abuses" of the regime and "never felt Mr Wolfowitz was on their side." They pointed out further that Wolfowitz "remained a defender of the Suharto regime through the 1990s," well past the time when this world-class mass murderer, torturer, and robber had been overthrown from within.[65]

The record of Wolfowitz's "passion" for human rights and democracy goes back to his early days in Reagan's State Department and continues to the present, without notable change. Regional academic specialist Joseph Nevins writes that, throughout his tenure as ambassador and since, Wolfowitz consistently "championed policies that undermine democracy and human rights in the sprawling archipelago," and supported the appalling atrocities carried out by the Indonesian army (TNI) in occupied East Timor. In early 1999, Nevins writes, "when it looked as if Indonesia might consider leaving East Timor, Wolfowitz argued against US policies promoting such a scenario.

Employing language long utilized by Jakarta, he predicted that if Indonesia were to withdraw, East Timor, due to tribal and clan-based tensions, would descend into civil war. Only the TNI had prevented such an outcome, according to Wolfowitz." At that time, the TNI was escalating its atrocities, and soon practically destroyed what little remained of the tortured country in a final paroxysm of violence. "Human rights groups report continuing widespread military atrocities," Nevins continues, "especially in Aceh and West Papua." Indonesian political and military leaders were absolved from responsibility in East Timor in fraudulent trials condemned by human rights organizations, but easily tolerated by Western participants in their crimes. Visiting Jakarta in January 2005, Wolfowitz called for increasing the US military aid and training that have plagued Indonesians and others within the reach of the TNI for the past forty years. The "humanitarian guise" of his mission was tsunami relief, Nevins writes, but its "real significance lies in his effort to strengthen US ties with Indonesia's brutal military, TNI, a role that he has long played."[66]

Bush and associates continued to pursue the president's democratizing mission in the traditional domains of US power as well. In 2002, they supported a military coup to overthrow the elected government of Venezuela, headed by Hugo Chávez, but had to slink away in the face of overwhelming condemnation in Latin America, where democracy is not considered as "quaint" and "obsolete" as it is in Washington. After a popular uprising restored the government, Washington turned to subversion, under the guise of "supporting democracy"—a familiar pattern. Thus, after decertifying Venezuela for alleged noncooperation with US drug operations in the region, Washington "waived the cuts in US foreign aid usually attached to 'decertification' so that it can continue to support Venezuelan pro-democracy groups that oppose the leftist Chávez."[67]

The concept is interesting. While Washington's right to support anti-Chávez groups in Venezuela cannot be questioned, there might perhaps be some eyebrows raised if Iran were funding anti-Bush groups in the United States, particularly if it did so right after having supported a military coup to overthrow the government. It is also ap-

parently taken to be a logical impossibility that some groups supporting Chávez might be "pro-democracy." That is proven by Washington's opposition to the government. Accordingly, it can have no
relevance that Chávez has repeatedly won monitored elections and
referenda despite overwhelming and bitter media hostility, that his
popularity ratings are at 80 percent, or that Latin America's major
polling organization, Latinobarómetro, found in 2004 that while sat-
isfaction with democracy continues its ominous decline throughout
Latin America (in striking parallel to the march of neoliberal programs that undermine functioning democracy), there were three exceptions: leading the list was Venezuela, where support for democracy
climbed from 64 percent to 74 percent between 1997 and 2004. The
country now leads all countries in Latin America in support for its
elected government.[68]

In contrast, most US citizens believe that the public has little influence on government decisions and few believe that Congress will conform to "the decisions the majority of Americans would make." US
citizens rank their own government below Britain, Sweden, Canada,
and others on the scale ranging from not democratic at all to completely democratic.[69]

Further proof of the antidemocratic character of Chávez supporters in Venezuela was his performance at the September 2005 UN Summit, where he "generated the loudest burst of applause for a world
leader at the summit with his unbridled attack on what he characterized as US militarism and capitalism." This outlandish characterization of the United States as capitalist and militaristic reveals that he
has "taken on the mantle of the bad boy of UN summitry." Off the
radar screen is what Americans can read in Ireland's leading journal
by the veteran Latin American correspondent Hugh O'Shaughnessy,
which helps explain the basis for the applause without resort to Bush-
style wailing about how the world hates us because we are so good:

> In Venezuela, where an oil economy has over the decades pro-
> duced a sparkling elite of super-rich, a quarter of under-15s go
> hungry, for instance, and 60 per cent of people over 59 have no

income at all. Less than a fifth of the population enjoys social security. Only now under President Chávez, the former parachute
colonel elected to office in 1998, has medicine started to become
something of a reality for the poverty-stricken majority in the
rich but deeply divided—virtually non-functioning—society.
Since he won power in democratic elections and began to transform the health and welfare sector which catered so badly to the
mass of the population progress has been slow. But it has been
perceptible—not least because Venezuela has joined with Cuba
in a joint health strategy which has brought perhaps 20,000
Cuban doctors and other health professionals here and spread
them around the country from Caracas to remote spots where
Venezuelan doctors refuse to serve.

"Operation Miracle" is spreading the model to the Caribbean, with
significant impact among the poor majority, it appears.[70]

In March 2004, concerned that elections in El Salvador might come
out the wrong way, the democracy promotion missionaries warned
that if Salvadorans made the wrong choice, the country's lifeline—
remittances from the United States, a crucial pillar of the "economic
miracle"—might be cut, among other consequences. They also clari-
fied their mission by offering their achievements in El Salvador as a
model for Iraq. In reaction to the favorable coverage of this audacious
stand, one of the leading academic specialists on Central America,
Thomas Walker, distributed an op-ed to newspapers around the country describing the "free elections" under US domination hailed by
Cheney, Rumsfeld, and others. These elections, he reminds us, "were
held against a backdrop of state-sponsored terror which had taken the
lives of tens of thousands of innocent civilians, crippled civil society,
and completely silenced the opposition media." The candidates, more-
over, were limited to "a narrow spectrum from center to far right";
voter abstention was threatened with murder, and votes were cast using sequentially numbered, identifiable ballots "deposited in clear plas-
tic boxes in front of armed soldiers—so translucent that [the ballots]
could be read even when duly folded."[71]

This was clearly the wrong story; the op-ed was rejected. That came as no surprise to Walker. He is also the author of the major scholarly studies of Nicaragua, and through the 1980s, when Nicaragua was the top story of the day, he sent several op-eds a year to the *New York Times*. None appeared. Again, the wrong story. A review of op-eds and editorials in the liberal national press at the peak moments of coverage of Nicaragua revealed the familiar split between hawks and doves, about fifty-fifty, demonstrating the balance and openness in the free press. The hawks called for escalating the international terrorist assault. The doves countered that violence was not succeeding, so the United States should find other means to compel Nicaraguans to adhere to the "Central American mode" and adopt the "regional standards" of Washington's preferred states, El Salvador and Guatemala, then engaged in gruesome state terror. Walker and Latin American specialists generally fell outside of this spectrum and thus were virtually ignored, sometimes in startling ways. One example, again bearing on "democracy promotion," was the 1984 Nicaragua elections, which had doctrinally unacceptable results—the Sandinistas won—and therefore *did not take place*, though they were closely observed and generally approved, including by hostile observers and a delegation of specialists on Nicaragua sent by the professional association of Latin America scholars, all suppressed. One of those observers was José Figueres of Costa Rica, who joined in pronouncing the 1984 elections fair by Latin American standards and was also ignored. More generally, though passionately anti-Communist and anti-Sandinista, and a strong supporter of Washington and US corporate investors, he felt that Nicaraguans should be left to deal with their own problems in their own way. Consequently, the leading figure of Central American democracy was barred from the press throughout the years of Reagan's terrorist wars in the region, or in the preferred version, the years of dedication to "democracy promotion." A familiar practice, as we have seen.[72]

In praising the Salvadoran model, Bush administration democracy-promoters failed to mention one of the important contributions of Reagan's "war on terror." In Iraq, the private security firms that are the second-largest component of the "coalition of the willing are dipping into experienced pools of trained fighters," almost 70 percent from El Salvador, it is estimated. The trained killers from the Reagan-run state terrorist apparatus can earn better pay pursuing their craft in Iraq than in what remains of their societies at home.[73]

The familiar patterns have been followed from the traditional domains of US power in the Western Hemisphere to the newer ones in Central Asia. After the May 2005 massacres in Uzbekistan, "US officials have walked a fine line, saying they were 'deeply disturbed' over [the] killings but also express[ing] alarm over anti-government violence. Taking a more assertive stand, British, French and European Union officials have denounced the deadly crackdown and called for international observers to be let in to investigate." Washington distanced itself even from Europe's light tap on the wrist, preferring more open support for the tyrant Islam Karimov, who enjoys such pleasures as murdering dissidents by boiling them to death, according to former British ambassador Craig Murray. Murray was recalled to London for such indiscretions, not to speak of his description of Karimov as "George Bush's man in central Asia," praised by senior members of the Bush administration and backed "to the hilt" because of Uzbekistan's significant reserves of oil and gas. In his cables to London in 2002 and 2003, Murray had written: "US plays down human rights situation in Uzbekistan. A dangerous policy: increasing repression combined with poverty will promote Islamic terrorism." And: "As seen from Tashkent, US policy is not much focused on democracy or freedom. It is about oil, gas and hegemony. In Uzbekistan the US pursues those ends through supporting a ruthless dictatorship." The State Department gave Uzbekistan a favorable human rights assessment, Murray said, in order to free up hundreds of millions of dollars in aid. In a secret letter on March 18, 2003, as Bush and Blair were launching the Iraq war, Murray wrote: "Last year the US gave half a billion dollars in aid to Uzbekistan, about a quarter of it military aid. Bush and Powell repeatedly hail Karimov as a friend and ally. Yet this regime has at least seven thousand prisoners of conscience; it is a one-party state without freedom of speech, without freedom of media, without freedom of movement, without freedom of assembly, without freedom of religion. It practices, systematically, the most hideous tortures on thousands. Most of the population live in conditions precisely analogous with medieval serfdom."[74]

Karimov was not backed enthusiastically enough for his taste, however. Dissatisfied, he compelled Washington to shift its air bases to neighboring tyrannies. "The US is trying to cover its retreat behind a smokescreen of belated concern for human-rights abuses in Uzbekistan," Murray wrote. "Suddenly one of their most intensively courted allies has been discovered—shock horror—to be an evil dictator. (Remember Saddam?)" The dictator, it turned out, preferred the style of Russian president Vladimir Putin to that of his Western suitors, though not all are withdrawing: "Of all western ministers, the most frequent guest in Uzbekistan, who most uncritically praises the regime, is Joschka Fischer, the trendy German foreign minister" and former 1960s radical.[75]

Prior to Karimov's slap in Washington's face, it was widely expected that the United States might be "the saviour of this dying autocratic regime," writes David Wall of the Royal Institute of International Affairs, noting Washington's "increase in funding for the Uzbek government" and the fact that "independent observers inside Uzbekistan say that US presence in the country is up to twice as large as Washington is willing to admit." At the same time, "Secretary of State Condoleezza Rice exercised a waiver to allow continued military aid to nearby Kazakhstan on national security grounds despite what the State Department acknowledged were 'numerous steps backward' on human rights." Washington "will stay 'fully engaged' despite what [Rice] outlined as Kazakhstan's many recent regressions"—from a starting point that was not exactly elevated. US military aid "enhances democracy," Rice said, intoning rhetoric that is as familiar as its grim meaning.[76]

In neighboring Azerbaijan, at the opening of a pipeline that will carry Caspian oil to the West on a route that avoids Russia and Iran, the US energy secretary delivered a ringing message from President Bush: "As Azerbaijan deepens its democratic and market economic reforms, this pipeline can help generate balanced economic growth, and provide a foundation for a prosperous and just society that advances

the cause of freedom." A few days earlier, the *New York Times* reported, "the Azerbaijani police beat pro-democracy demonstrators
with truncheons when opposition parties, yelling 'free elections,' defied the government's ban on protests against President Ilham Aliyev,"
a US ally who had just "won a highly suspect election to succeed his
father, a former Soviet strongman." Much the same is true in Turkmenistan, which Human Rights Watch describes as "one of the most
repressive countries in the world."[77]

"In a region of bases, energy and big-power rivalries, ideals require
patience," the *New York Times* explains. Therefore Washington has
to temper its passion for democracy and human rights.[78]

There are good reasons for the imperial powers and their acolytes
to insist that we should forget about the past and move forward: the
familiar refrain of "change of course" that is invoked every few years.
But those who prefer to understand the world, the victims included,
will recognize that history teaches many important lessons. "All of
this matters," two scholars write in *Foreign Affairs*, "because national
historical memory—or amnesia—can have concrete political consequences. How states and societies engage their pasts affects how they
develop." We understand that very well, and rightly find it deeply disturbing, when the charge of amnesia is directed against antagonists, as
in this case: they are discussing how "national historical memory" in
Russia has failed to come to terms with Bolshevik crimes. Deep concern has also been expressed, repeatedly, about Japan's limited recognition of its past atrocities, among other cases selected according to
the same very clear criterion.[79]

Preserving "historical memory" unsullied by apologetics is no less
important for the permanent victors, who can be called to account
only by their own citizens. That is particularly true when the institutional roots of past practices persist. Those who want to understand
today's world will take note of Britain's actions from the days when it
created modern Iraq for its own convenience, ensuring Iraq's dependency. And they will not overlook Britain's practices until the regime it
imposed and supported was overthrown in 1958. Nor will they overlook the conclusion of the Foreign Office in July of that year that in
British-dominated Iraq, "Wealth and power have remained concen-

trated in the hands of a few rich landowners and tribal sheikhs centered round the Court in a brutally repressive society."[80]

The overthrow of the British-backed Iraqi regime by Abdul Karim Qasim in 1958 was the first break in the Anglo-American condominium over the world's major energy resources. The United States and United Kingdom reacted at once, both with military action in Lebanon and Jordan and with secret joint plans to resort to violence if necessary to ensure that the virus of independent nationalism did not infect others—"ruthlessly to intervene," in their words, whatever the source of the threat to dominance. This planning was highly relevant to the 1991 war.[81]

Concerns over the Qasim regime were enhanced by the evaluations of close imperial observers. An official of the British corporation that controlled Iraq's oil informed the Foreign Office that Qasim's goals went well beyond "political independence, dignity and unity, in brotherly cooperation with other Arabs." He also wanted "to increase and distribute the national wealth, . . . to found a new society and a new democracy, [and] to use this strong, democratic, Arabist Iraq as an instrument to free and elevate other Arabs and Afro-Asians and to assist the destruction of 'imperialism,' by which he largely meant British influence in the underdeveloped countries."[82]

As if that were not ominous enough, there was concern that Qasim might adopt Gamal Abdel Nasser's "plans to use Saudi petrodollars to improve the living standards of poor Arabs everywhere." One Nasser was bad enough: "an expansionist dictator somewhat of the Hitler type," Secretary of State Dulles railed, a power-hungry monster whose *Philosophy of the Revolution* was barely distinguishable from *Mein Kampf*. He was capturing "Arab loyalty and enthusiasm throughout the region," President Eisenhower observed with dismay, warning that he was trying "to get control of [Middle East oil]—to get the income and the power to destroy the Western world." Eisenhower assured Congress that the coup in Iraq and disturbances in Lebanon and Jordan were "being fomented by Nasser under Kremlin guidance." Intelligence reported that "popular feeling in the Arab world, even in such states as Saudi Arabia and Kuwait, is generally favorable to the Iraqi coup and hostile to US and UK intervention [so] there is a strong possibility that the revolutionary infection will spread" even to the US-backed tyrannies that controlled the world's main oil resources, possibly even to Libya, another important oil producer then firmly under a US-backed dictator. Washington toyed with the idea that Qasim might be a counter to "Communism," but it is unlikely that any such thoughts survived his 1961 decision that "took away over 99.5 percent of the concession area" of the multinational that controlled Iraq's oil, including both proven reserves and possible fields that were still unexplored but assumed to be huge.[83]

The virus was evidently dangerous and had to be destroyed. And it was, in 1963. According to former National Security Council staffer Roger Morris, confirmed by other sources, "The Central Intelligence Agency, under President John F. Kennedy, conducted its own regime change in Baghdad, carried out in collaboration with Saddam Hussein" and the Baath Party. It was " 'almost certainly a gain for our side,' National Security Council aide Robert Komer informed Kennedy the day of the takeover." The usual hideous atrocities followed, including a slaughter of "suspected Communists and other leftists," using lists provided by the CIA, much as in Guatemala in 1954 and in Indonesia two years after the overthrow of Qasim. "The Baathists systematically murdered untold numbers of Iraq's educated elite," Morris continues, including "hundreds of doctors, teachers, technicians, lawyers and other professionals as well as military and political figures." There followed further crimes that we need not recount, with ample support when considered useful by London, Washington, and other willing participants. Reviewing the story on the eve of the US and UK invasion of Iraq in 2003, Morris commented perceptively: "If a new war in Iraq seems fraught with danger and uncertainty, just wait for the peace." There appear to have been many such warnings from knowledgeable analysts, disregarded by Rumsfeld, Wolfowitz, and associates.[84]

It is notable that fear of Iraqi democracy persisted without change even when Saddam became an enemy in 1990. In the following months and through the war, the democratic opposition within Iraq was not only barred from Washington but by the media as well.[85]

Suppose, however, that we adopt the convention of dispatching the inconvenient past to the memory hole and dismissing its rather clear lessons as old-fashioned irrelevancy, adopting the comforting posture of "historical amnesia" that we deplore among enemies. Let us then assume that a miraculous conversion has taken place in Washington and London, as often proclaimed before, but this time in reality: the United States will promote (or at least tolerate) a moderately independent and sovereign Iraq, departing from its consistent record there and elsewhere. A rational observer might nevertheless conclude that the declarations of the foreign minister of Iran are more credible than those emanating from Washington and London. Iran could live with a more or less democratic and sovereign Iraq. It is hard to imagine how Washington and London could do so.

Consider the policies that Iraq would be likely to adopt. Iraqis may have no love for Iran, but they would prefer friendly relations with their powerful neighbor to antagonism and conflict, and would be likely to join in the efforts to integrate Iran into the region, which were under way long before the US and UK invasion. Furthermore, the Shiite religious and political leadership in Iraq has very close links with Iran. Shiite success in Iraq is already invigorating the pressures for freedom and democracy among the bitterly oppressed Shiite population of Saudi Arabia just across the border, tendencies that would only increase if Iraq were to be granted a measure of sovereignty. The efforts of the Saudi Shiites go back many years, and elicited a harsh crackdown when they sought to overthrow the brutal US-backed monarchy in the early 1980s. "They believe that Osama bin Laden and his ilk created an important opening," the *New York Times* reports, "with the royal family now casting about for ways to limit the Wahhabi extremism that it has encouraged but which now seeks to overthrow Saudi rule." For the first time, "the Shiites of eastern Saudi Arabia, the only part of the kingdom where they are a majority, are preparing to win a small measure of political power." That is also the region where most Saudi oil happens to be.[86]

The outcome could be a loose Shiite-dominated alliance comprising Iraq, Iran, and the oil regions of Saudi Arabia, independent of Washington and controlling the bulk of the world's energy resources. Washington's ultimate nightmare—almost. It could get worse. It's not unlikely that an independent bloc of this kind might follow Iran's lead in developing major energy projects jointly with China and India, perhaps even allying with the Asian Energy Security Grid and the Shanghai Cooperation Organization. This bloc might also move toward a basket of currencies for denomination of oil, rather than relying primarily on the US dollar, a step that could have a major impact on the US and global economy. A side issue is that if the United States cannot control Iraq, there is no guarantee that Iraqis in charge of the country's immense oil resources will give preferential treatment to favored energy corporations.[87]

Even the very limited degree of sovereignty that the Iraqi government enjoyed after the January 2005 elections gives a foretaste of what might lie ahead. On an official visit to Tehran, the Iraqi minister of defense and his Iranian counterpart announced "a new chapter" in their relations, including cross-border military cooperation and Iranian help with training and upgrading Iraq's armed forces, displacing US-Coalition advisers, a move that apparently took Washington by surprise. The Iraqi minister dismissed US concerns about Iranian meddling in the region, saying, "Nobody can dictate to Iraq its relations with other countries." Meanwhile, "the once libertine oil port of Basra," deep in the south near the Iranian border, "is steadily being transformed into a mini-theocracy under Shiite rule," Edward Wong reports. "The growing ties with Iran are evident. Posters of Ayatollah Ruhollah Khomeini, the leader of the 1979 Iranian revolution, are plastered along streets and even at the provincial government center. The Iranian government opened a polling station downtown for Iranian expatriates during elections in their home country in June. The governor also talks eagerly of buying electricity from Iran, given that the American-led effort has failed to provide enough of it." The provincial council is dominated by clerics close to the anti-occupation Sadr movement and to the Supreme Council for the Islamic Revolution (SCIRI), the major Shiite faction, formed by Shiite exiles in Iran. SCIRI also controls the Badr militia, which runs much of the southern region and has traditionally close relations with Iran, where it was organized and trained. Returning from a visit to Iran, the head of SCIRI, Abdul Aziz al-Hakim, praised the proposal to buy electricity from Iran, and called for closer ties to "the great Islamic Republic, [which] has a very honorable attitude toward Iraq."[88]

Peter Galbraith writes that "it may be the ultimate irony that the United States, which, among other reasons, invaded Iraq to help bring liberal democracy to the Middle East, will play a decisive role in establishing its second Shiite Islamic state."[89] It would indeed be the ultimate irony, in fact almost incomprehensible stupidity, if a goal of the invasion had been "to help bring liberal democracy to the Middle East" in any meaningful sense—yet another reason for skepticism about the claim, which remains free from any taint of supporting evidence, apart from the well-timed declarations of leaders, and has to face mountains of counterevidence, some already sampled. Additional reasons for skepticism are that an independent Iraq, or an Arab Iraq if Iraq fractures, might seek to recover its leadership role in the Arab world, therefore rearming to confront the regional enemy, Israel, and quite possibly developing a nuclear deterrent.

We are therefore being asked to believe that the United States will stand by quietly watching a serious challenge to Israel, its primary regional client, as well as the takeover of the world's major energy reserves by a Muslim bloc free from US control, and the displacement of the Saudi royal family, long allied with the United States in opposing secular Arab nationalism. Those who have jumped enthusiastically on the "democratization bandwagon" are suggesting that Washington would politely observe such not unlikely developments. Perhaps, but the prospects appear rather remote.[90]

These are among the many reasons why a rational observer might be inclined to share Iraqi skepticism about the sudden and timely conversion to the messianic mission, and why such an observer might give considerable weight to the conclusion that, among the difficulties that have stood in the way of democratic transformation for many years in the Middle East, today too the "final barrier [is that] the world's sole superpower does not really want it to happen, pious neoconservative rhetoric notwithstanding."[91]

These are also among the many reasons why comparisons between Vietnam and Iraq are so misleading. In Vietnam, Washington planners could fulfill their primary war aims by destroying the virus and inoculating the region, then withdrawing, leaving the wreckage to enjoy its sovereignty. The situation in Iraq is radically different. Iraq cannot be destroyed and abandoned. It is too valuable, and authentic sovereignty and even limited democracy would be too dangerous to be easily accepted. If at all possible, Iraq must be kept under control, if not in the manner anticipated by Bush planners, at least somehow. For the same reasons, the many proposals for an "exit strategy" are quite odd.[92] Planners surely do not need the advice. They can figure out these simple exit strategies for themselves. And no doubt they want to withdraw—but only once an obedient client state is firmly in place, the general preference of conquerors, leaving just military bases for future contingencies.

In discussing these matters, it is important to bear in mind some fundamental principles. Crucially, occupying armies have no rights, only responsibilities. Their primary responsibility is to withdraw as quickly and expeditiously as possible, in a manner to be determined primarily by the occupied population. Unless there is strong popular support for their presence, they have no right to remain. If these principles are not observed, proposals for an "exit strategy" are more a reflection of imperial will than an expression of concern for the victims. As we shall see, Iraqi opinion, insofar as information is available, overwhelmingly calls for withdrawal. Furthermore, since shortly after the invasion, a large majority of people in the United States have held that the UN, not Washington, should take the lead in working with Iraqis to transfer authentic sovereignty, as well as in economic reconstruction and the maintenance of civic order. That could be a sensible stand if Iraqis agree, though the General Assembly, less directly controlled by the invaders, is preferable to the Security Council as the responsible transitional authority. The disgraceful economic regime imposed by the occupying authorities should be rescinded, along with the harsh antilabor laws and practices of the occupation. Reconstruction should be in the hands of Iraqis, not designed as a means of controlling them in accord with Washington's announced plans.[93] Reparations—not just aid—should be provided by those responsible for devastating Iraqi civilian society by cruel sanctions and military actions, as well as for supporting Saddam Hussein through his worst atrocities and well beyond. That is the minimum that decency requires. One way to evaluate the entire discussion of democracy promotion is to ask how these issues are dealt with, or if they are even raised—questions that regrettably do not require much inquiry.

THE "STRONG LINE OF CONTINUITY"

The strongest witnesses for the defense of the authenticity of President Bush's messianic mission should be the leading scholars and most enthusiastic advocates of "democracy promotion." None is as prominent as the director of the Democracy and Rule of Law Project at the Carnegie Endowment, Thomas Carothers, who identifies his stand as neo-Reaganite. A year after the invasion of Iraq, and after the messianic mission had replaced the "single question," he published a book reviewing the record of democracy promotion since the end of the Cold War, now "much in the news [with the] strenuous effort by the United States and its coalition partners to carry off a democratic transformation of Iraq." Carothers found a "strong line of continuity" running through all administrations in the post–Cold War era, Bush II included: "Where democracy appears to fit in well with US security and economic interests, the United States promotes democracy. Where democracy clashes with other significant interests, it is downplayed or even ignored." All administrations are "schizophrenic" in this regard, Carothers observes, with puzzling consistency—commonly called "inconsistency."[94]

Carothers also wrote the standard scholarly work on democracy promotion in Latin America in the 1980s. The topic is of particular contemporary significance because of the widely held thesis that Washington's traditional idealistic dedication to promoting democracy gained "particular salience" during the Reagan years, and has since been taken up with even greater force by the present administration, with its Reaganite roots. Carothers writes in part from an insider's perspective, having served in Reagan's State Department in the programs of "democracy enhancement." He regards these programs as having been sincere, though a failure, and a systematic one. Where US influence was least, in South America, progress toward democracy

was greatest, particularly in the early 1980s when "the Reagan administration was trying to support the military governments that were on
the way out [and] if anything, the US policy of that period worked
against the democratic trend." Where US influence was strongest, in
the regions nearby, progress was least. The reason, Carothers explains, is that Washington sought to maintain "the basic order of
what, historically at least, are quite undemocratic societies" and to
avoid "populist-based change in Latin America—with all its implications for upsetting economic and political orders and heading off in a
leftist direction." The Reagan administration "came to adopt
prodemocracy policies as a means of relieving pressure for more radical change, but inevitably sought only limited, top-down forms of
democratic change that did not risk upsetting the traditional structures of power with which the United States has long been allied." The
proudest achievement was El Salvador, now offered by Washington as
a model for Iraq. Here, the Reagan administration sought two goals:
"ensuring that technically credible elections were held and that the
Christian Democratic candidate . . . won." The administration "could
not conceive of an El Salvador in which the military was not the dominant actor, the economic elite no longer held the national economy in
its hands, the left was incorporated into the political system, and all
Salvadorans actually had both the formal and substantial possibility of
political participation. In short, the US government had no real conception of democracy in El Salvador."[95]

While "democracy enhancement" was proceeding in this manner,
the state terrorists supported by Washington were slaughtering the opposition by the tens of thousands, carrying out hideous torture and
other atrocities, destroying the independent press, and leaving behind
a "culture of terror [that] domesticates the expectations of the majority" and undermines aspirations toward "alternatives that differ from
those of the powerful," in the words of the Salvadoran Jesuits; those
who survived, that is.

The Reaganite conception of democracy is illustrated as well by
their favorite figures in Central America. Among them was the worst
of Guatemala's gang of extraordinary murderers, Rioss Montt, who
was getting a "bum rap" and was "totally dedicated to democracy,"

Reagan explained. Another was Brigadier General Gustavo Álvarez Martínez of Honduras, chief of the Honduran armed forces. His career is of particularly pertinence today because he operated under the protection of John Negroponte, who is now in charge of counterterrorism, and was then ambassador to Honduras, running the world's largest CIA station. Known as the "pro-consul," Negroponte "was essentially managerially in charge of the Contra war in an extraordinary way for a diplomat," Peter Kornbluh observes, relying in part on secret documentation obtained by the National Security Archives, where he is a senior analyst. Negroponte's responsibilities took a new turn after official funding for Reagan's international terrorist operations was barred in 1983, and he had to implement White House orders to bribe and pressure senior Honduran generals to step up their support for these operations with funds from other sources, later also using funds illegally transferred from US arms sales to Iran.

Chief of the Honduran armed forces, General Álvarez was the most important and also the most vicious of the Honduran killers and torturers protected by Negroponte. Álvarez received strong American support, a *Baltimore Sun* investigation discovered, even after he told Carter administration ambassador Jack Binns that "he intended to use the Argentine method of eliminating suspected subversives." Negroponte, Binns's successor, regularly denied gruesome state crimes in Honduras to ensure that military aid would continue to flow for the international terrorist operations he was managing. The *Sun* reported that "by 1983, when Alvarez's oppressive methods were well known to the US Embassy, the Reagan administration awarded him the Legion of Merit medal for 'encouraging the success of democratic processes in Honduras.'" Negroponte praised Álvarez's "dedication to democracy," following the same script as Reagan. The elite unit responsible for the worst crimes in Honduras was Battalion 3-16, organized and trained by the United States and Argentine neo-Nazis, the most barbaric of the Latin American killers that Washington had been supporting. Honduran military officers in charge of the battalion were on the CIA payroll. When the government of Honduras finally tried to deal with these crimes and bring the perpetrators to justice, the Reagan-Bush administration refused to allow Negroponte to testify, as the courts requested.[96]

All worth remembering, along with a treasure trove of other examples, when we read about the Reaganite passion for "democracy
promotion."

In short, the "strong line of continuity" goes back a decade earlier,
to the Reagan years. In fact, far beyond. Democracy promotion has
always been proclaimed as a guiding vision. But it is not even controversial that the United States often overthrew democratic governments, often installing or supporting brutal tyrannies: Iran, Guatemala,
Brazil, Chile, and a long list of others. The Cold War pretexts regularly collapse under investigation. What we do find, however, is the operative principle that Carothers describes: democracy is a good thing *if*
and only if it is consistent with strategic and economic interests.

Putting aside doctrinal blinders, it is hard to disagree with Latin
American scholar Charles Bergquist that "rather than promoting
democracy" in Latin America, consistent and often brutal US opposition to struggles for reform of deeply unjust and undemocratic societies "has historically subverted [democracy], both at home and
abroad" while serving "the 'security interests' of privileged elites in
the hemisphere, who have benefited most from the social status quo."
Serious mainstream scholarship has long recognized that "while paying lip-service to the encouragement of representative democracy in
Latin America, the United States has a strong interest in just the reverse," apart from "procedural democracy, especially the holding of
elections—which only too often have proved farcical." Functioning
democracy may respond to popular concerns, while "the United
States has been concerned with fostering the most favourable conditions for her private overseas investment." Accordingly there is "no
serious question of [US] intervention in the case of the many right-
wing military coups"—except, one may add, intervention to support
or initiate them—but matters are different "when her own concept of
democracy, closely identified with private, capitalistic enterprise, is
threatened by communism," commonly a cover term for the threat of
independent development. The record is not fundamentally different
outside of Latin America, as one would expect from the nature of the
institutions that set the basic framework for policy choices. Nor is it

surprising that policies continue today, reflecting the same "schizo-phrenia."[97]

Carothers hopes that democracy promotion will mature into a "proto-science," though the process is slow: "Democracy promotion is not a young field when one considers the efforts by the United States in the early twentieth century to construct democratic governments in Central America and the Caribbean after its various military interventions there."[98] A competent scholar, Carothers is well aware of the nature of these efforts, well illustrated by the three leading targets of US military intervention: Haiti, Guatemala, and Nicaragua. In these cases, as in others, we find that policies did not materially change with the onset of the Cold War, and that during the Cold War years the conflict was rarely relevant beyond providing misimpressions. What we find throughout is the operative principle that Carothers describes.

Woodrow Wilson invaded Haiti, the prototypical "failed state," in 1915, sending his troops to dissolve the National Assembly "by genuinely Marine Corps methods," in the words of the marine commander, Major Smedley Butler. The reason was the assembly's refusal to ratify a US-designed constitution that gave US corporations the right to buy up Haiti's lands—regarded by the invaders as a "progressive" measure that Haitians could not comprehend. A marine-run plebiscite remedied the problem: the constitution was ratified by a 99.9 percent majority, with 5 percent of the population participating. Thousands of Haitians were killed resisting Wilson's invaders, who also reinstituted virtual slavery, leaving the country in the hands of a vicious National Guard after nineteen years of Wilsonian idealism. Horrors continued unabated, along with US support, until Haiti's first democratic election in 1990.

The outcome set off alarm bells in Washington. Grassroots organizing in the slums and hills, to which few had paid attention, permitted an authentic election. Against enormous odds, the population chose their own candidate, the populist priest Jean-Bertrand Aristide, while the US-approved candidate, former World Bank official Marc Bazin, received 14 percent of the vote. Washington moved immediately to reverse the scandal. Aid for "democracy promotion" sharply increased, directed to antigovernment, probusiness groups, mainly through the US Agency for International Development (USAID), also the National Endowment for Democracy and AIFLD (the AFL-CIO affiliate with a notorious antilabor record throughout the Third World). One of the closest observers of Haiti, Amy Wilentz, wrote that USAID's huge "Democracy Enhancement" project was "specifically designed to fund those sectors of the Haitian political spectrum where opposition to the Aristide government could be encouraged." Other US policy choices were also directed to containing the threat of democracy that had made the wrong decisions. When a military coup took place a few months later, the Organization of American States imposed an embargo. Bush I announced that he would violate it, exempting US firms. Under Clinton, trade increased still further. Bush and particularly Clinton also authorized the Texaco oil company to supply the military junta and its wealthy supporters with oil in violation of presidential directives, thus rendering the OAS blockade almost entirely meaningless.[99]

After three years of horrendous state terror, Clinton allowed the elected president to return, but on a crucial condition: that he adopt the program of the defeated US candidate in the 1990 election. As predicted at once, the harsh neoliberal programs dismantled what was left of economic sovereignty and drove the country into chaos and violence, accelerated by Bush's banning of international aid on cynical grounds. In February 2004, with French support, the United States spirited Aristide out of the country, which fell back into the hands of the traditional predators, including elements of the army that Aristide had disbanded. Nine months later, investigations by the University of Miami School of Law found that "many Haitians, especially those living in poor neighborhoods, now struggle against inhuman horror. Nightmarish fear now accompanies Haiti's poorest in their struggle to survive in destitution [in] a cycle of violence [fueled by] Haiti's security and justice institutions."[100]

Meanwhile the main Haitian architect of the terror, who bears major responsibility for thousands of deaths, lives peacefully in New York (Emmanuel Constant, who headed the terrorist force FRAPH). Repeated requests by the elected government of Haiti for his extradition were rejected by Washington, or simply ignored—in one striking case, right in the midst of the furor over the unwillingness of the Taliban to follow Washington's orders to turn over 9/11 suspects without evidence. The reason, it is widely assumed, is concern that, if tried, Constant might reveal CIA connections during the terror.[101]

The virus of popular democracy once again was destroyed, along with hopes for some measure of social justice in a country that has been crushed under the boots of the great powers for centuries. There is no further interest in Washington, which has been in charge of the operation for the past century. What survives in the doctrinal system is that Haiti has been "battered by storms of [its] own making," and that the despair of Haitians over their wrecked country is "a sorry comment on the failed governments" since Aristide assumed office in 1991.[102] Washington's dedication to democracy promotion could not overcome the deficiencies of the society it so fervently sought to help.

In Guatemala, Washington's destruction of the elected government "triggered a ghastly, four-decade-long cycle of terror and repression that led to the death of perhaps two hundred thousand Guatemalans," facts well enough known despite Reagan administration efforts to protect state power from US citizens by blocking the regular declassification procedure covering atrocities there, "an appalling incident in the history" of the State Department's Office of the Historian.[103] Guatemala's hopeful decade of democracy was crushed with resort to Cold War pretexts that would be disgraceful even if they had been valid. The real reasons, as extensively documented in the internal record, were fear of Guatemalan democracy and the risk that the "infection" of highly popular social and economic reforms there would spread in the region. When there finally was an independent accounting by Truth Commissions in El Salvador and Guatemala, the scenes of the worst terrorist crimes of the Reagan years, the atrocities were almost entirely attributed to state terrorists, as had been evident all along.

In Nicaragua, the US military occupation created the National Guard that brutalized the population for decades under the rule of the murderous Somoza family dictatorship, which Washington supported until the latest tyrant was overthrown by an internal revolt in 1979. When Somoza could no longer be sustained, Washington tried to preserve its National Guard, then turned to a terrorist war, which raged until 1990, when voters chose a candidate of Washington's choice with "a gun to their heads," as Thomas Walker writes in his standard history. The death toll was equivalent in per capita terms to 2.25 million in the United States, greater than all wars in American history combined, including the Civil War.[104]

After the United States regained control in 1990, Nicaragua declined to become the second poorest country in the hemisphere, after Haiti—which also holds the prize as the prime target of US intervention in the past century; Nicaragua is second. Within a decade, a large part of the working population had emigrated to carry out the dirty work elsewhere to provide the remittances on which families survive. Most went to Costa Rica, the one functioning country in Central America (and the only one not to have experienced direct US intervention). Health officials reported in 2003 that 60 percent of children under two suffer from anemia due to malnutrition, with likely mental retardation. In 2004, malnourishment increased, mainly among children, while life expectancy declined. Close to 70 percent of rural inhabitants live in a state of chronic or extreme hunger, with more than 25 percent unable to eat more than one meal a day, and 43 percent unable to eat more than two meals. The public health system is in a state of collapse, and environmental catastrophes resulting largely from desperate poverty (deforestation, and so on) made Nicaragua "worthy of the title the ultimate laboratory of social vulnerability" in 2004, the year-end summary in *La Prensa* observed. Sixty percent of children and adolescents are not in school. The average number of years of formal education is 4.6, dropping to only 2 years in the countryside, and the quality is extremely poor because of lack of resources. International relief goes largely to paying debt, mostly to the mafia-style financial system that developed after the victory of Washington's terrorist war and economic strangulation in the 1980s.[105]

The victory of US terror was so complete that the "democracy" that emerged from the wreckage—a "Victory for US Fair Play," as a *New York Times* headline enthusiastically proclaimed after the 1990 election—has been considerably more willing to follow IMF–World Bank directives than its neighbors. The results show, for example, in the energy sector, where the privatization demanded by the international financial institutions tends to correlate with disaster for the population. Nicaragua was the most obedient, and the disaster is worst. Access to electricity is far lower in Nicaragua than its neighbors, and prices (which generally correlate with privatization) are far higher, as is dependence on imported oil instead of internal resources. (Costa Rica has been able to shift almost completely to hydroelectric power.) In 1996, before the neoliberal dictates were followed in Nicaragua, its electrification rate was the same as Guatemala's; now it is just over half as high. Nicaragua has plenty of reserve capacity, but there is no profit incentive to supply it to rural regions or the great mass of poor people. The familiar and quite natural outcome of neoliberal programs.[106]

At the liberal extreme of US journalism, commentators puzzle about the "anti-American screeds" in Nicaragua "as the country tries to recover from 25 years [sic] of failed revolution and economic stagnation." Perhaps Nicaraguans suffer from the irrationality that has always caused such frustration in the civilized West, much like the Iraqis who today find it "entirely incomprehensible that foreigners have been unselfishly expending their own blood and treasure to help them."[107]

The substantial progress of the early years in Nicaragua after the overthrow of the US-backed dictatorship, which greatly impressed development agencies and international institutions, has been sharply reversed. The miserable conditions in Nicaragua could be significantly alleviated in very conservative ways. A start would be for the United States to pay the reparations ordered by the highest international authorities, the World Court and Security Council. That would more than overcome the debt strangling the country since the years of the US terrorist attack, though much more would have to be done to restore a viable society from the wreckage of the Reaganite assault.

In 2003, Colin Powell visited Nicaragua to make sure that it was cooperating properly with the US "war on terror" that was redeclared after 9/11. Powell was speaking from experience, having helped direct the first phase of the "war on terror" in the 1980s, which specifically targeted Nicaragua. No eyebrows were raised. As Powell arrived to deliver his injunction, the US embassy in Managua released a briefing memo to journalists reporting that "Nicaragua crawls along as the second-poorest country in the hemisphere after Haiti, battered by storms of nature and *their own making*, with little hope of changing things in the future" (my emphasis). Nicaraguans appeared unreceptive to Powell's message. Perhaps the explanation is provided by the memo, "written in a disdainful tone," which "said most Nicaraguans had little interest in the world beyond their shores."[108] For some strange reason.

Powell faced problems in delivering his message elsewhere in Latin America as well. At the annual meeting of the Organization of American States in June 2003, "Mr. Powell was nearly alone in focusing on the triple scourge he described as 'tyrants, traffickers and terrorists.' For the most part, representatives of the 33 other nations taking part emphasized the need for social justice, warning that democracy itself could be threatened by mounting economic difficulties and inequality," in no small measure a consequence of US military intervention, terror, and economic doctrines and policies.[109]

Washington's redeclared "war on terror" also has limited resonance in other regions; in Iraq, for example. "The Iraqi people need no lessons on the topic of terrorism," the Bush administration's former special envoy for Afghanistan explains: "they have lost more compatriots to the scourge over the past year than Americans have in all the terrorist incidents of their history combined." Relative to population, "Iraq suffers every month—sometimes every week—losses comparable to those of the September 11, 2001, attacks inflicted on the United States. Unfortunately, Iraqis are as likely to attribute those losses to the US-sponsored war on terrorism as to the terrorists themselves." Some possible reasons come to mind. One, perhaps, is that they are aware—as is, surely, the director of international security and defense policy at the Rand Corporation—that increases in terror and chaos were widely anticipated consequences of the invasion of Iraq.[110]

Apparently, there will be some barriers to the maturation of the protoscience of democracy promotion.

Some of the more careful scholarship that jumps on the bandwagon does intimate that something may be amiss. That includes the scholarly articles cited at the outset of this chapter. Jonathan Monten's study of "the roots of the Bush doctrine," after invoking the conventional mantra, observes that it is not entirely an innovation. Throughout American history, democracy promotion has been "central to US political identity and sense of national purpose" and to the way "the United States defines its political interests." It has been the heart of "American exceptionalism." Monten's lengthy and careful review of this defining property of American exceptionalism skirts any evidence that the policy was ever pursued, keeping to numerous declarations. A footnote explains that at issue are not the historical facts, "but the extent to which the United States' historical perception of itself as exceptional has influenced foreign policy"—more accurately, influenced its rhetorical framework. So understood, "promotion of democracy is central" to Bush strategy in a kind of postmodern interpretation, in which we restrict attention to narrative and text, recoiling from "Truth," perhaps a social construction.

Of the articles cited, only Katarina Delacoura's makes an effort to provide some reasons to believe that democracy promotion has actually guided policy, restricting herself to the Bush II years and the Middle East. Apart from rhetoric, she gives several examples: the Bush administration's encouragement of "economic liberalization" (which for the region means effective takeover of the economies by Western corporate power); new radio stations aimed at "initiating [younger audiences] into American culture and winning them over to American values" (comment unnecessary); the invasion of Iraq, to which we will turn directly; and several specific measures that she criticizes because, though "introduced with much fanfare," they were much like earlier ones and were scarcely funded. She also criticizes the "*inconsistency*" in US efforts at democracy promotion, which leads to a "problem of *credibility*" (her emphasis): namely, the same "strong line of continuity" that Carothers found, which, in reality, is highly consistent. Somehow, the persistence of these policies through the Bush years leads to skepticism in the Middle East about Washington's motives, and to a search for a "hidden agenda, for example to help Israel control the Palestinians, to control Iraqi oilfields, or generally to extend American hegemony." But, Delacoura argues (conventionally), "this is an inaccurate description of the US position and that the Bush administration is serious about democracy." All that is missing is evidence.

Carothers predicted, with regret, that Washington's Iraq policies would extend the strong line of continuity: they will "likely exhibit similar contradictions between stated principles and political reality." His predictions were being fulfilled as his book went to press. The occupation authorities worked assiduously to avert the threat of democracy, but were compelled, with great reluctance, to abandon their plans to impose a constitution and to prevent elections. Few competent observers would disagree with the editors of the *Financial Times* that "the reason [the elections of January 2005] took place was the insistence of the Grand Ayatollah Ali Sistani, who vetoed three schemes by the US-led occupation authorities to shelve or dilute them." Middle East scholar Alan Richards observes that "although the United States initially opposed early elections in Iraq, after Ayatollah Sistani turned huge numbers of his followers out in the streets to demand such elections, Washington had little choice but to agree." The *Wall Street Journal* explained that Sistani "gave his marching orders: Spread the word that Ayatollah Sistani insists that the new government be chosen through a direct election, not by the US or US-appointed Iraqi leaders," as Washington had sought. Veteran correspondent Patrick Cockburn adds that "it was only when it became clear that the US could not withstand a Shia uprising that elections turned out to have been an immediate American goal all along."[111]

Once it became clear that US and UK efforts to bar elections could not be sustained, the invaders of course took credit for them. The elections and the background soon settled comfortably into "the American-sponsored electoral process," much as the Israel-Palestine "peace process" that the United States has impeded for thirty years has been transmuted into the "halting American-led process to make peace between Israelis and Palestinians."[112]

In Iraq, though compelled to tolerate elections, the occupying forces sought to subvert them. The US candidate, Iyad Allawi, was given every possible advantage: state resources and access to TV, as well as the support of the military occupation. He ran a distant third, with about 12 percent of the vote. To ensure that elections would be free, the most important independent media were expelled from the country, notably the Qatar-based channel Al-Jazeera, which is despised by the ruling tyrants in the region because it has been a leading force for democratization in the Arab world. That alone makes its presence before elections in Iraq inappropriate, and the background tells us more about the nature of the messianic mission.

For years, high officials—Cheney, Rumsfeld, Rice, Powell—had pressured Qatar to curtail the channel's reporting. The United States bombed its facilities in Kabul and Baghdad (killing a Jordanian correspondent there). US pressure was "so intense," according to a senior Qatari official, that "the government is accelerating plans to put Al Jazeera on the market, though Bush administration officials counter that a privately owned station in the region may be no better from their point of view."[113]

We thus have another demonstration of the Bush vision of democracy in the Middle East: no media can be tolerated that are not under US control, whether public or private. Also very familiar practice, and entirely understandable.

Washington complains that Al-Jazeera inflamed opinion by direct reporting that "emphasized civilian casualties" during the US destruction of Falluja, and that it "reports passionately about the Palestinian conflict." Another departure from journalistic standards is that the channel showed "taped messages by Osama bin Laden," which are apparently considered newsworthy in the Muslim world, as they are among people everywhere concerned with the threat of terror.[114]

There was much derision, along with sober expressions of concern over Moscow's moves "to tighten state control over the news media," when Russia barred ABC News after it recorded an interview with the Chechen leader "who has ordered or carried out some of the worst terrorist acts in the country's history," including the school siege in Beslan that left 330 people dead. Such selective reactions are standard practice, sometimes reaching extraordinary levels. Thus Nicaragua, under intense US attack, was bitterly condemned for censorship, with scrupulous care to suppress the fact that its major newspaper was openly supporting overthrow of the government by terrorist forces of the superpower that was also funding the journal. The condemnation kept under wraps the incomparably worse record of Washington's Israeli client at the same time and under nothing like comparable threat, and of course the shameful record of the United States under little direct threat at all, all easily demonstrated. In Washington's regional client regimes, independent media were blown up by state terrorists, who also murdered editors and journalists or forced them to flee, arousing scarcely any notice in the country that bears primary responsibility for the crimes.[115]

Returning to the January 2005 Iraq election, it was, "in effect," an "ethnic census," with Shiites mostly voting for Sistani's Shiite list, Kurds for the Kurdish list, and Sunnis boycotting. Nevertheless, the election was a major triumph of mass nonviolent resistance to the US occupation, celebrated on election day with great enthusiasm and courage by Shiites and Kurds, who saw themselves as coming to the polls "to claim their rightful power in the land."[116]

The fundamental problem facing Washington was reported regularly as the United States sought to block Iraqi democracy. On the eve of the election, two experienced correspondents wrote that "the one thing every Iraqi agrees upon is that occupation should end soon," which would be in direct conflict with the US objective of constructing "a US-friendly democracy that would allow America to replace its military presence in Saudi Arabia . . . with one in Iraq that would allow America to keep shaping the regional balance of power." As in the traditional domains of US control, "democracy" will be welcomed as long as it is of the conventional "top-down" form that leaves elites supportive of US goals in power. Washington's problem was summarized by *Wall Street Journal* correspondent Yochi Dreazen: "the men likely to lead Iraq's next government promise to demand withdrawal as soon as they take power after Sunday's national elections." Even the US-backed candidate, Iyad Allawi, was compelled to indicate support for withdrawal. But that is unacceptable. There would have been no point to the invasion if the United States could not maintain a dependable client state and military basing rights. Accordingly, Dreazen reports, Washington hopes, and expects, that the dominant Shiite alliance "would accept vague promises to withdraw rather than a firm time line." Not an easy task, because whatever the Iraqi leadership may want, "they could find publicly defending any US troop presence difficult."[117]

The major task in the subversion of Iraqi democracy is to pressure political elites to accept "vague promises" and to retain as much as possible of the illegal economic regime imposed by the invaders, based on the standard principle of opening the country and its resources to foreign control (primarily US and UK), under the guise of "economic liberalism." The struggle is far from over—either in Iraq or in the home countries of the invaders.

The occupiers did not waste a moment in declaring their intentions to subvert the elections they had worked so hard to prevent. A long interview with Prime Minister Blair opens with the statement that "Tony Blair says there is no way that the US and UK will set out a timetable for the withdrawal of their troops from Iraq," whatever Iraqis may think about it—which is nowhere mentioned. "Mr Blair is still angered by the suggestion that the US and UK are occupying Iraq"—the opinion of the overwhelming majority of Iraqis, as he surely knows: 81 percent of Iraqi Arabs a year after the invasion. Blair insists that the "coalition is in Iraq [by] permission" of the interim Iraqi government that it installed, and that the "enhanced legitimacy" of the elected government "will make the coalition's presence more defensible." Washington's statements were hardly different, apart from a few ritual phrases about dedication to democracy.[118]

What Iraqis think about such matters we cannot know with great confidence. A Zogby International poll released on the day of the election found that 82 percent of Sunnis and 69 percent of Shiites "favor US forces withdrawing either immediately or after an elected government is in place." Similar results have been found in Western-run polls since shortly after the invasion. In one of the most in-depth polls, Oxford Research International found in fall 2003 that "less than 1% worry about occupation forces actually leaving." It found further that "people have no confidence in US/UK forces (79%) and the Coalition Provisional Authority—CPA (73%) [while] 8% say they have a 'great deal' of faith in US/UK troops." Military and Middle East specialist Andrew Cordesman reports that more than 70 percent of all Iraqis wanted US forces out by fall 2003, a figure that rose to more than 80 percent by mid-2004. The newly elected parliament's National Sovereignty Committee issued a report that "called for setting a timetable for the troops to go home," referring to them as "occupation forces." A spokesman for SCIRI, the largest Shiite Muslim party, said, "British troops should withdraw to their barracks, and come out only at the request of Iraqi forces." At a meeting in Cairo of all Iraqi factions, a prominent member of the Central Council of SCIRI, Dr. Ali al-Adad, stated that "all Iraqi forces, Shiite, Sunni and Kurds, want a timetable for the withdrawal of foreign troops," and agreed that it should be the "first demand" on their political program. The closing statement of Sunni, Shiite, and Kurdish leaders attending "demands a withdrawal of foreign troops on a specified timetable, dependent on an immediate national program for rebuilding the security forces." It also added that "national resistance is a legitimate right of all nations," though not terror.[119]

Polling on these crucial matters virtually ended after the elections, or at least was not reported. Two knowledgeable commentators write that "American polling agencies in Iraq basically stopped asking Iraqis what they thought of the US and its troops when unpopularity approached 90 percent in Iraq in the spring of 2004." According to Steven Kull, a leading authority on public opinion studies, the International Republican Institute began to withhold polling data from Iraq, which was showing that "the findings were getting pretty negative toward the US presence there." One poll, a very important one, did reach the public—in England: a poll undertaken for the British Ministry of Defence in August 2005, carried out by Iraqi university researchers and leaked to the British press. It found that 82 percent are "strongly opposed" to the presence of coalition troops, less than 1 percent believe they are responsible for any improvement in security, over 70 percent do not have confidence in them, and 67 percent feel less secure because of the occupation. "For Iraq as a whole, 45 per cent of people feel attacks [against occupying forces] are justified"; the proportion rises to 65 percent in one British-controlled province and is 25 percent even in Basra, which is mostly run by Shiite militias. If the poll really covered "Iraq as a whole," then the percentages must be considerably higher where the occupying forces are actually operating, in Arab Iraq. The reconstruction effort "appears to have failed, with the poll showing that 71 per cent of people rarely get safe clean water, 47 per cent never have enough electricity, 70 per cent say their sewerage system rarely works and 40 per cent of southern Iraqis are unemployed." The regular Brookings Institute review of "The State of Iraq" reported that 80 percent of Iraqis favored "Near Term US Troop Withdrawal" in November 2005, confirming the British Defence Ministry poll.[120]

Independent polling may have become virtually impossible. The catastrophe created by the occupying army is so extreme that reporters are far more restricted than in other conflict zones in the past. We can only guess the impact on Iraqi opinion of the brutality of the occupation and what it evoked, and of the stimulation of ethnic-religious conflict as the occupying armies sought to impose their will. We can, however, be reasonably confident that the occupiers will seek to bar the threat of a sovereign Iraq that is "democratic" in more than the traditional sense of US and UK practice in their domains.

The Iraqi calamity again illustrates "the strong line of continuity," much as Carothers feared. That should come as little surprise given the unusual significance of Iraq in geopolitical and economic terms, though the scale of the catastrophe could hardly have been anticipated.

Chapter 5

Supporting Evidence: The Middle East

Beyond declarations of leaders, and the self-refuting case of Iraq, several additional bits of evidence have been adduced to justify the faith in the sincerity of the messianic mission: the most important are Lebanon, Egypt's Kifaya ("Enough") movement, and Palestine. Let us examine each in turn.

The case of Lebanon can be dismissed, unless the CIA decides to take credit for the bombing that killed Lebanese prime minister Rafik Hariri, which set off the anti-Syrian demonstrations that have led to a complex but significant opening of the society. Though it is hardly credible, one can imagine why the story might have some resonance in Beirut. Perhaps the Lebanese have not consigned to oblivion the most horrendous car bombing in Beirut, in 1985, a huge explosion killing eighty people and wounding two hundred, mostly women and girls leaving the mosque exit where the bomb was placed. The attack, aimed at a Muslim cleric who escaped, was traced to the CIA and Saudi intelligence, apparently operating with British help. Accordingly, it is out of Western history.[1]

The year 1985 is identified by scholarship and media as the peak of Middle East terror during Reagan's "war on terror." By far the most significant acts of terror that year were the Beirut bombing, Shimon Peres's vicious Iron Fist operations targeting "terrorist villagers" in

Israeli-occupied Lebanon, and Israel's bombing of Tunis, murdering seventy-five Tunisians and Palestinians with extreme brutality, according to the report from the scene by Israeli journalist Amnon Kapeliouk. The United States assisted by refusing to inform its ally Tunisia that the bombers were on the way, though the Sixth Fleet certainly knew. The attack was praised by Secretary of State George Shultz, then unanimously condemned by the UN Security Council as an "act of armed aggression" (United States abstaining). The pretext for the bombing was retaliation for the killing of three Israelis in Cyprus, apparently traced to Syria, but Tunis was a defenseless and ideologically more useful target, housing the headquarters of the PLO. The Cyprus killings were in turn retaliation for regular kidnappings and killings on the high seas by Israeli naval forces attacking ships in transit between Cyprus and northern Lebanon, with many of those captured brought to Israel and kept in prison without charge as hostages.[2]

In accord with the reigning single standard, the major terrorist atrocities—or worse, aggression—are excluded from the canon of international terrorism. The special status of 1985 as the peak year of the "plague spread by depraved opponents of civilization itself" is conferred by two events in each of which a single American died. The most famous is the *Achille Lauro* hijacking, in retaliation for the Tunis bombing, during which a crippled American, Leon Klinghoffer, was brutally murdered. That was undoubtedly a shocking crime, which finds its place alongside the murder of the crippled Palestinians Kemal Zughayer and Jamal Rashid by Israeli forces during their destruction of the Jenin refugee camp. Zughayer was shot dead carrying a white flag as he tried to wheel himself away from Israeli tanks, which apparently drove over him, ripping his body to shreds. Rashid was crushed in his wheelchair when one of Israel's huge US-supplied bulldozers demolished his home with the family inside. Thanks to prevailing moral standards, such acts are also excluded from the canon of terrorism (or worse, war crimes), by virtue of wrong agency.[3]

The *Achille Lauro* hijacking and Klinghoffer's murder have become the very symbol of the bestiality of Palestinian terrorism. Typical is a careful study by a member of Reagan's National Security Council staff, Michael Bohn, who was director of the White House

Situation Room and therefore well informed about the events. He reviews the hijacking and Klinghoffer's murder in two hundred pages of meticulous detail. The review contains a few sentences on the Tunis bombing to illustrate "the complexity of the Middle East peace process," omitting all the crucial facts (such as those just mentioned).[4]

The irrational people of the Middle East, however, do not seem to share the perceptions of the world refracted through the ideological prisms of Western intellectual and moral culture, and may even fail to admire the "moral clarity" of its divinely guided leaders. Perhaps that has some relation to the fact that while 61 percent of Lebanese oppose Syrian interference in their country, 69 percent oppose US interference.[5]

There are other divergences between Lebanese and official US opinion on democracy. Attitudes toward Hezbollah are an illustration. Hezbollah has gained considerable support in Lebanon, particularly in the south, where its candidates won 80 percent of the vote in the June 2005 elections. In March 2005, by a vote of 380 to 3, the US House of Representatives passed a resolution condemning "the continuous terrorist attacks perpetrated by Hezbollah" and urging the European Union to "classify Hezbollah as a terrorist organization." The Senate followed with unanimous endorsement of a similar resolution. Middle East scholar Stephen Zunes contacted scores of congressional offices asking for examples of terrorist attacks by Hezbollah in the past decade, but no one was able to cite any. Rather than welcome Hezbollah's transformation into a political party, thus supporting Lebanese democracy, Congress preferred to follow the president's lead, continuing to punish Hezbollah for its real crime. Organized in 1982 in response to Israel's US-backed invasion of Lebanon, Hezbollah drove the invader from the country. For twenty-two years Israel had defied Security Council orders to withdraw, in the process carrying out many terrible atrocities with impunity, thanks to US support. As Zunes comments, "That virtually the entire United States Congress, including erstwhile liberal Democrats, would collude with such an agenda is yet another frightening example of how far to the right political discourse in this country has evolved."[6]

In any event, it seems safe to remove Lebanon from the canon. Let's turn to Egypt, the leading recipient of US military aid after Israel, and therefore of particular concern to Americans apart from its very significant role in the region.

There have long been internal pressures for democratization in Egypt. In the past few years, the leading force in opposition to the US-backed Hosni Mubarak dictatorship has been Kifaya, the popular "movement for change." Kifaya was formed in 2000, when it challenged the country's emergency laws. It was largely sparked by the Palestinian Intifada; its leading elements were Palestinian solidarity groups. Although such events mean little by Western standards, in Egypt and elsewhere there were strong reactions to what took place in the occupied territories immediately after the Israeli actions that provoked the al-Aqsa Intifada. In its first month, Israel killed seventy-five Palestinians (with four Israelis killed), in response mostly to stone-throwing, using US helicopters to attack apartment complexes and other civilian targets. Clinton responded by making the biggest deal in a decade to send new military helicopters to Israel. The US population was protected from that information by the press, which refused—not failed, but refused—to publish it. This is not terror, or even misdeed, according to the reigning Western conventions, not shared by Egyptian democracy activists. Subsequent atrocities in the occupied territories stimulated the Egyptian reform movement further, and it was then joined by the mass opposition to the war in Iraq. The spokesperson for Kifaya, Abdel-Hakim Qandil, stresses that it is an anti-imperial movement, with goals extending beyond the democratization of Egypt.[7]

The democratization movement in Egypt does not seem a very good candidate for the messianic mission and its impact. That leaves Israel-Palestine, a more intricate case, to which we turn directly.

Elsewhere in the region the strong line of continuity persists. Iranian reformists have repeatedly warned that Washington's harsh stand is strengthening hard-line opponents of democracy, helping to create an atmosphere in which "democracy is killed." But for Washington, democracy promotion ranks low in comparison with the need to punish Iran for overthrowing the murderous tyrant, the shah, imposed in 1953 by the US and UK coup that destroyed the Iranian parliamentary system. What remains in historical memory is the 1979 hostage crisis. The preceding quarter century did not occur. Iranians may disagree.[8]

In the Arab and Muslim worlds, there is a long history of attempts to advance democracy and human rights, often blocked by Western imperial intervention. In recent years, probably the most important democratizing force has been Al-Jazeera, as noted earlier, the primary reason why it is so despised by the Arab tyrannies and Washington.

A contribution to democratization in a different domain is the series of *Arab Development Reports* produced under the auspices of the United Nations Development Program (UNDP), which inquire into the "issue of freedom in the Arab world, and its relationship to good governance and human development," to quote the focus of the 2004 report. Correspondent Ian Williams writes that the report and its predecessors contribute to "the debate in the region that is an essential prerequisite of positive change there." He adds that the authors of the report "are serious about Arab democracy, while Bush is only kidding." The report does not spare its criticism, internally or externally. It charges that the Israeli occupation of Palestine, the US occupation of Iraq, and Arab terrorism have "adversely influenced" human development. It condemns the "Arab despots [who rule] oppressively, restricting prospects of their countries' transition to democracy," and the support for them by "major world powers." It also deplores "The US' repeated use or threat of use of the veto [which] has limited the effectiveness of the Security Council in establishing peace in the region."[9]

In Iraq, the record of struggle for democracy and justice traces to the constitutional movements and contested elections of a century ago, though political development was set back, in the usual way, by the British occupation after World War I. Political scientist Adeed Dawisha writes that "the British were singularly hostile to democratic practices if they were perceived to be impeding British interests." Nor were "Americans any more enamored with the democratic process." Nevertheless, despite Britain's heavy hand, Iraqis did develop "relatively liberal and democratic institutions and practices, which could contribute to a democratic future [if] contemporary leaders are genuine about following the democratic path." After the US and UK invasion, as already discussed, the flight to religion resulting from the brutal sanctions regime they imposed accelerated further, along with a reversal of secular democratic tendencies that had existed prior to the 1963 Baathist takeover that they had supported. But even if Iraqis can recover what they had accomplished despite imperial dominance, it takes impressive faith to believe that the current hegemons will permit such options in more than the traditional sense of "top-down" rule by elites linked to US power, with democratic forms of little substance—unless they are compelled to do so, by their own populations in particular.[10]

ISRAEL-PALESTINE

Washington's commitment to "democracy promotion" for Palestine is complex enough to merit separate treatment. The efforts were kept on hold until the November 2004 death of Yasser Arafat, which was hailed as an opportunity for the realization of Bush's "vision" of a democratic Palestinian state—a pale and vague reflection of the international consensus that the United States has blocked for thirty years. The reasons for the new hopes were explained in a front-page *New York Times* think piece, under the headline "Hoping Democracy Can Replace a Palestinian Icon." The first sentence reads: "The post-Arafat era will be the latest test of a quintessentially American article of faith: that elections provide legitimacy even to the frailest institutions." In the final paragraph on the continuation page, we read: "The paradox for the Palestinians is rich, however. In the past, the Bush administration resisted new national elections among the Palestinians. The thought then was that the elections would make Mr. Arafat look better and give him a fresher mandate, and might help give credibility and authority to Hamas."[11]

In brief, the "quintessential article of faith" is that elections are fine, as long as they come out the right way. A year after the formal announcement of the messianic mission that set off the rush to the "democratization bandwagon," the strong line of continuity is revealed once again, along with its paradoxical quality: inexplicably, deeds consistently accord with interests, and conflict with words—discoveries that must not, however, weaken our faith in the sincerity of the declarations of our leaders.

The quintessential faith was shared by President Bush's regional ally in democracy promotion. In September 2005, Prime Minister Ariel Sharon informed the United Nations that Israel would use its ample means to disrupt Palestinian elections if Hamas were permitted to run, because of Hamas's commitment to violence. By the same logic, Hamas should disrupt Israeli elections if Likud, the new Sharon-Peres Kadima Party, or Labor run; Iran should disrupt US elections; and so on. Israel's stand undercut the efforts of Palestinian prime minister Mahmoud Abbas "to ease [Hamas and Islamic Jihad] away from violence [by bringing] them into the political mainstream," Joel Brinkley reported. Washington again adhered to its quintessential article of faith: "worried that Palestinian militants will gain a foothold in legislative elections, [Washington is] pressing Mahmoud Abbas to require that candidates renounce violence and 'unlawful or nondemocratic methods' "—a condition that would save the United States and Israel the trouble of even running elections. Meanwhile Sharon explained that Israel was abandoning its commitments to freeze settlement at the first stage of the "road map," reiterating "that Israel would never give up the large West Bank settlement blocks where the vast majority of settlers live" and noting that "last year President Bush acknowledged in a letter to him that 'demographic realities' would have to be taken into account in determining the border between Israel and a future state of Palestine."[12]

Arafat had been elected president in 1996 in elections deemed acceptable by Washington, which, however, later turned against him, so their legitimacy was retrospectively revoked. Middle East specialist Gilbert Achcar points out that "Arafat, having been democratically elected by universal suffrage, repeatedly demanded the right to organise new Palestinian elections. But he was denied that right, simply because the Palestinians would certainly have elected him again." Bush's announcement of his mission to bring democracy to the Arab world was soon followed by his endorsement of the imprisonment of the one elected Arab leader in his compound in Ramallah by Ariel Sharon. Meanwhile, Bush designated Sharon a "man of peace," easily dismissing his record of a half century of extreme terrorist violence against civilians and outright aggression, continuing to the present moment.[13]

With Arafat safely imprisoned, Bush and Sharon demanded that he be replaced by Mahmoud Abbas, the new hope for democracy in Palestine. The press reported that "unlike Mr. Arafat, Mr. Abbas does not have a popular following, and competitors in his own generation may resist his new authority"—another indication of the solemnity of the administration's commitment to democracy.[14]

We learn more about this vision of democracy by looking at the coverage of the death of Arafat, keeping just to the newspaper of record.

Arafat was "both the symbol of the Palestinians' hope for a viable, independent state and the prime obstacle to its realization." He was never able to reach the heights of President Anwar Sadat of Egypt, who won "back the Sinai through a peace treaty with Israel" because he was able to "reach out to Israelis and address their fears and hopes" with his visit to Jerusalem in 1977 (quoting Shlomo Avineri, an Israeli political philosopher and former government official).[15]

Turning to fact, six years earlier, in February 1971, Sadat had offered a full peace treaty to Israel in return for Israeli withdrawal from the occupied territories, specifically the Egyptian Sinai. The Golda Meir Labor government rejected Sadat's offer, preferring to expand into the Sinai, where troops under the command of General Sharon were driving thousands of Bedouins into the desert and demolishing their towns in order to build the all-Jewish city of Yamit along with kibbutzim and other Jewish villages. Sadat's offer was closely in accord with official US policy, but Washington decided to back Israel's rejection of it, adopting Kissinger's policy of "stalemate": no negotiations, only force. US-Israeli rejection of diplomacy led directly to the 1973 war, which was a very close call for Israel, and the world; the United States declared a nuclear alert. Kissinger realized that Egypt could not simply be dismissed and agreed to pursue a diplomatic path, which led finally to the Camp David accords of 1979, in which the United States and Israel accepted the offer that Sadat had made in 1971. The accords appear in history as a US diplomatic triumph. In reality, Washington's performance was a diplomatic disaster, causing immense suffering and even danger of global war.

In 1971, Sadat's peace offer said nothing about Palestinian rights, which were not yet on the international agenda. By the mid-1970s that had changed, and Sadat insisted on Palestinian national rights in the occupied territories, the international consensus that the United States and Israel have rejected, virtually alone. Hence the Egyptian offer to which the United States and Israel agreed at Camp David was harsher, from their point of view, than the one they had rejected eight years earlier. Acceptance of Sadat's 1971 offer would have effectively ended the international conflict. There might have been progress toward settlement of the Israel-Palestine conflict as well, had the United States and Israel been willing to contemplate the possibility. General Shlomo Gazit, military commander of the occupied territories from 1967 to 1974, reports in his memoirs that Palestinian leaders proposed various forms of local autonomy in the territories during these years. These were transmitted sympathetically by Israeli military intelligence but rejected or ignored by the higher political echelons, which insisted on "substantial border changes" and had no intention of reaching any agreement, acting "with determination to thwart any Palestinian hopes in that direction [while] Israel forbade any political activity."[16]

By adopting this extreme rejectionist stance, Gazit believes, the US-backed Labor governments of the early 1970s bear significant responsibility for the rise of the fanatic Gush Emunim settler movement, and eventually the Palestinian resistance that developed many years later in the first intifada—after years of state terror, settler brutality, and steady takeover of valuable Palestinian lands and resources. Along with arable land, the most important of these resources is water, leaving Palestinians under occupation "the most water-deprived people in the entire region; indeed one of the most deprived in the world," while Israel takes for itself 80 percent of the water extracted from West Bank aquifers, arrangements now consolidated by the "Separation Wall" on transparently fraudulent security grounds. In further robbery and humiliation, Israel plans to take the West Bank's largest quarry for illegal transfer of garbage from Israel, depriving Palestinians of its use and jeopardizing remaining Palestinian water resources, according to pollution experts.[17]

While keeping largely to political and diplomatic history, we should not overlook the human reality of the occupation, described succinctly by Israeli historian Benny Morris:

> Israelis like to believe, and tell the world, that they were running an "enlightened" or "benign" occupation, qualitatively different from other military occupations the world had seen. The truth was radically different. Like all occupations, Israel's was founded on brute force, repression and fear, collaboration and treachery, beatings and torture chambers, and daily intimidation, humiliation, and manipulation. True, the relative lack of resistance and civil disobedience over the years enabled Israelis to maintain a facade of normalcy and implement their rule with a relatively small force, consisting of a handful of IDF battalions, a few dozen police officers (rank-and-file policemen were recruited from among the Palestinians), and a hundred or so General Security Service (GSS) case officers and investigators.[18]

There is good reason to believe that prior to the October 1973 war, Israel could have moved toward some sort of federal arrangement in mandatory Palestine (cis-Jordan, the river to the sea), with two partially autonomous regions, predominantly Jewish and Arab. The Palestinian proposals that were dismissed by the political leadership could have been steps in this direction. A federal solution could have led to further integration of the two societies, as circumstances permitted, leading to the kind of binational arrangement that has significant roots in prestate Zionism and is quite natural in that region—in fact more generally. There are many models of multinational states, some reasonably successful, often considerably more so than the state systems that have largely been imposed by violence and have often led to horrendous atrocities. Anyone familiar with cis-Jordan knows that any line drawn through it is highly artificial, though certainly superior to military occupation. During those years, there was some—if limited—public advocacy of such moves, but after the 1973 war the opportunity was lost, and the only serious short-term option became the two-state settlement of the international consensus that the United States and Israel have blocked.[19]

The basic facts are clear. It was not the villain Arafat who was "the prime obstacle to [the] realization" of a Palestinian state, but rather the United States and Israel, with the help of media and commentary that suppressed and distorted what was taking place. That conclusion is even more sharply drawn when we look at the actual record since the issue of Palestinian national rights reached the international agenda in the mid-1970s. In 1976, the United States vetoed a Syrian-initiated resolution calling for a two-state settlement on the international borders backed by the major Arab states and Arafat's PLO, and incorporating the crucial wording of UN Security Council Resolution 242, recognized on all sides to be the basic diplomatic document. In the years that followed, the United States, virtually alone, blocked the very broad international consensus on a similar diplomatic resolution, while supporting Israel's expansion into the occupied territories. The legal status of the takeover of lands and resources is not seriously in question. The prominent Israeli legal scholar David Kretzmer, professor of international law at the Hebrew University, observes that the illegality of the settlements "has been accepted by the United Nations Security Council, the International Committee of the Red Cross (ICRC), the states parties to the Geneva Conventions," along with foreign governments and academic writers and, more recently, by the International Court of Justice, unanimously, including US justice Buergenthal.[20]

The United States continues to block a diplomatic resolution. One important recent example was the presentation of the Geneva Accord in December 2002. These detailed proposals for a two-state solution, formulated by unofficial but prominent Israeli and Palestinian negotiators, were supported by the usual broad international consensus, with the usual exception: "The United States conspicuously was not among the governments sending a message of support," the New York Times reported in a dismissive article. Israel rejected the accord.[21]

This is only a small fragment of a diplomatic record that is so consistent, so dramatically clear, and so extensively documented that it takes real diligence to misread it. But the history conflicts radically with the righteousness of our leaders, so it must be discarded as politically incorrect. Arafat must be the "prime obstacle" to the sincere dedication of Washington to a Palestinian state and to democracy.

The lengthy obituary of Arafat by *New York Times* Middle East specialist Judith Miller proceeds in the same vein. According to her version, "Until 1988, [Arafat] repeatedly rejected recognition of Israel, insisting on armed struggle and terror campaigns. He opted for diplomacy only after his embrace of President Saddam Hussein of Iraq during the Persian Gulf war in 1991." Turning to actual history, through the 1980s Arafat repeatedly offered negotiations leading to a diplomatic settlement, while Israel—in particular the dovish "pragmatists"—flatly refused any discussions, a position backed by Washington. *New York Times* Jerusalem correspondent Thomas Friedman regularly misrepresented the ongoing record, and the press generally refused to publish the facts readily available in the Israeli press.[22]

Miller presumably mentions 1988 (without explanation) because that is the year the Palestinian National Council officially called for a two-state settlement in terms of the international consensus, having "implicitly posited" the idea at its 1974 meeting, Benny Morris observes, concurring with other historians of the period. A year later, in May 1989, the Israeli coalition government headed by Yitzhak Shamir and Shimon Peres reaffirmed the Israeli political consensus in its peace plan. The first principle was that there could be no "additional Palestinian state" between Jordan and Israel—Jordan already being a "Palestinian state." The second was that the fate of the territories will be settled "in accordance with the basic guidelines of the [Israeli] government." The Israeli plan was accepted without qualification by the United States, becoming "the Baker Plan" (December 6, 1989). As I wrote at the time, it is much as if someone were to argue that "the Jews do not merit a 'second homeland' because they already have New York, with a huge Jewish population, Jewish-run media, a Jewish mayor, and domination of cultural and economic life." The Baker Plan also allowed Palestinians selected by the United States and Israel to attend a "dialogue" on the Israeli plan, but on condition that they keep solely to its provisions, which requires an extension of the analogy.[23]

The same day that Washington announced its renewed endorsement of Israel's extreme rejectionism, the UN General Assembly once again called for an international peace conference under UN supervision. Its announced goal was to lay the basis for a diplomatic settlement on the international (pre–June 1967) borders, with guarantees for the security of all states in the region "within secure and internationally recognized borders," and with the new Palestinian state "under the supervision of the United Nations for a limited period, as part of the peace process." The vote was 153 to 3, with the United States, Israel, and Dominica opposed and one abstention (Belize). About as usual since the 1970s.[24]

Exactly contrary to Miller's account and standard doctrine, it was only after the 1991 Gulf war that *Washington* was willing to consider negotiations, recognizing that it was now in a position to impose its own terms unilaterally. US-Israeli rejectionism continued after the 1993 Oslo agreements, which said nothing about Palestinian national rights. Under Oslo, Arafat was assigned the role of being Israel's policeman in the occupied territories. Prime Minister Rabin could hardly have been clearer about that. As long as Arafat fulfilled this task, he was a "pragmatist," approved by the United States and Israel with no concern for his corruption, violence, and harsh repression. It was only after he could no longer keep the population under control while Israel took over more of their lands and resources that he became an archvillain, blocking the path to peace. Israel's first official mention of the possibility of a Palestinian state was apparently made by the ultra-right Benjamin Netanyahu government, which agreed that Palestinians can call whatever fragments of Palestine are left to them "a state" if they like, or they can call it "fried chicken" (in the words of David Bar-Illan, director of communications and policy planning in the prime minister's office). In May 1997, the Labor Party, apparently for the first time, recognized "the Palestinians' right to self-determination [and did] not rule out in this connection the establishment of a Palestinian state with limited sovereignty" in areas excluding "major Jewish settlement blocs."[25]

The goals of the Israeli doves were outlined in a 1998 academic publication by Shlomo Ben-Ami, who went on to become Ehud Barak's chief negotiator at Camp David in 2000. The "Oslo peace process," Ben-Ami wrote, was to lead to a "permanent neocolonial dependency" for the Palestinians in the occupied territories, with some form of local autonomy. Israeli settlement and cantonization of the occupied territories proceeded steadily through the 1990s, with full US support. The highest rate of post-Oslo settlement expansion was in 2000, the final year of Clinton's term, and Labor prime minister Barak's.[26]

Miller's version reaches the standard denouement: at Camp David in mid-2000, Arafat "walked away" from the magnanimous Clinton and Barak offer of peace, and later refused to join Barak in accepting Clinton's December 2000 "parameters," thus proving conclusively that he insisted on violence, a depressing truth with which the peace-loving states, the United States and Israel, would somehow have to come to terms.

In the real world, the Camp David proposals could not possibly be accepted by any Palestinian leader (including Abbas, who rejected them). That is evident from a look at the maps that were easily available from standard sources, though apparently are nowhere to be found in the US mainstream. In the most careful analysis by Israeli scholars, Ron Pundak and Shaul Arieli conclude that Barak's opening offer left Israel in control of 13 percent of the West Bank, and that a day before the end of the summit the Israeli side still held that position, though Barak's final offer reduced it to 12 percent. The most authoritative map, which Pundak provides in another analysis, reveals that the US-Israeli proposal established three cantons in the remnants of the West Bank left to Palestinians. The three are formed by two Israeli salients, extending from Israel well into the West Bank.

One salient, including the town of Ma'aleh Adumim, stretches from the greatly expanded Jerusalem area that Israel would take over, past Jericho far to the east, and on to the "security zone" under Israeli control at the Jordan River, thus effectively bisecting the West Bank. This salient also extends well to the north to virtually encircle Ramallah, the main Palestinian city in the central canton. The northern salient extends more than halfway through the West Bank to unsettled areas, including the town of Ariel and Shiloh to its east. The effect is largely to separate the southern and central cantons from the northern one. Along with other significant expansion, the proposals effectively cut off the major Palestinian towns (Bethlehem, Ramallah, Nablus)

Palestinian Sovereignty

Israeli Sovereign Areas

Security Zone under
Temporary Israeli Control

Mediterranean Sea

REHAN

Jenin

Tulkarm

Nablus

Kalkilya

SHOMRON
SETTLEMENTS

ELKANA   ARIEL

SHILO

Tel Aviv-
Jaffa

OFARIM

W E S T   B A N K

Jordan

MODI'IN
ILLIT

OFRA

Ramallah   BET
EL

GIV'AT
ZE'EV

Jericho

Jerusalem

MA'ALE
ADUMIM

Old City

Abu
Dis

Bethlehem

K. ETZION

Dead Sea

Hebron

I   S   R   A   E   L

J   O   R   D   A   N

IISS*maps*

| 0 | | 10km |
| 0 | | 5 miles |

© Jan de Jong

from one another. And all Palestinian fragments are largely separated from the small sector of East Jerusalem that is the center of Palestinian commercial, cultural, religious, and political life and institutions.[27]

After the collapse of the Camp David negotiations, Clinton recognized that Arafat's objections had merit, as demonstrated by his famous parameters of December 2000, which went farther toward a possible settlement—thus undermining the official story that Miller repeats. Clinton described the reaction to his parameters in a talk to the Israeli Policy Forum on January 7, 2001: "Both Prime Minister Barak and Chairman Arafat have now accepted these parameters as the basis for further efforts. Both have expressed some reservations." Again, the standard version is undermined.[28]

High-level Israeli-Palestinian negotiators took the Clinton parameters as "the basis for further efforts," addressing their "reservations" at meetings in Taba in late January 2001. These negotiations met some of the Palestinian concerns, thus again undermining the standard version. Problems remained, but the Taba negotiations might have led to peace. At Taba, Pundak and Arieli observe, Israel reduced its demands by 50 percent beyond Camp David. They admonish those who claim that Israel reached its "Red Lines" at Camp David, presenting "the most far-reaching offer that can be conceived," to attend to "the distance between a map that annexes 13 percent at Camp David and the 6–8 percent that Israelis proposed before and during the Taba negotiations." They may have had in mind such well-known Israeli doves as novelist Amos Oz, who informed a Western audience that at Camp David Israel offered "a peace agreement based on the 1967 borders with minor mutual amendments, [the] most far-reaching offer Israel can make," and that Israel did so "at the price of an unprecedented chasm within Israeli society, at the price of a political earthquake," but Palestinians rejected the offer, insisting on "eradicating Israel." Accordingly, Oz said, Israel's peace movement should now "reconsider its stance" that occupation was the central issue, now that Israel's government was agreeing to terminate the occupation and Palestinians had refused. The truth, well known in Israel, is sharply different.[29]

The Taba negotiations were called off by Israeli prime minister

Barak on January 27, earlier than planned and ten days prior to the Israeli elections scheduled for February 6. So their outcome cannot be
known. At their final press conference, the two parties issued a joint
statement declaring that they "have never been closer to reaching an
agreement and it is thus our shared belief that the remaining gaps
could be bridged with the resumption of negotiations following the Israeli elections." A detailed report by European Union envoy Miguel
Moratinos, suggesting the same optimistic conclusions, was accepted
as accurate by both sides, and prominently reported in Israel, though
ignored in the United States. When asked why he had called off the
negotiations four days early, Barak "simply denied" that there was
any hope for progress and stated, "It doesn't make any difference why
I ended it. It had to end because it wasn't going anywhere." Barak informed Israeli historian Ahron Bregman that he had told Clinton at
once that he rejected the Clinton parameters and that he did "not in-
tend to sign any agreement before the elections."[30]

Unofficial negotiations nevertheless continued, with several outcomes, the most detailed being the Geneva Accord that Israel rejected
and the United States dismissed in December 2002.

Reviewing the failure of these efforts, Pundak concludes that prior
to Camp David both sides failed to live up to their commitments, "but
the Israeli breaches were both more numerous and more substantive in
nature," even putting aside the obvious imbalance. "The Palestinian
leadership had been able to contain the violence which might have easily erupted during Netanyahu's tenure" as prime minister from 1996
to 1999, while "Netanyahu sabotaged the peace process relentlessly."
Barak's election in 1999 raised expectations, but they were dashed by
his refusal to transfer authority to Palestinian villages around Greater
Jerusalem even after the transfer was approved by the Israeli government, and by actions on the ground: the increase in harassment, collective punishment, poverty, water shortages, and settlement while
Palestinians were confined to "Bantustan-like enclaves," as well as
support for ugly settler actions by the army and civil authorities. At
Camp David, the Palestinian leadership and the majority of the public
were ready to make "necessary concessions," but needed some indication that the relation of occupier and occupied would change. That

Barak did not provide. Pundak dismisses the versions that were pub-licly reported (an offer of 95 percent of the West Bank, and so on) as "an attempt at rewriting history."

During the intifada that followed the breakdown of Camp David, Pundak writes, "in reality, the Palestinians had not altered the basic position they had held since 1993: a two-state solution, with a non-militarized Palestinian state along 1967 borders, and a pragmatic so-lution to the refugee problem." The Taba negotiations came close to a solution on the territorial issue, the "main basis for any agree-ment." On the refugee issue, often brought up in an effort to blame Palestinian intransigence for failure of the peace efforts, Pundak writes that the position of the Palestinian negotiators at Camp David was "moderate and pragmatic," and remained so throughout. The Taba draft had a "clear emphasis that its implementation would not threaten the Jewish character of the State of Israel." In the end, Pun-dak concludes that, though none are blameless, Netanyahu's insincer-ity and Barak's mismanagement "were the two main obstacles to reaching an agreement." Palestinians naturally take a harsher view, but in the context of the present discussion, what is most relevant is the interpretation by the most knowledgeable observers who basically adopt Israel's stand.[31]

Miller's version is based on a widely praised book by Clinton's Middle East envoy and negotiator Dennis Ross. As every serious com-mentator must be aware, any such source is highly suspect, if only be-cause of its origins. And even a casual reading suffices to demonstrate that Ross's account is worth very little. Its eight hundred pages consist mostly of admiration of Clinton's (and his own) efforts, based almost entirely on "quotations" of what he claims was said in informal dis-cussions. There is scarcely a word on what everyone knows to have been the core issue all along: the programs of settlement and infra-structure development in the territories that continued with US sup-port through the Oslo years, peaking in 2000. In Ross's version, Arafat is the villain who refused a magnanimous peace offer at Camp David and rejected Clinton's later parameters though Barak accepted them; false, as just reviewed. Ross handles the Taba negotiations sim-ply: by terminating the book immediately before they began (which also allows him to omit Clinton's evaluation of the reaction to his parameters by the two sides, just quoted). Thus he is able to avoid the fact that his primary conclusions were instantly refuted. It is clear that the book has little value apart from what it tells us about one of the participants. "In the final analysis," Middle East scholar Jerome Slater writes, Ross's "account amounts to a clever but quite unpersuasive brief for Israel, the Clinton administration, and indeed himself."[32]

Not worthless, however, is crucial evidence that escapes notice. One important example is the final assessment by high-level Israeli intelligence officials, among them Amos Malka, head of Israeli military intelligence; Ami Ayalon, who headed the General Security Services (Shin Bet); Matti Steinberg, special adviser on Palestinian affairs to the head of the Shin Bet; and Ephraim Lavie, the research division official responsible for the Palestinian arena. As Malka presents their consensus, "The assumption was that Arafat prefers a diplomatic process, that he will do all he can to see it through, and that only when he comes to a dead end in the process will he turn to a path of violence. But this violence is aimed at getting him out of a dead end, to set international pressure in motion and to get the extra mile." Essentially Pundak's conclusion.[33]

In addition to Miller's obituary, the *Times* published one major op-ed on Arafat's death, by Benny Morris. The first comment captures the tone: Arafat was a deceiver who spoke about peace and ending the occupation but really wanted to "redeem Palestine." This demonstrates Arafat's irremediably savage nature. Here Morris is revealing his contempt not only for Palestinians, which is profound, but also for his American audience. He apparently assumes that they will not notice that he is borrowing the terrible phrase from Zionist ideology, whose core principle for over a century has been to "redeem The Land." The principle lies behind what Morris recognizes as a central theme of the Zionist movement from its origins: "transfer"—that is, expulsion—of the indigenous population to somewhere else so as to "redeem The Land" for its true owners, who are returning to it after two thousand years.[34]

Morris is identified as an Israeli academic and author of major studies on the Israel-Arab conflicts, in particular on the origins of the Palestinian refugee problem. That is correct. He has done the most extensive work on the Israeli archives and published valuable scholarly accounts. He also demonstrates in considerable detail the savagery of the Israeli operations in 1948 and 1949 that led to "transfer" of most of the population from what became Israel, including the part of the UN-designated Palestinian state that Israel took over, dividing it roughly in half with its tacit Jordanian partner. In Morris's own words, "Above all, let me reiterate, the refugee problem was caused by attacks by Jewish forces on Arab villages and towns and by the inhabitants' fear of such attacks, compounded by expulsions, atrocities, and rumors of atrocities—and by the crucial Israeli cabinet decision in June 1948 to bar a refugee return," leaving the Palestinians "crushed, with some 700,000 driven into exile and another 150,000 left under Israeli rule." Morris is critical of Israeli atrocities and "ethnic cleansing" (literally, "ethnic purification") of Palestinians. One reason is that it did not go far enough. Prime Minister David Ben-Gurion's great error, Morris feels, perhaps a "fatal mistake," was not to have "cleansed the whole country—the whole Land of Israel, as far as the Jordan River."[35]

To Israel's credit, Morris's stand on this matter has been bitterly condemned. In Israel. In the United States, he was considered the appropriate choice for the sole commentary on his reviled enemy.[36]

Though Palestinians are, of course, the prime victims of US and Israeli rejectionism, Israel has suffered, too, even during the several decades when it was surprisingly free from retaliation from within the territories, where the Palestinians silently endured brutality, torture, degradation, and robbery of their lands and resources. Israel's US-backed refusal to accept a peace settlement in 1971 led to much misery and near disaster. Its refusal since to accept a political settlement is driving it "on the road to catastrophe," four former heads of the Shin Bet security service have warned, calling for a peace agreement in which most of the settlements would be abandoned. Israel has been "behaving disgracefully" toward Palestinians, said Avraham Shalom, one of the four. An early opponent of the occupation, the renowned Orthodox scholar and scientist Yeshayahu Leibowitz, was famous for his prediction that oppressing another people would lead to serious moral degeneration, corruption, and internal decay. By now his warnings have entered the mainstream in Israel. One of Israel's leading legal analysts, Moshe Negbi, describes with despair Israel's descent to the condition of a "banana republic." Negbi reserves his most bitter scorn not just for the increasingly corrupt political leadership across the political spectrum, but also for Israel's courts. The courts, he writes, are capable of imposing a six-month sentence on an interrogator who tortured a prisoner to death or a Jew convicted of murdering an Arab child, of tolerating "secret prisons" where inmates "disappear" in the manner of neo-Nazi Argentina and the Soviet Union, and of innumerable other crimes that he sees as destroying Israeli democracy and the rule of law by acceding to the "thugs of the racist fundamentalist right."[37]

In a searing indictment of Israel's subordination to the settlers in the occupied territories from the earliest days of the occupation, diplomatic correspondent Akiva Eldar and historian Idit Zartel recount how the "ugly, racist" regime of "the Lords of the Land" not only "crushes the most elementary human rights" of the Palestinians but also "demolishes the basic norms of Israeli democracy." "Even more than their book infuriates," writes military-political analyst Reuven Pedatzur, "the book saddens anyone who cares for the fate, the image, and the future of Israeli democracy." Eldar and Zartel emphasize that "the development of the settlements would not have been possible without the massive assistance they received from the various political institutions, the authorization of the courts from which they benefited, and without the relations of sympathy and shared goals that were constructed between the settlers and the military command." From the Eshkol Labor government of 1967 to the governments of Rabin and Peres and on to the present, "none can escape responsibility" for the expansion of the settlements and the assault against human rights and Israeli democracy.[38]

Eldar and Zartel also stress the "particularly sad harm caused by the judicial authorities." They review shocking racist court judgments—among them very light sentences for the brutal murder of Arab children, and even court refusal to pass sentence on Jews by appeal to the saying that "you should not judge your neighbor unless you are in his place." Such stands have been "destroying the entire basis of the judicial system," Eldar and Zartel write. "It is only against this background," Pedatzur adds, that one can comprehend the decision of occupation authority official Pliya Albek, who, with the support of the courts, rejected the appeal of a Palestinian man for compensation after the border police had killed his wife, on the grounds that he "only gained from his wife's death because when she was alive he had to support her, but now he does not, and therefore the damage to him is at most zero." Benny Morris writes that "the work of the military courts in the territories, and the Supreme Court which backed them, will surely go down as a dark age in the annals of Israel's judicial system."[39]

Meanwhile, Eldar and Zartel conclude, "the lives of the large majority of Israelis within the green line [the international border] continue undisturbed, while the settlements [in the occupied territories] conquer the state of Israel on the one hand, and destroy the lives of the Palestinians on the other."

The reasons why Israelis continue their lives undisturbed are not hard to fathom. They are described by Israeli journalist Amira Hass, who has lived in and reported from the occupied territories for years. "There is a settler in every Israeli," she explains, at least in every relatively privileged one. "The West Bank settlement enterprise has become a means of socioeconomic advancement for many Israelis," who, thanks to government subsidies, can obtain lovely houses that they could never afford in Israel. "For them, this is a way of dealing with the gradual destruction of the welfare state," as Israel has adopted some of the worst features of its protector. Furthermore, the settlements ensure Israel's control over Palestinian resources, so "we, the Jews, can be wasteful, as if we lived in a land with abundant water," while Palestinians lack water to drink. And Jews can benefit from modern highways "built on lands stolen from the Palestinians, [which] serve not only the settlers, but also many [other Israelis], whose developing middle-class consciousness requires convenience, efficiency and time-saving." There is also a bonanza for the wide range of businesses that "benefit from the building boom," and, by guaranteeing a continuing security threat, the settlements "necessitate the growth of the security industry." It is no surprise, then, that the public is "not troubled by the question of what [settlement] is doing to the region's future." The crushing of the Palestinians and destruction of their society remains "invisible," and the future is for someone else to worry about.[40]

"Travel on the roads of Gaza, closed to Palestinian traffic for years, exposes the full dimensions of the physical destruction Israel left behind," Hass writes.

> A thousand words and a thousand images cannot describe it. That's not because of the weakness of words and photos, but because of the ability of most Israelis not to see and not to grasp the extent of the vineyards and groves and orchards and fields that the people's army of Israel turned into desert, the green that it painted yellow and gray, the sand turned over and the exposed land, the thorns, the weeds. To ensure the safety of the settlers . . . the IDF [Israeli Defense Forces] spent five years uprooting the green lungs of Gaza, mutilating its most beautiful areas and cutting off the livelihood of tens of thousands of families. The Israeli talent for ignoring the enormous destruction that we caused leads to the wrong political assessments. Ignoring it enables the IDF to continue destroying Palestinian territory in the West Bank. Along the [separation] fence, around the settlements, in the Jordan Valley, the destruction goes on as a means to continue creating facts on the ground and to guarantee that the future Palestinian entity remains as divided and split and territory-less as possible.[41]

The international consequences of Israel's decision to prefer expansion to security in 1971 extend well beyond the 1973 war of which it was the immediate cause. By refusing peace, Israel chose dependency on the United States, "the boss-man called 'partner,'" as one of Israel's leading political commentators describes the relationship. As long as Israel's actions conform to US objectives, it receives the diplomatic, military, and economic support that facilitates its takeover of valuable parts of the occupied territories and its development into a rich industrial society. But when the boss-man draws the line, Israel must obey. There have been repeated occasions. One arose in 2005, when the United States ordered Israel to terminate its sales of advanced military technology to China. Israel sought to evade or mitigate the restrictions, but in vain. The United States imposed sanctions. Pentagon officials refused even to meet with their Israeli counterparts, compelling Defense Minister Shaul Mofaz to cancel a trip to Washington. "Strategic dialogue" was effectively terminated. The United States demanded that the Knesset enact legislation tightening oversight of military exports, that Israel sign an official memorandum of understanding, and that the government and Mofaz present a written apology to the United States. "After Israel raised a white flag and acquiesced to most of the demands," Israel's leading military correspondent, Ze'ev Schiff, reported, "the US made additional, harsher demands, and was said to have shown contempt for the Israeli delegation."[42]

These are bitter blows to Israel. Apart from the direct insults, these sales are a crucial component of the militarized Israeli high-tech export economy. But Israel has no alternative when the boss-man speaks, and understands that it cannot rely on the domestic US lobby, which knows better than to confront state power on important matters. The choice of expansion and associated dependence has had deleterious effects on Israeli society, while foreclosing beneficial alternatives, and it risks consequences that could be quite serious in the unpredictable world of international affairs.

While contemplating his visions of democracy and justice, Bush is continuing to "crush the most elementary human rights of Palestinians and demolish the basic norms of Israeli democracy." The record of Security Council vetoes concerning Israel is another illustration. Bush II's seven vetoes of UN resolutions related to Israel match the seven under Bush I and Clinton combined (but do not reach Reagan's nineteen). The resolutions vetoed include the call for a UN observer force in the territories to reduce violence, condemnation of all acts of terror and violence and establishment of a monitoring apparatus, expression of concern over Israel's killing of UN employees and destruction of a UN World Food Program warehouse, reaffirmation of the illegality of deportation, expression of concern over the Separation Barrier cutting through the occupied West Bank, condemnation of the assassination of the quadriplegic cleric Sheikh Ahmed Yassin (and half a dozen bystanders) in March 2004, and condemnation of an Israeli military incursion into Gaza with many civilians killed and extensive property damage.[43]

Bush has also gone to new lengths in supporting the occupation by formally recognizing Israel's right to retain West Bank settlements and continuing to provide the needed support for Israel's expansion into the West Bank. That includes support for the Separation Barrier, designed to ensure that the comfortable Jewish suburbs in the West Bank will be effectively incorporated within Israel, along with some of the most arable land and main water resources of the region, while the remnants left to a "Palestinian state" will be fragmented and unviable. The Separation Barrier is to encompass all settlement blocs, creating "three Bantustans on the West Bank: first, Jenin-Nablus; second, Bethlehem-Hebron; and third, Ramallah," Meron Benvenisti writes. A particularly cynical component is the virtual encirclement of Palestinian towns and villages, separating residents from their lands, which will in the course of time become "state lands" in accord with the Ottoman laws that Israel has revived in an effort to disguise its theft of lands with a thin veil of legality. The wall around the town of Qalqilya at Israel's border increases cost and Israeli insecurity, but the town is dying, as intended by this act of supreme cynicism.[44]

The same fate awaits others. Many cases have been investigated by the Israeli human rights organization B'Tselem. To mention just one, the Separation Barrier around illegally annexed Greater Jerusalem, for which there is not even the slimmest pretext of "security" (in fact, it enhances insecurity by enclosing many Palestinians within the projected borders of Israel), "will result in the complete isolation of the village" of Sheikh Sa'ad, just east of the Jerusalem municipal boundary and physically connected to a neighborhood in East Jerusalem on which its residents depend "for all aspects of life: health, employment, secondary education, supply of food and other goods." Located on a cliff, the village has only one road for exit or entry, and that is blocked by the Israeli Defense Forces. Theoretically, residents can submit a request for a permit—which is routinely denied—if they can manage to enter Jerusalem illegally. In this and many other cases, the method is purposeful cruelty, designed so that the residents are "forced to decide between living in a prison and abandoning their homes to live elsewhere." Those familiar with the history of Zionism will recognize the method, dating back to the 1920s: "dunam after dunam," arousing as little attention as possible. More generally, as Moshe Dayan put the matter to the Labor cabinet in the 1970s, we must tell the Palestinian refugees in the territories that "we have no solution, you shall continue to live like dogs, and whoever wishes may leave, and we will see where this process leads." But quietly, step by step, so that apologists can deny the facts.[45]

The Separation Barrier adopts the basic logic of the Clinton and Barak proposals at Camp David but goes beyond. In October 2005, Ha'aretz published a map of "the division of the West Bank into 'blocs.'" The map shows that the northern (Ariel) salient is also to extend to the Israeli-controlled Jordan valley, just as the southern (Ma'aleh Adumim) salient does. The goal is to "sever the northern West Bank [including Nablus and Jenin] from its central region," blocking Palestinian traffic, part of "the big picture of creating three separate blocs in the West Bank." A few weeks later Sharon informed reporters that Israel "intended to keep control of the Jordan Valley in the occupied West Bank, signaling its insistence on retaining settlements there under any future peace deal." It follows that the three cantons are completely contained by Israel. Infrastructure development is another device to destroy the remnants of Palestinian society. The authoritative Foundation for Middle East Peace review of events in the territories reports that the road system that has been carefully planned since 1970 is to be extended with the aim of "consolidating Israel's permanent hold on about half of the West Bank and its strategic domination of the remaining territories conquered in June 1967." The plans ensure that "the core north-south transit way through Jerusalem . . . is closed to Palestinians," who are restricted to a barely passable road from Bethlehem to the north (it is an experience to drive on it, hoping not to fall into the nearby wadi). The system is to be funded by the United States and the international community.[46]

With a wink from Washington, Israel is closing the vise further. Citing the Israeli daily Ma'ariv, Chris McGreal reports that "the government quietly gave the military the go-ahead earlier this week for a plan to culminate in barring all Palestinians from roads used by Israelis in the West Bank." *Ma'ariv* reports that "the purpose is to reach, in a gradual manner, within a year or two, total separation between the two populations. The first and immediate stage of separation applies to the roads in the territories: roads for Israelis only and roads for Palestinians only," but the longer-term goal "is to turn the separation fence into a line to completely prevent Palestinians from entering Israeli territory"—meaning occupied territory to be eventually incorporated within Israel. The roads for Israelis will be well-built highways, McGreal continues, "while Palestinians will be confined to secondary routes, many little better than dirt tracks or roads which have yet to be built."[47]

Israeli journalist Gideon Levy, whose reporting from the territories is difficult to match in quality anywhere, provides a graphic account of the details: "every journey in the West Bank" is "a continuous nightmare of humiliation and physical anxiety." When settlers are not traveling,

> most of the roads in the West Bank are desolate, with no people or cars . . . ghost roads. . . . If you strain your eyes, you will notice at the sides of the road the traffic lanes assigned to the Palestinians: pathways through the terraces winding up the hills, goat paths on which cars are sputtering, including those carrying the sick, women in labor, pupils, and ordinary citizens who decide to place their life in their hands in order to travel for two to three hours to reach the neighboring village.

The security pretext is frivolous: "A terrorist wishing to enter Israel will find a way to do so, as evident in the large number of Palestinians who manage to do this without a permit. The fact that the trip from Hebron to Bethlehem takes hours does not prevent terrorism; it encourages it. And if the goal is to 'respond to' and 'punish' every attack, why weren't the residents of [the Jewish West Bank settlement] Tapuah denied the freedom of movement after the terrorist Eden Natan-Zada set out for [Palestinian] Shfaram to kill its residents?"—as he did.[48]

The claims by supporters of Israeli expansion that Palestine would retain "contiguity" by some contrived transportation network is a shameful exercise in deceit, as anyone familiar with the area and the plans is aware. It suffices to ask how the same apologists would react to the proposal, surely fair enough, that Israel (with half the population on 78 percent of cis-Jordan) would be subjected to the same plans as Palestine (on the remaining 22 percent). That test is quite enlightening more generally.

The year 2004, according to the Israeli Interior Ministry, showed a 6 percent increase in the number of Israelis moving to settlements in the occupied territories, apart from more than 200,000 Jews in East Jerusalem. Israel continued its E-1 development project connecting the West Bank town of Ma'aleh Adumim to Jerusalem, periodically delayed when investigated, then resumed. The E-1 project is now attributed to Sharon, and the claim is made that "US officials have opposed the plan for years." In fact, the E-1 project and development of Ma'aleh Adumim were high priorities for the official doves and were implemented with US support. They are designed to effectively bisect the West Bank and to solidify the barriers separating Palestinians from whatever may remain to them in East Jerusalem.[49]

The centerpiece of the Sharon-Bush programs in the occupied territories in 2005 was presented as a "disengagement plan" offering new hopes for peace, but that is highly misleading. It is true that sane US-Israeli rejectionists wanted Israel's illegal settlements removed from Gaza, which has been turned into a disaster area under occupation, with a few thousand Jewish settlers, protected by a substantial part of the Israeli army, taking much of the land and scarce resources. Far more reasonable for US-Israeli goals is to leave Gaza as "the largest and most overcrowded prison in the world," in which over a million Palestinians can rot, largely cut off from contact with the outside by land or sea, and with few means of sustenance.[50]

That the Gaza pullout was in reality an expansion plan was hardly concealed. As the plan was made public, Finance Minister Netanyahu announced that "Israel will invest tens of millions of dollars in West Bank settlements as it withdraws from the Gaza Strip." When the government approved the plan, Sharon and Defense Minister Shaul Mofaz "met to discuss another matter: bolstering West Bank settlement blocs that are slated to be annexed to Israel under a final agreement."

Sharon also approved 550 new apartments in Ma'aleh Adumim, informing the ministers that there is no "political problem" despite assurances (with a wink) to Condoleezza Rice. Elliott Abrams, Bush's Middle East adviser, let Israelis understand that the United States was concerned about the "media blitz"—but not about the projects themselves, which may therefore proceed in accord with the principle of "building quietly." Abrams's qualifications for his position are that he is a pro-Israel hawk who received a presidential pardon from Bush I after being convicted of lying to Congress about Washington's terrorist war against Nicaragua, part of Bush's final cover-up of the Iran-contra affairs. Sharon also approved " 'declaration of state lands'—the first step in establishing a settlement" between Ma'aleh Adumim and Jerusalem, and also near the town of Efrat, which is to be expanded northward, all within the Separation Barrier. "The proximity in timing between approving the disengagement and construction plans is no coincidence," political commentator Aluf Benn writes: "From the day he presented the disengagement plan [in December 2003], Sharon made it clear that withdrawal from the Gaza Strip and [isolated outposts in] northern Samaria [the northern West Bank] is just one side of a triangle whose other sides are completing the separation fence in the West Bank and 'strengthening control' over the settlement blocs."[51]

The unilateral Israeli "disengagement plan"—pointedly rejecting any Palestinian participation—was explicit about intentions: "In any future permanent status arrangement," the plan states, "it is clear that in the West Bank, there are areas which will be part of the State of Israel, including major Israeli population centers, cities, towns and villages, security areas and other places of special interest to Israel." Palestinian concerns are as irrelevant as international law. Harvard Mideast scholar Sara Roy, one of the leading academic specialists on the occupation, writes that "under the terms of disengagement, Israel's occupation is assured. Gazans will be contained and sealed within the electrified borders of the Strip, while West Bankers, their lands dismembered by relentless Israeli settlement, will continue to be penned into fragmented geographic spaces, isolated behind and between walls and barriers." That appears unavoidable, as long as the

United States backs Israel's takeover of anything of value to it in the West Bank.[52]

The "media blitz" on disengagement was quite impressive, manufacturing one of the lead stories of the year. There were pages and pages of photos and reports of the pathos of the families forced to leave their homes and greenhouses, the weeping children trying vainly to hold back the soldiers, and the anguish of soldiers who were ordered to evict Jews from their homes and to remove the thousands of protesters who flooded to the settlements to resist the evacuation (by means that would lead to instant death for any Palestinian), miraculously evading the military forces that keep an iron grip on Palestinians. The Israeli Physicians for Human Rights was appalled that the enormous coverage of the trauma of disengagement somehow missed "the human catastrophe taking place today in the Gaza Strip." Amira Hass, who has done the major reporting from Gaza for many years, summarizes the reality kept in the shadows: "For the sake of about half a percent of the population of the Gaza Strip, a Jewish half-percent, the lives of the remaining 99.5 percent were totally disrupted and destroyed." Those who matter lived "in a flourishing park and splendid villas just 20 meters from overcrowded, suffocated refugee camps." They could "turn on the sprinklers on the lawns, while just across the way, 20,000 other people are dependent on the distribution of drinking water in tankers."[53]

Also ignored was the fact, plain enough, that disengagement on August 15 required no army intervention. The government could have simply announced that on that date the IDF would leave the Gaza Strip. A week before, the settlers would have quietly departed in the lorries provided to them, with compensation to resettle. But that would not have entrenched the right message: *Never again* must Jews suffer such a terrible fate; the West Bank must be theirs.

Also missing was the fact that the melodrama was a rerun of what the most prestigious Hebrew daily had called "Operation National Trauma '82," the evacuation of the settlers from Yamit in the Egyptian Sinai. That performance was described by Israeli journalist Amnon Kapeliouk as "one of the largest brain-washing operations conducted by the government in order to convince the Israeli people that they have suffered a 'national trauma the effect of which will be felt for generations.' " The well-orchestrated trauma was intended to create "a national consensus opposed to similar withdrawals in the remaining occupied territories"—and, crucially, to establish the same commitment among the paymasters overseas. General Haim Erez, who commanded the 1982 operation, said, "Everything was planned and agreed from the beginning" with the settlers, who were to offer a show of resistance. One consequence, Kapeliouk writes, is that "while the hospitals of the West Bank were full of scores of Palestinian victims of 'trigger happy' Israeli soldiers, a miracle occurred in Yamit: no demonstrators required even first-aid attention."[54]

Operation National Trauma 2005 reached far more elevated heights of drama, with the same miracle: only soldiers appear to have been injured. Describing the "agony and the ecstasy," Orit Shohat summarizes the clear message:

> Everything was staged down to the last detail. The settlers wanted to come out of it big-time, evacuated by force but without violence, and that is just what they did. . . . Religious Zionism shaped the visual national memory of the past week and strengthened the IDF, which emerged from the operation sensitive, determined and value-minded only thanks to the rabbis. The settlers reinforced their hold in the West Bank, reinforced the separation between the beloved IDF and the hated Ariel Sharon, reinforced the bond between religion and state, between religion and army, between religion and settlement, between religion and Zionism. . . . The settlers and the act of settlement became more deeply rooted in the people's hearts. It was television that did the work. Who can now conceive of an evacuation of the West Bank settler outposts, or the evacuation of more settlements, when we are in the stage of "healing" and "reconnecting"? Only the totally wicked.[55]

One of the most prominent academic specialists on Israeli society, Baruch Kimmerling, describes the "absurd theater" as "the largest show ever produced in Israel and perhaps the entire world, . . . a well-directed play [in which] tears flow like water and the supposed rivals embrace and fall on each other's shoulders, like a Latin soap opera." The show of force was plainly unnecessary if the goal had simply been to evacuate Gaza, Kimmerling observes, nor would there have been any need for "a cast of several thousand backup players" to enhance the drama. Announcement of the evacuation date and minimal preparations would have sufficed without "the grandiose production being presented to us. But then, who would have needed an evacuation?" The proper lesson of this "educational production par excellence" is conveyed by "the professional lamenters [who] weep and shout slogans aimed at shocking the Israeli people, employing an endless reservoir of symbols of the Holocaust and destruction," while intellectuals and writers "mobilize to aggrandize the collective mourning." The purpose is "to demonstrate to everyone that Israel is incapable of withstanding additional evacuations. That is, if the state's maximum resources needed to be mobilized to evacuate about 7,000 people, there is no possibility of evacuating 100,000–200,000 or more."[56]

Prime Minister Sharon rose to the occasion. "After directing the highly emotional evacuation of nearly 9,000 settlers from Gaza last month," Joel Brinkley reported, "Sharon asserted that he could not conceive of taking a similar step in the West Bank anytime soon." In Sharon's own words, "There are about a quarter million Jews living in these areas. There are many children there, religious families with many children. What am I supposed to say, 'You cannot live there anymore'? You were born there. You were born there!"[57]

The settlers, many from the United States, were amply subsidized to take over Gaza's scarce arable land and resources in gross violation of international law, and to enjoy a pleasant lifestyle near the festering refugee camps and towns devastated by Israeli army attacks and closures. They were then amply subsidized to resettle in Israel or the illegally occupied West Bank and Golan Heights. But the compensation laws are carefully honed. The settlements were highly productive, thanks in part to cheap Palestinian labor. "But neither the state nor their employers are compensating [Palestinian workers] for losing their jobs," Hass reports. "The Evacuation Compensation Law passed by the Knesset provides two benefits for people whose jobs are terminated by the evacuation. . . . But the new law specifically grants these benefits to Israelis only," and Palestinian workers are also unable to obtain back wages due from employers who are leaving. The workers who built the settlements and produced the export crops may now enjoy their freedom in the world's largest prison.[58]

Meanwhile, the takeover of the West Bank continues. Haim Ramon, minister in charge of Greater Jerusalem, conceded that the goal of the Jerusalem segment of the Separation Barrier is to guarantee a Jewish majority. The barrier was therefore constructed to cut off over 50,000 Palestinians from Jerusalem and include Jewish "neighborhoods" extending well into the West Bank. Israel's annexation of Jerusalem immediately after the June 1967 war was immediately condemned by the UN Security Council, which *"urgently calls upon* Israel" to rescind any measures taken with regard to the legal status of Jerusalem and to take no further measures (Resolution 252 of May 21, 1968). The annexation is officially recognized almost nowhere outside of Israel, where state law stipulates that "Jerusalem is the capital of Israel, East Jerusalem is Israel's territory and Israel is sovereign to act there regardless of international law" (Aharon Barak, the chief justice of Israel's Supreme Court). The expansion and reconstruction of Greater Jerusalem for Israeli interests proceeds with US funding and diplomatic support, also regardless of international law. In December 2002, Bush for the first time reversed official US opposition to the annexation, voting against yet another General Assembly resolution condemning it. If that move was intended seriously, it virtually ends the possibility of a resolution of the conflict, except by force.[59]

Ramon's rare acknowledgment of the truth about the Separation Barrier was amplified by Meron Benvenisti, who knows Jerusalem and the West Bank very well. The Palestinians seriously harmed are not just the officially cited 55,000 within the barrier, but also another 50,000 "who live in satellite communities of East Jerusalem and migrated to them because they could not find housing inside the city, due to the expropriation of [Palestinian] land and building restrictions" imposed on Palestinians, designed to turn Jerusalem into a Jewish city. "This means that the fence harms over 40 percent of East Jerusalem's 240,000 Arab residents." Deputy Prime Minister Ehud

Olmert, formerly mayor of Jerusalem, announced that he would allow twelve crossings for Palestinians, but immediately "made [this plan's] implementation dependent on international funding, 'since the crossings serve the Palestinians.'" As Benvenisti puts it: "first he surrounds them with a fence, and then he cynically claims that the crossing is 'in the interest' of those who are imprisoned." Benvenisti believes "there is a chance that the 'soft transfer'—which is an unavoidable result of the 'fence' surrounding Jerusalem—will achieve its goal, and that Jerusalem will in fact be 'more Jewish,' at the expense of the disintegration of the Palestinian community. For the first time since East Jerusalem was annexed, and after repeated and unsuccessful attempts to break the spirit of the Palestinian community in the city, there is now a real danger to the future of this community as a vital and vibrant body." The "human disaster" being planned will also "turn hundreds of thousands of people into a sullen community, hostile and nurturing a desire for revenge," once again sacrificing security to expansion. Correspondent Danny Rubinstein, who has covered the occupation with distinction for years, writes that "the elimination of East Jerusalem as a metropolitan center for its Arab hinterlands is proceeding apace, . . . creating facts [that] will, to an extent, obliterate the option of East Jerusalem as the Palestinian capital" while severely limiting freedom of movement to the West Bank for Jerusalem's Palestinian inhabitants.[60]

On the final day of Operation National Trauma 2005, Israeli officials confirmed that Israel is confiscating more land to extend the Separation Barrier around Ma'aleh Adumim, where 3,500 new houses and apartments would be built. The barrier will "cut deep into the West Bank, sealing off Palestinians in East Jerusalem," and virtually separating the southern canton from the remainder of the fragmented West Bank. The announcement was followed by the usual evasions under questioning, while Ehud Olmert informed the press that "it is absolutely clear that at a certain point in the future, Israel will create continuity between Jerusalem and Ma'aleh Adumim, and so there is not even an argument that at the end we will have to build the project." Shortly after, Sharon reiterated the same conclusion, while outgoing US ambassador Daniel Kurtzer amplified Bush's commitment to

Israel's retention of West Bank settlements, stating that "in the context of a final status agreement, the United States will support the retention by Israel of areas with a high concentration of Israeli population": the settlement blocs that create the "three Bantustans" referred to by Benvenisti and others who attend to the facts, barely linked to whatever is left of Palestinian Jerusalem.[61]

While these views are attributed to the far right, they simply carry forward the plans of the dovish Peres government, supported throughout by President Clinton. In February 1996, Peres's minister of housing and construction Benjamin ("Fuad") Ben-Eliezer explained, "It is no secret that the government's stand, which will be our ultimate demand, is that as regards the Jerusalem areas—Ma'aleh Adumim, Givat Ze'ev, Beitar, and Gush Etzion—they will be an integral part of Israel's future map. There is no doubt about this." There is, to be sure, a difference between hawks and doves, also explained frankly by Ben-Eliezer: "I build quietly. My goal is to build and not to encourage opposition to my efforts. . . . What is important to me is to build, build, build, and build some more." Quietly, though, so the master can pretend he does not see. Others have no difficulty in seeing, however. A confidential European Union report, attributed to the British Foreign Office, observes that a variety of Israeli programs quietly under way—including expansion of Ma'aleh Adumim to the E-1 area and incorporation of large areas around Greater Jerusalem within the separation wall—will allow Israel effectively to separate East Jerusalem from its Palestinian satellite cities of Bethlehem and Ramallah, and the rest of the West Bank beyond. The actions will have serious economic, social, and humanitarian consequences for the Palestinians, and will signal the virtual end of any hope for a viable Palestinian state, which would depend crucially on preservation of organic links between East Jerusalem, Ramallah, and Bethlehem.[62]

With Operation National Trauma 2005 successfully completed, Israel continued, with US backing, "to redraw Israel's borders deep inside the Palestinian territories . . . building quietly and quickly," with settlement and land takeovers rapidly increasing, particularly "in the Ariel and Maale Adumim blocks that penetrate deep into the occupied territories." In the first nine months of 2005, an estimated 14,000 settlers moved to the West Bank while 8,500 left Gaza, and more land was taken in the West Bank than was abandoned in the entire Gaza prison left behind. The general picture suggests that Sharon and Bush now sense that the final victory is in sight: the "vision" of the former Palestine cleansed of the alien growth, apart from some unviable fragments that remain, perhaps called "a democratic state"—or perhaps "fried chicken."[63]

Without proceeding further, even the bare outlines make it clear that Israel-Palestine joins the other illustrations of Bush's messianic mission to bring peace and democracy to the Middle East.

Though they have been subjected to disgraceful treatment, the Palestinians in East Jerusalem are fortunate in comparison with those who are less visible, and therefore can be killed, tortured, humiliated, and driven from their destroyed homes and lands virtually at will. It is, in fact, astonishing that their spirit has not been broken. One can say much the same about many other miserable victims throughout the world. I have been in many awful places, but have never seen such fear as in the eyes of those who were trying to survive in Haiti's indescribable slums during the Clinton-backed terror. Or such misery as among poor peasants in southern Colombia driven from their devastated lands by US chemical warfare ("fumigation"). And much more like it around the world. Even after violence achieves its goals and is relaxed, it leaves a residual "culture of terror," as the surviving Salvadoran Jesuits observed. Yet somehow communities endure and survive. This virtual miracle is the topic of sober reflections by *New York Times* columnist Benedict Carey, who marvels at the capacity of "fragile societies" to recover from terror and violence—referring to London, Tel Aviv, New York, but not to the *unpeople* of the world whose trauma at the hands of their foreign oppressors is immeasurably worse.[64]

The comparison may be unfair, however, mere sentimentality. As Reagan's UN ambassador thoughtfully explained, "Because the miseries of traditional life are familiar, they are bearable to ordinary people who, growing up in the society, learn to cope, as children born to untouchables in India acquire the skills and attitudes necessary for survival in the miserable roles they are destined to fill." Hence we need not be overly concerned about their fate at our hands.[65]

THE PERCEPTIONS OF THE *UNPEOPLE*

It is comforting to attribute the alleged "clash" between Islam and the West to their hatred of our freedom and values, as the president proclaimed after 9/11, or to our curious inability to communicate our true intentions. A *New York Times* headline reads: "US Fails to Explain Policies to Muslim World, Panel Says," referring to a study by the Defense Science Board, a Pentagon advisory panel, in December 2004. The conclusions of the panel, however, were quite different. "Muslims do not 'hate our freedom,' but rather they hate our policies," the study concluded, adding that "when American public diplomacy talks about bringing democracy to Islamic societies, this is seen as no more than self-serving hypocrisy." As Muslims see it, the report continues, "American occupation of Afghanistan and Iraq has not led to democracy there, but only more chaos and suffering."[66]

The Defense Science Board study was reiterating conclusions that go back many years. In 1958, President Eisenhower puzzled about "the campaign of hatred against us" in the Arab world, "not by the governments but by the people," who are "on Nasser's side," supporting independent secular nationalism. The reasons for the "campaign of hatred" were outlined by the National Security Council: "In the eyes of the majority of Arabs the United States appears to be opposed to the realization of the goals of Arab nationalism. They believe that the United States is seeking to protect its interest in Near East oil by supporting the status quo and opposing political or economic progress." Furthermore, the perception is understandable: "Our economic and cultural interests in the area have led not unnaturally to close US relations with elements in the Arab world whose primary interest lies in the maintenance of relations with the West and the status quo in their countries," blocking democracy and development.[67]

Much the same was found by the *Wall Street Journal* when it surveyed the opinions of "moneyed Muslims" immediately after 9/11. Bankers, professionals, businessmen, committed to official "Western values" and embedded in the neoliberal globalization project, were dismayed by Washington's support for harsh authoritarian states and the barriers it erects against development and democracy by "propping up oppressive regimes." They had new grievances, however, beyond those reported by the National Security Council in 1958: Washington's sanctions regime in Iraq and its support for Israel's military occupation and takeover of the territories. There was no survey of the great mass of poor and suffering people, but it is likely that their sentiments are more intense, coupled with bitter resentment of the Western-oriented elites and the corrupt and brutal rulers backed by Western power who ensure that the enormous wealth of the region flows to the West, apart from enriching themselves. The Iraq invasion only heightened these feelings, much as anticipated.[68]

Writing about the same 2004 Defense Science Board study, David Gardner observes that "for the most part, Arabs plausibly believe it was Osama bin Laden who smashed the status quo, not George W. Bush, [because] the 9/11 attacks made it impossible for the west and its Arab despot clients to continue to ignore a political set-up that incubated blind rage against them." Saudi Shiites share that belief, as the *New York Times* reported.[69]

The evidence concerning Washington's actual stance and role, virtuous declarations aside, is clear and compelling, surely by the standards of complex world affairs. Nonetheless, it is always possible that Washington's actions might have an incidental positive effect. It is hard to predict the consequences of striking a system as delicate and complex as a society with a bludgeon. This is often true of even the worst crimes. As noted, Osama bin Laden's atrocities are reported to have had a positive effect in spurring democratization in the Arab world. The terrible crimes of imperial Japan led to the expulsion of the European invaders from Asia, saving many millions of lives—in India, for example, which has been spared horrifying famines since the British withdrew and was able to begin to recover from centuries of imperial domination. Perhaps what many Iraqis and others see as another Mongol invasion will end up having positive consequences as well, though it would be disgraceful for privileged Westerners to leave that possibility to chance.

THE PERSISTENCE OF the "strong line of continuity" to the present again reveals that the United States is very much like other powerful states, pursuing the strategic and economic interests of dominant sectors to the accompaniment of rhetorical flourishes about its exceptional dedication to the highest values. It should come as no surprise that the evidence for Washington's dedication to the proclaimed messianic mission reduces to routine pronouncements, or that the counterevidence is mountainous. The reaction to these facts is of no slight significance for those concerned with the state of US democracy, as noted at the outset. Abroad, democracy is fine as long as it takes the "top-down form" that does not risk popular interference with primary interests of power and wealth. Much the same doctrine holds internally, a topic to which we now turn.

Chapter 6

Democracy Promotion at Home

The concept of democracy promotion at home may seem odd or even absurd. After all, the United States was the first modern (more or less) democratic society, and has been a model for others ever since. And in many dimensions crucial for authentic democracy—protection of freedom of speech, for example—it has become a leader among the societies of the world. There are, however, quite good reasons for concern, some already mentioned.[1]

The concern is not unfamiliar. The most prominent scholar who concentrates on democratic theory and practice, Robert Dahl, has written on seriously undemocratic features of the US political system, proposing modifications. Thomas Ferguson's "investment theory" of politics is a searching critique of deeper institutional factors that sharply restrict functioning democracy. The same is true of Robert McChesney's investigations of the role of the media in undermining democratic politics, to the extent that by the year 2000 presidential elections had become a "travesty," he concludes, with a reciprocal effect on deterioration of media quality and service to the public interest. Subversion of democracy by concentrations of private power is, of course, familiar: mainstream commentators casually observe that "business is in complete control of the machinery of government" (Robert Reich), echoing Woodrow Wilson's observation, days before he took office, that "the masters of the government of the United States are the combined capitalists and manufacturers of the United States." America's leading twentieth-century social philosopher, John Dewey, concluded that "politics is the shadow cast on society by big business" and will remain so as long as power resides in "business for private profit through private control of banking, land, industry, reinforced by command of the press, press agents and other means of publicity and propaganda." Accordingly, reforms will not suffice. Fundamental social change is necessary to bring meaningful democracy.[2]

"THE NEW SPIRIT OF THE AGE"

The political system that is the subject of these critiques bears some resemblance to the initial design, though the framers would surely have been appalled by many subsequent developments, in particular the radical judicial activism that granted rights of persons to "collectivist legal entities" (corporations), rights extended far beyond those of persons of flesh and blood in recent international economic arrangements (mislabeled "free trade agreements"). Each such step is a severe attack against classical liberal principles, democracy, and markets. The enormously powerful immortal "persons" that have been created are, furthermore, required by law to suffer from moral deficiencies that we would regard as pathological among real people. A core principle of Anglo-American corporate law is that they must be dedicated single-mindedly to material self-interest. They are permitted to do "good works," but only if these have a favorable impact on image, hence profit and market share. The courts have sometimes gone further. The Chancery Court of Delaware observed that "contemporary courts recognize that unless corporations carry an increasing share of the burden of supporting charitable and educational causes . . . the business advantages now reposed in corporations by law may well prove to be unacceptable to the representatives of an aroused public." The powerful "means of publicity and propaganda" of which Dewey spoke must be deployed to ensure that an "aroused public" does not come to understand the workings of the state-corporate system.[3]

The initial design was articulated clearly by the most influential of the framers, James Madison. He held that power should be in the hands of "the wealth of the nation . . . the more capable set of men." People "without property, or the hope of acquiring it," he reflected at the end of his life, "cannot be expected to sympathize sufficiently with its rights, to be safe depositories of power over them." The rights are not those of *property*, which has no rights, but of property *owners*, who therefore should have extra rights beyond those of citizens generally. In his "determination to protect minorities against majority infringements of their rights," the prominent Madison scholar Lance Banning observes, "it is absolutely clear that he was most especially concerned for propertied minorities among the people." Madison could hardly have been unaware of the force of Adam Smith's observation that "civil government, so far as it is instituted for the security of property, is in reality instituted for the defence of the rich against the poor, or of those who have some property against those who have none at all." Warning his colleagues at the Constitutional Convention of the perils of democracy, Madison asked them to consider what would happen in England "if elections were open to all classes of people." The population would then use its voting rights to distribute land more equitably. To ward off such injustice, he recommended arrangements "to protect the minority of the opulent against the majority," subsequently implemented.[4]

The problem Madison posed was an old one, tracing back to the first classic of political science, Aristotle's *Politics*. Of the variety of systems he surveyed, Aristotle found democracy "the most tolerable," though of course he had in mind a limited democracy of free men, much as Madison did two thousand years later. Aristotle recognized flaws in democracy, however, among them the one that Madison presented to the convention. The poor "covet their neighbours' goods," Aristotle observed, and if wealth is narrowly concentrated, they will use their majority power to redistribute it more equitably, which would be unfair: "In democracies the rich should be spared; not only should their property not be divided, but their incomes too . . . should be protected. . . . Great then is the good fortune of a state in which the citizens have a moderate and sufficient property; for where some possess much, and others nothing, there may arise an extreme democracy" that does not recognize the rights of the rich, perhaps deteriorating even beyond.

Aristotle and Madison posed essentially the same problem, but drew opposite conclusions. Madison's solution was to restrict democracy, while Aristotle's was to reduce inequality, by what amount to welfare-state programs. For democracy to function properly, he argued, "measures therefore should be taken which will give [all people] lasting prosperity." The "proceeds of the public revenues should be accumulated and distributed among its poor" to enable them to "purchase a little farm, or, at any rate, make a beginning in trade or husbandry," along with other means, such as "common meals" with costs defrayed by "public land."[5]

In the century that followed the establishment of the American constitutional system, popular struggles greatly expanded the scope of democracy, not only by political changes like extension of the franchise, but also by establishing the much more far-reaching concept that "self-directed work defined the democrat," a principle taken to be "the norm for all men" in the nineteenth century, historian Robert Wiebe writes. Wage labor was considered hardly different from chattel slavery. By the mid-nineteenth century, working people bitterly denounced the rising industrial system that forced them to become "humble subjects" of "despots," reduced to a "state of servitude" with "a moneyed aristocracy hanging over us like a mighty avalanche threatening annihilation to every man who dares to question their right to enslave and oppress the poor and unfortunate." They deplored "the New Spirit of the Age: Gain Wealth, forgetting all but Self" as a cruel attack on their dignity and freedom and culture.[6]

It has taken massive efforts to try to drive such sentiments from the mind, to bring people to accept "the New Spirit of the Age" and the fact—in Woodrow Wilson's words—that "most men are servants of corporations . . . in a very different America from the old." In this new America—"no longer a scene of individual enterprise, . . . individual opportunity, and individual achievement"—"small groups of men in control of great corporations wield a power and control over the wealth and business opportunities of the country." As the process of corporatization gained force, undermining markets and freedom, the era of "self-rule" came to an end, Wiebe writes. "The lights dimmed in the great showcase of nineteenth century democracy," he continues, a process abetted by "drives for conformity and control expressing themselves in [World War I] wartime patriotism, [Wilson's] Red Scare," and other devices "to regiment the lower class."[7]

While popular struggle over centuries has gained many victories for freedom and democracy, progress does not follow a smooth upward trajectory. There has been a regular cycle of progress under popular pressure, followed by regression as power centers mobilize their considerable forces to reverse it, at least partially. Though over time the cycle tends to be upward, sometimes regression reaches so far that the population is almost completely marginalized in pseudo-elections, most recently the "travesty" of 2000 and the even more extreme travesty of 2004.

DEMONIC MESSIANISM

The opening remarks of this chapter reviewed some of the critique of corporatized state capitalist democracy, in its relatively stable form. But in specific reaction to Bush administration policies, more imminent concerns have been voiced, sometimes in ways that have few if any precedents. Cautious voices in scholarly journals have questioned the very "viability . . . of the United States political system" unless it can face threats to survival posed by current policies. Some have turned to Nazi analogues in discussing Bush's Justice Department; others have compared administration policies to those of fascist Japan. The measures currently being used to control the population have also aroused bitter memories. Among those who remember well is the distinguished scholar of German history Fritz Stern. He opens a recent review of "the descent in Germany from decency to Nazi barbarism" with the comment: "Today, I worry about the immediate future of the United States, the country that gave haven to German-speaking refugees in the 1930s," himself included. With implications for here and now that no reader can fail to discern, Stern reviews Hitler's demonic appeal to his "divine mission" as "Germany's savior" in a "pseudoreligious transfiguration of politics" adapted to "traditional Christian forms," ruling a government dedicated to "the basic principles" of the nation, with "Christianity as the foundation of our national morality and the family as the basis of national life." Hitler's hostility toward the "liberal secular state," shared by much of the Protestant clergy, drove forward "a historic process in which resentment against a disenchanted secular world found deliverance in the ecstatic escape of unreason."[8]

It should not be forgotten that the rapid descent to the depths of barbarism took place in the country that was the pride of Western civilization in the sciences, philosophy, and the arts; a country that before the hysterical propaganda of World War I had been regarded by many American political scientists as a model of democracy. One of Israel's most prominent intellectuals, Amos Elon, now self-exiled in despair over Israel's social and moral decline, describes the German Jewry of his youth as "the secular elite of Europe. They were the essence of modernism—leaders who made their livelihood from brainpower and not from brawn, mediators and not workers of the land. Journalists, writers, scientists. If it all hadn't ended so horribly, today we'd be singing the praises of Weimar culture. We'd be comparing it to the Italian Renaissance. What happened there in the fields of literature, psychology, painting and architecture didn't happen anywhere else. There hadn't been anything like it since the Renaissance." Not an unreasonable judgment.[9]

It may be recalled that Nazi propaganda techniques were borrowed from business doctrines and practices that were mostly pioneered in the Anglo-American societies. These techniques were based on resort to simple "symbols and slogans" with "tremendously reiterated impressions" that appeal to fear and other elementary emotions in the manner of commercial advertising, a contemporary review observes. "Goebbels conscripted most of the leading commercial advertising men in Germany for his propaganda ministry," and boasted that "he would use American advertising methods" to "sell National Socialism" much as business seeks to sell "chocolate, toothpaste, and patent medicines." These measures were frightfully successful in bringing about the sudden descent from decency to barbarism that Fritz Stern describes with an ominous warning.[10]

Demonic messianism is a natural device for leadership groups that are at the extreme of the spectrum in their dedication to the short-term interests of narrow sectors of power and wealth, and to global domination. It takes willful blindness not to see how these commitments guide current US policy. The goals pursued and programs enacted are opposed by the public in case after case. That impels the need for mass mobilization, employing the skills of the huge industries that have been created in a business-run society to influence attitudes and beliefs. The need for such measures has taken on special importance during the past several decades, a highly unusual period of American economic history. When neoliberal-style programs began to take shape in the 1970s, real wages in the United States were the highest in the industrial world, as one would expect in the richest society in the world, with incomparable advantages. The situation has now drramatically changed. Real wages for the majority have largely stagnated or declined and are now close to the lowest level among industrial societies; the relatively weak benefits system has declined as well. Incomes are maintained only by extending working hours well beyond those in similar societies, while inequality has soared. All of this is a vast change from the preceding quarter century, when economic growth was the highest on record for a protracted period and also egalitarian. Social indicators, which closely tracked economic growth until the mid-1970s, then diverged, declining to the level of 1960 by the year 2000.[11]

Edward Wolff, the leading specialist on wealth distribution, writes that "living conditions stagnated in the 1990s for American households in the middle, while rapid advances in wealth and income for the elite briskly pulled up the averages." From 1983 to 1998, average wealth of the top 1 percent rose "a whopping 42%," while the poorest 40 percent "lost 76 percent of their (very modest) wealth." He concludes that even "the boom of the 1990s has bypassed most Americans. The rich have been the main beneficiaries," in a continuation of tendencies that go back to the late 1970s. The Bush administration's

dedication to wealth and privilege accelerated these tendencies, leading to a surge in "corporate profits, professionals' incomes, gains
from investments and executive compensation," while, by mid-2005,
"average hourly wages for production and non-supervisory workers"
had yet to rise to the low point of the 2001 recession. Census Bureau
2004 figures revealed that for the first time on record, household incomes failed to increase for five straight years. Median pretax real
income was at its lowest point since 1997, while the poverty rate increased for the fourth consecutive year, to 12.7 percent. Median
earnings for full-time workers "dropped significantly," for men, by
2.3 percent. Inequality continued to rise to "near all-time highs," not
including "gains from stock holdings, which would further increase
inequality," given the extremely narrow concentration of stock
ownership. The Labor Department reports an additional decline in
real wages in 2004 for most workers, apart from a small percentage
of the highly skilled. Economist Dean Baker reported in October
2005 that "the economy went through its longest period of job loss
since the Great Depression following the 2001 recession. The employment to population ratio is still almost 2 percentage points below its pre-recession level. Using the recovery of the labor market as
a metric, the economy has never been less resilient throughout the
post-war period."[12]

The number of people who go hungry because they cannot afford
to buy food rose to over 38 million in 2004: 12 percent of households,
an increase of 7 million in five years. As the government released the
figures, the House Agricultural Committee voted to remove funding
for food stamps for 300,000 people, and cut off school lunches and
breakfasts for 40,000 children, only one of many illustrations.[13]

The results are hailed as a "healthy economy" and a model for
other societies. Alan Greenspan is treated with reverence for having
presided over these achievements, which he attributes in part to "atyp-
ical restraint on compensation increases [which] appears to be mainly
the consequence of greater worker insecurity," an obvious desidera-
tum for a healthy economy. The model may in fact be without many
precedents in harming the "underlying population" while benefiting
the "substantial people," in Thorstein Veblen's acid terminology.[14]

To keep the underlying population in line in the face of the daily realities of their lives, resort to "pseudoreligious transfiguration" is a natural device, exploiting features of popular culture that have sharply diverged from the rest of the industrial world for a long time, and have been manipulated for political gain particularly since the Reagan years.[15]

Another device that is regularly exploited is the fear of imminent destruction by an enemy of boundless evil. Such perceptions are deeply rooted in American popular culture, coupled with faith in nobility of purpose—the latter, as close to a universal as history provides. In an enlightening review of popular culture from the earliest years, Bruce Franklin identifies such leading themes as the "Anglo-American syndicate of War" that will impose its "peaceful and enlightened rule" by threatening "annihilation" of those who stand in the way, bringing "the Spirit of Civilization" to backward peoples (1889). He also reviews the remarkable choice of demons about to destroy us, typically those whom Americans were crushing under their boots: Indians, blacks, Chinese workers, among others. Participants in these exercises included leading progressive writers, such as Jack London, who wrote a 1910 story in a popular journal advocating the extermination of the Chinese by bacteriological warfare to undercut their nefarious secret scheme to overwhelm us.[16]

Whatever the roots of these cultural features may be, they can easily be manipulated by cynical leaders, often in ways that are hard to believe. During the Reagan years, Americans were supposed to cower in fear before images of Libyan hit men seeking to assassinate our leader; an air base in the nutmeg capital of the world that Russia might use to bomb us; the ferocious Nicaraguan army only two days from Harlingen, Texas; Arab terrorists lurking everywhere; crime in the streets; Hispanic narco-traffickers—anything that could be conjured up to mobilize support for the next campaign at home and abroad, commonly with domestic victims alongside those abroad who suffered far greater blows.

ELECTIONS 2004

The results of the 2004 elections led to exultation in some quarters, despair in others, and much concern about the United States becoming a "divided nation." The outcome has policy consequences, harmful to the general population at home and threatening for the world and future generations. The elections also provide useful insight into the growing democratic deficit, a criterial feature of "failed states." But they tell us little about the state of the country or the popular mood. There are, however, other sources from which we can learn a great deal about these critical matters. Public opinion in the United States is intensively monitored and, while caution and care in interpretation are always necessary, these studies are valuable resources. Results of polls that are unwelcome to powerful interests are often kept under wraps by the doctrinal institutions. The practice applied again to highly informative studies of public opinion released right before the 2004 elections, to which I will return.[17]

Immediately after the 2004 elections, Colin Powell informed the press that "President George W. Bush has won a mandate from the American people to continue pursuing his 'aggressive' foreign policy." That is far from true. It is also very far from what the population believed. After the elections, Gallup asked whether Bush "should emphasize programs that both parties support," or whether he "has a mandate to advance the Republican Party's agenda," as Powell and others claimed. Sixty-three percent chose the former option, 29 percent the latter.[18]

The elections conferred no mandate for anything; in fact, they barely took place, in any serious sense of the term *election*. Though the 2004 election was extreme in this respect, many of its features have become familiar. Analyzing Reagan's victory in 1980, Thomas Ferguson and Joel Rogers concluded that it reflected "the decay of organized party structures, and the vast mobilization of God and cash in the successful candidacy of a figure once marginal to the 'vital center' of American political life." The election revealed "the continued disintegration of those political coalitions and economic structures that have given party politics some stability and definition during the past generation."[19]

In the same valuable collection of essays on the 1980 elections, Walter Dean Burnham described these elections as further evidence of a "crucial comparative peculiarity of the American political system: the total absence of a socialist or laborite mass party as an organized competitor in the electoral market," a lack that accounts for much of the "class-skewed abstention rates" and the downplaying of issues. Thus of the 28 percent of the electorate who voted for Reagan, 11 percent gave as their primary reason "he's a real conservative." In his "landslide victory" of 1984, just under 30 percent of the electorate voted for Reagan. Of these, 4 percent gave as their primary reason that he's a real conservative. Therefore, 1 percent of the electorate voted for a "real conservative" in what was described as a powerful mandate for "conservatism." Furthermore, polls showed that by 3 to 2, voters hoped that Reagan's legislative program would not be enacted. As before, polls revealed that the public favored tax increases devoted to New Deal and Great Society programs. Support for equal or greater social expenditures was about 80 percent in 1980, and increased in 1984. Cuts in Social Security were opposed with near unanimity, cuts in Medicare or Medicaid by well over 3 to 1. The public preferred cuts in military spending to cuts in health programs by about 2 to 1. Large majorities supported government regulations to protect worker health and safety, protection of consumer interests, help for the elderly, the poor, and the needy, and other social programs.[20]

But none of this matters as long as elections are skillfully managed to avoid issues and marginalize the underlying population, again in Veblen's terminology, freeing the elected leadership to serve the substantial people. As it did.

Ferguson and Rogers were describing early effects of the powerful coordinated backlash against the "crisis of democracy" of the 1960s that deeply concerned the Trilateral Commission, which coined the phrase. The commission consisted of prominent liberal internationalists from the three major industrial regions: North America, Europe, and Japan. Their general perspective is illustrated by the fact that the

Carter administration was mostly drawn from their ranks. The worri-some crisis under discussion was that the 1960s had given rise to what they called "an excess of democracy": normally passive and marginal-ized sectors—women, youth, elderly, labor, minorities, and other parts of the underlying population—began to enter the political arena to press their demands. The "crisis of democracy" was regarded as even more dangerous by the components of the elite spectrum to the right of the commission and by the business world in general. The "excess of democracy" threatened to interfere with the well-functioning sys-tem of earlier years, when "Truman had been able to govern the coun-try with the cooperation of a relatively small number of Wall Street lawyers and bankers," so the American rapporteur at the Trilateral Commission proceedings, Samuel Huntington, recalled with a trace of nostalgia and pardonable exaggeration. Among the immediate re-actions to the "crisis" were a dramatic increase in corporate lobbying and the proliferation of right-wing think tanks to ensure control of legislative programs and doctrinal institutions, along with other de-vices to restore order and discipline. Such "drives for conformity and control" (Wiebe) are normal reactions of concentrated power to the "crises of democracy" that erupt when the public seeks to enter the public arena: Wilson's Red Scare and the massive post–World War II corporate propaganda offensive are two of the well-documented ex-amples. Both achieved at least short-term discipline, but the popular forces unleashed in the 1960s have been far harder to tame, and in fact have continued to develop, sometimes in unprecedented ways.[21]

The project of restoring order and discipline was also advanced by the neoliberal measures instituted in the 1970s, enforced more rigidly in later years, with economic as well as political consequences. The former, which would hardly surprise economic historians, are summa-rized by José Antonio Ocampo, the executive secretary of the Eco-nomic Commission for Latin America and the Caribbean: "The period of fastest growth in the developing world in the postwar pe-riod, and most prolonged episodes of rapid growth (the East-Asian or the most recent Chinese and Indian 'miracles' or, in the past, the peri-ods of rapid growth in Brazil or Mexico) do not coincide with phases or episodes of extensive liberalization, even when they involved a large scale use of the opportunities provided by international markets." The same, we may add, applies to the industrial powers.

Reviewing the neoliberal experience of a quarter century, a study of the Center for Economic and Policy Research shows that it has been accompanied by much slower rates of growth and reduced progress on social indicators for countries in every quintile, rich to poor. There are exceptions to the general tendency: high growth rates were recorded among those who ignored the rules (and with tremendous inequality and other severe side effects in China and India). "The overall growth pattern is unambiguous," economist Robert Pollin found in a detailed analysis: "there has been a sharp decline in growth in the neoliberal era relative to the developmental state period" that preceded it, a decline of over half, a trend that "is even more dramatic" when measured per capita, with increase in inequality and little or no reduction of poverty (when China is excluded), and devastating side effects among the most vulnerable. Political economist Robert Wade observes that "one of the big—and underappreciated facts of our time [is the] dramatic growth slowdown in developed and developing countries" in the quarter century of neoliberal economic policy, including, probably, an increase in poverty and in-country and between-country inequality when China (which rejected the policies) is removed and realistic poverty measures are used. The facts are sometimes obscured by the observation that conditions have generally improved under the neoliberal regime (as they almost invariably do over time under any economic regime), or by resort to a concept of "globalization" that muddles export orientation with neoliberalism, so that if a billion Chinese experience high growth under export-oriented policies that radically violate neoliberal principles, the increase in average global growth rates can be hailed as a triumph of the principles that are violated. While too little is understood to be confident about causation, it is difficult to ignore the fact that the strong and harmful tendencies associated with neoliberal policies are quite consistent with economic history over a much longer term, facts well known to economic historians.[22]

The "reforms" had predictable political consequences as well. A prime target of neoliberal measures is national autonomy, which,

Ocampo observes, "is the only system that is consistent with the promotion of democracy." Evidently, democracy reduces to empty form "if the representative and participatory processes at the national level are given no role in determining economic and social development strategies." It should be clear that undermining that role is an unconcealed objective of the "reforms" and the "free trade agreements" that institutionalize them. As "free trade" is construed in these arrangements, it incorporates monopoly pricing rights and other highly protectionist devices to benefit multinationals. It also bans the measures that have been used by the industrial societies to achieve their current state of economic development, including government efforts, responding to public will, to privilege popular concerns over investor rights. It guarantees free movement of capital while dismissing free movement of labor, a core principle of free trade for Adam Smith. It also defines *trade* in expansive ways, including, for example, transfers internal to a firm that happen to cross international borders, a very substantial component of "trade." Apart from having only a limited relation to free trade, these "agreements" are certainly not agreements, at least not if citizens, who are generally opposed, are regarded as part of their countries. The "agreements" are reached only by secrecy and other devices to marginalize the annoying public. In the term "North American Free Trade Agreement" (NAFTA), the only accurate words are "North American." Other agreements are generally no different.[23]

As Ocampo observes, the neoliberal reforms are antithetical to promotion of democracy. They are not designed to shrink the state, as often asserted, but to strengthen state institutions to serve even more than before the needs of the substantial people. A dominant theme is to restrict the public arena and transfer decisions to the hands of unaccountable private tyrannies. One method is privatization, which removes the public from potential influence on policy. An extreme form is privatization of "services," a category that encompasses just about anything of public concern: health, education, water and other resources, and so on. Once these are removed from the public arena by "trade in services," formal democratic practices are largely reduced to a device for periodic mobilization of the public in the service of elite interests, and the "crisis of democracy" is substantially overcome.

Much the same is true of the financial liberalization instituted from the early 1970s on. As well understood by international economists, these measures create a "virtual Senate" of investors and lenders who can exercise "veto power" over government decisions by threat of capital flight, attacks on currency, and other means. Such measures for undermining democracy were restricted under the Bretton Woods system established after World War II by the United States and Britain (Harry Dexter White and John Maynard Keynes), responding to powerful public pressures. Keynes considered the most important achievement of Bretton Woods to be establishment of the right of governments to restrict capital movement; in sharp contrast, the US Treasury now regards free capital mobility as a "fundamental right," unlike such alleged rights as decent employment.[24] The Bretton Woods rules also restricted financial speculation and attacks on currencies. The effect was to allow a form of "embedded liberalism," as it is sometimes called, in which social democratic policies could be pursued. The outcome is often termed the "golden age" of capitalism (more accurately, state capitalism), with unprecedented economic growth that was also egalitarian, and enactment of significant welfare-state measures to benefit the general population. All of this has been reversed in the neoliberal period.

In earlier years the public had not been much of a problem. In his history of the international monetary system, Barry Eichengreen explains that before government policy became "politicized by universal male suffrage and the rise of trade unionism and parliamentary labor parties," the severe costs of financial rectitude imposed by the virtual Senate could be transferred to the underlying population. But with the radicalization of the general public during the Great Depression and the anti-fascist war, that luxury was no longer available to private power and wealth. Hence in the Bretton Woods system "limits on capital mobility substituted for limits on democracy as a source of insulation from market pressures."[25] With the dismantling of the system from the 1970s, substantive democracy is reduced, and it becomes necessary to divert and control the public in some fashion.

"TO DECEIVE AND OPPRESS THE PUBLIC"

In the 2004 elections, Bush received the votes of just over 30 percent of the electorate, Kerry a bit less. Voting patterns resembled those of 2000, with virtually the same distribution of "red" and "blue" states (whatever significance that may have). A small change in voter preference would have put Kerry in the White House. Either way, the outcome tells us very little about the country and public concerns. Congressional voting patterns make that even clearer. In the Senate, only one of twenty-six incumbents lost, Democrat Tom Daschle of South Dakota, a state with a population of about 770,000. In the House, had it not been for gerrymandering by anti-democratic Texas Republicans led by majority leader Tom DeLay, only eight seats would have changed hands, an all-time low, and Republicans would have lost seats overall; outside of Texas they lost three. The limited competition for House seats reached the lowest level on record. And Bush had the lowest approval rating of any reelected president for whom data are available.[26]

Not much of a mandate. The results, however, significantly understate the meaninglessness of the electoral results, as we see when we look beyond electoral statistics.

As usual in recent years, the 2004 electoral campaigns were run by the public relations industry, which in its regular vocation sells toothpaste, lifestyle drugs, automobiles, and other commodities. Its guiding principle is deceit. The task of advertising is to undermine the free markets we are taught to admire: mythical entities in which informed consumers make rational choices. In such systems, businesses would simply provide information about their products: cheap, easy, simple. But it is hardly a secret that they do nothing of the sort. On the contrary, business spends hundreds of billions of dollars a year projecting imagery to delude consumers. Uncontroversially, that is the goal of advertising—not providing information. The automobile industry does not simply make public the characteristics of next year's models. Rather, it devotes huge efforts to deception, featuring sex objects, cars climbing sheer cliffs to a heavenly future, and so on. Furthermore, as Veblen pointed out long ago, one of the primary tasks of business propaganda is the "fabrication of consumers," a device that helps induce "all the classic symptoms of state-based totalitarianism: atomization, political apathy and irrationality, the hollowing and banalization of purportedly democratic political processes, mounting popular frustration, and so forth."

The basic observation is as old as Adam Smith, who warned that the interests of merchants and manufacturers are "to deceive or even to oppress the public," as they have done "on many occasions." By now they are served by major industries that have been created for this purpose. Informed consumer choice is about as realistic as the famed "entrepreneurial initiative" and "free trade." Except for temporary advantage, the fanciful markets of doctrine and economic theory have never been welcomed—or long tolerated—by those who dominate society.[27]

Sometimes the commitment to deceit takes extreme forms. One illustration is the US-Australia negotiations on a "free trade agreement" from 2003. These were held up by Washington's concern that Australia follows "evidence-based" procedures and prohibits "direct-to-consumer marketing for prescription drugs," while US "manufacturers would prefer a system in which they have the freedom to market their products and set prices according to the market's willingness to pay." Australia engages in unacceptable market interference, US government negotiators objected. Pharmaceutical corporations are deprived of their legitimate rights if they are required to produce evidence when they claim that their latest product is better than some cheaper alternative, or run TV ads in which some sports hero or movie actress tells the audience to "ask your doctor whether this drug is right for you (it's right for me)," sometimes not even revealing what the drug is supposed to be for. The right of deceit must be guaranteed to the immensely powerful and pathological immortal "persons" that have been created by radical judicial activism.[28]

Australia's health care system is perhaps the most efficient in the world. In particular, drug prices are a fraction of those in the United States: the same drugs, produced by the same companies, earning substantial profits though nothing like those in the United States, where such profits are commonly justified on the dubious grounds that they are needed for research and development (R&D). Economist Dean Baker finds that savings to consumers would be immense if public funding increased to 100 percent of R&D, thus eliminating the drug companies' justifications for monopoly pricing rights. The public already plays a much greater role than acknowledged, since the development of drugs relies on fundamental science, virtually all of which is funded by the public. Even with what is counted, corporate R&D concentrates more toward the marketing end: major US drug companies spend more than twice as much on marketing, advertising, and administration as on any kind of R&D, while reporting huge profits.[29]

One reason for the efficiency of the Australian system is that, like other countries, Australia relies on the practices that the Pentagon employs when it buys paper clips: the government uses its purchasing power to negotiate prices, actions barred by legislation for drugs in the United States. Another reason is Australia's reliance on evidence-based procedures: "In order to charge the Australian Government a high price for a new drug," the US pharmaceutical corporations "actually have to provide evidence that the new drug has demonstrable benefits, [which] is considered to be a barrier to trade by the US." The US drug industry also objects to the Australian requirement that the companies "must demonstrate significant clinical advantages" and "satisfactory cost-effectiveness" in comparison with available drugs, as well as to Australia's "overriding focus on cost-effectiveness" generally. The industry denounces such measures as "insidious"—as they are, in interfering with the right of deceit that is central to really existing markets.[30]

When assigned the task of selling candidates, the PR industry naturally resorts to the same techniques as in marketing commodities. Deceit is employed to undermine democracy, just as it is a natural device to undermine markets. Voters appear to be aware of the travesty. On the eve of the 2000 elections, a large majority of the electorate dismissed them as an extravaganza run by rich contributors, party managers, and the PR industry, which trains candidates to project images and produce empty phrases that might win some votes. Pollsters found only one issue on which more than half of respondents could identify the stands of the candidates: Gore on prescription drugs. More than 60 percent of regular voters felt that "politics in America is generally pretty disgusting." The director of Harvard's Vanishing Voter Project reported that "Americans' feeling of powerlessness has reached an alarming high," well beyond earlier levels.[31]

Very likely, these are among the reasons why the population at large seemed to have little interest in the "stolen election" that exercised educated sectors. And it may be why they paid little attention to charges about fraud in 2004. If one is flipping a coin to pick the king, it is of no great concern if the coin is biased.

In 2000, "issue awareness"—knowledge of the stands of the candidates—reached an all-time low. It may have been even lower in 2004. In 2004, about 10 percent of voters, in an open question, chose the candidate's "agendas/ideas/platforms/goals" as a prime reason for their votes (Bush 6 percent, Kerry 13 percent). National security appeared to be the top concern: 22 percent "volunteered something about the situation in Iraq and 12 percent mentioned terrorism."[32] Many voted for what the public relations industry calls "qualities" or "values," which are designed and projected with great care and have about as much authenticity as imagery in toothpaste ads. News commentary focused on "style," "likability," "bonding," and "character," and on such flaws as Bush's occasional "testiness" or Kerry's getting the name of a football stadium wrong. Pollster Daniel Yankelovich reported that "the views of Americans who frequently attend religious services and the views of Americans who do not mirror those of Republicans and Democrats, respectively." Churchgoing white evangelical Protestants are a particularly powerful Republican voting bloc. "This constituency sees the president as a man of strong character: honest, simple, straight-talking, determined, no-nonsense, God-fearing," a man of "sincerity and clarity of moral purpose" who is "on the side of good," a major triumph of marketing, which permits the leadership to carry out its programs without concern for public opinion.[33]

Extremist religious beliefs have a long history in the United States, going back to the early colonists and those who settled the continent. There have been periodic religious revivals since, notably during the 1950s, which historian Seth Jacobs suggests may have been the most religious decade in American history. Jacobs attributes the Eisenhower administration's decision to install the devout Catholic Ngo Dinh Diem to run its client state in South Vietnam, despite his recognized unpopularity and incompetence, to the great religious revival in the United States at the time. Writing in 1980, Walter Dean Burnham found "the pervasiveness of religious cognitions in American political life [to be] yet another—and very important—comparative peculiarity of this country in the cosmos of advanced industrial societies," alongside the class bias noted earlier. By and large, intensity of religious belief correlates negatively with economic development, but the United States is off the chart. It is, however, only in the past quarter century that party managers have recognized that this voting bloc can be organized to shift elections to "cultural issues," while the leadership carries out programs favoring business and the wealthy to which the public is opposed but that do not come up in elections. By 1980, some close observers were already noticing parallels between the mobilization of religious extremism in the rise of the Nazis (the German Christian Church) and a potential "Christian fascism" in the United States—the words of Dr. James Luther Adams of the Harvard Divinity School, who spoke from personal experience, having worked with Dietrich Bonhoeffer's underground anti-Nazi church in Germany in 1935–36. Fritz Stern's observations on the descent to barbarism, quoted earlier, reflect the increasing significance of these warnings. Journalist Chris Hedges reports that "Christian fundamentalists now hold a majority of seats in 36 percent of all Republican Party state committees, or 18 of 50 states," as well as "large minorities in 81 percent of the rest of the states," with George Bush playing—or being used to play—an important role in the mobilization. The importance of the phenomenon has long been recognized, particularly in Israel, recently by Israel's English-language newspaper, the *Jerusalem Post*, which is launching a special edition directed to the Christian right, the most powerful voting bloc supporting Israeli aggressiveness and expansionism.[34]

The most careful studies in 2004 confirmed that on matters that particularly concerned voters, they had little idea of the candidates' stands. Bush voters tended to believe that he shared their views on major issues, even when the Republican Party explicitly rejected them, as in the case of the Kyoto protocols already mentioned. Investigating the sources used in the studies, we find that the same was largely true of Kerry voters, unless we give highly sympathetic interpretations to vague statements that most voters probably never heard. Kerry was hardly responding to the concerns of his constituency either on international or domestic issues. The latter were supposed to be the focus of the final presidential debate, a few days before the election. For most of the population, the health crisis is at or near the top of domestic issues. In the debate, the press reported, Kerry "took pains . . . to say that his plan for expanding access to health insurance would not create a new government program," because "there is so little political support for government intervention in the health care market in the United States."[35]

The comment is interesting. A large majority of the population supports extensive government intervention, it appears. An NBC–*Wall Street Journal* poll found that "over ⅔ of all Americans thought the government should guarantee 'everyone' the best and most advanced health care that technology can supply"; a *Washington Post*–ABC News poll found that 80 percent regard universal health care as "more important than holding down taxes"; polls reported in *Business Week* found that "67% of Americans think it's a good idea to guarantee health care for all U.S. citizens, as Canada and Britain do, with just 27% dissenting"; the Pew Research Center found that 64 percent of Americans favor the "U.S. government guaranteeing health insurance for all citizens, even if it means raising taxes" (30 percent opposed). By the late 1980s, more than 70 percent of Americans "thought health care should be a constitutional guarantee," while 40 percent "thought it already was." One can only imagine what the figures would be if the topics were not virtually off the public agenda.[36]

The facts are sometimes acknowledged, with an interesting twist. The rare allusions to public support for guaranteed health care describe the idea as lacking "political support," or "politically impossible" because of "tangled politics." These are polite ways of saying that the pharmaceutical and financial industries and other private powers are strongly opposed. The will of the public is banned from the political arena.[37]

As in the markets constructed by the PR industry, so also in the democratic elections they run, a primary task is to delude the public by carefully constructed images that have only the vaguest resemblance to reality. Not surprisingly, voters disapprove. Large majorities believe "the nation would be better off if its leaders paid more attention to the views of the public and to public opinion polls." But the public can be ignored as long as "consumer choice" can be barred in the political arena by the carefully honed means used to undermine markets.[38]

Bush won large majorities of those concerned with the threat of terror and "moral values." These results, again, tell us very little. Popular judgments about terror are another tribute to effective marketing by government and media. The public is hardly aware of the preference of Bush planners for policies that increase the threat of terrorism, which is not a high priority for them, as already reviewed. As for "moral values," we learn what we need to know from the business press the day after the election, reporting "the air of euphoria" in board rooms and corporate lobby offices—not because CEOs oppose gay marriage, but because "US business expects a clear run" now that the "political landscape [is tilted] in favour of corporate America more dramatically than at any period in modern American history."[39]

We learn more about the guiding moral values of Bush and associates from their unconcealed efforts to transfer to future generations the costs of their dedicated service to privilege and wealth. By running persistent budget deficits, the Organization of Economic Cooperation and Development (OECD) warns, leading countries, primarily the United States during the Bush years, "are 'sacrificing' their children." The OECD's chief economist informed the business press that "the current generation will probably survive, [but] we are going to bequeath to our children a capital stock which will be grossly undersized." The second of the "twin deficits," the huge trade deficit, has also greatly concerned economists and others who care about the future, though it should be mentioned that the scale of the deficit depends on how we define "the country." Analysts "conclude record trade deficits aren't as threatening as they appear," the *Wall Street Journal* reports, "because they are being driven in part by increasingly profitable U.S. companies producing [abroad] and shipping their goods and services back to the U.S., [helping] to keep overall corporate profits strong." By 2005, "earnings overseas account[ed] for 40% of profit growth for all corporations," along with $2.7 trillion in stock-market capitalization that greatly benefits the tiny percentage of the population who dominate shareholding. If we understand the country to be US-based corporations rather than the population, the trade-deficit accounting thus shifts markedly.[40]

Bush's "signature" program for improving education revealed a similar disregard for our children and the health of the society. It concentrated on testing rather than education. The heart of any serious educational program is fostering the ability to "inquire and create," as discussed by one of the founders of classical liberalism and of the modern university system, Wilhelm von Humboldt. Focus on testing does not advance, and probably harms, such objectives, for which quite different initiatives would be required.

To paraphrase the title of Bush's educational program, virtually "no opportunity is left behind" to transfer costs to future generations in other ways. Anyone familiar with the US economy is aware of what the journal of the American Academy for the Advancement of Science calls "the essential role of government-sponsored university-based research in producing the ideas and people that drive innovation" in information technology (IT), the specific topic of these comments. The journal warns that changes in funding policy under Bush "have put this innovation pipeline at risk," with funding for IT halved, threatening to "derail the extraordinarily productive interplay of academia, government, and industry in IT."[41] The interplay extends well beyond, hence also the risk posed by Bush funding policy to the "innovation pipeline": the creation and development of computers, the Internet, satellites, telecommunication, along with much of the rest of electronics-based and, more recently, biology-based industry. Government funding is either direct (government laboratories, universities) or indirect, through support for the private sector by subsidy, procurement, and, when needed, protection.

Even putting aside the clear and consistent evidence about the guiding moral values, it means little to say that people vote on the basis of moral values. The question is what they mean by the phrase "moral values." The limited indications are of some interest. In one poll, "when the voters were asked to choose the most urgent moral crisis facing the country, 33 percent cited 'greed and materialism,' 31 percent selected 'poverty and economic justice,' 16 percent named abortion, and 12 percent selected gay marriage." In another, "when surveyed voters were asked to list the moral issue that most affected their vote, the Iraq war placed first at 42 percent, while 13 percent named abortion and 9 percent named gay marriage." Other studies reveal that most of the large majorities that favor national health insurance regard it as a "moral issue."[42]

Whatever voters meant, it could hardly have been the operative moral values of the administration that were celebrated by the business press.

PUBLIC OPINION AND PUBLIC POLICY

The most serious evidence about public opinion is provided by the studies cited earlier that were released shortly before the elections by two of the most respected and reliable institutions that regularly monitor public opinion. Evidently, such information is of crucial importance for a functioning democratic society, which is not a collection of isolated atoms but a community of people who interact in forming opinions and policies. In the world of politics, as in science or any other endeavor, or for that matter in everyday life, knowing what others think is an important factor in reaching one's own conclusions. That seems close to a truism. Independently, such information permits us to determine how well the political system succeeds in allowing the will of the public to enter into the formation of public policy, a defining property of democratic societies. To evaluate the state of American democracy, then, we will of course want to know what public opinion is on major issues, how it relates to public policy, and how information about it was made available to the public on the eve of a presidential election. The studies were scarcely reported, cited only in a few local press reports and scattered opinion pieces, one in the national press (*Newsweek*). The information kept from the public, some already mentioned, is enlightening.[43]

A large majority of the public believe that the United States should accept the jurisdiction of the International Criminal Court (ICC) and the World Court, sign the Kyoto protocols, allow the United Nations to take the lead in international crises, and rely on diplomatic and economic measures more than military ones in the "war on terror." Similar majorities believe the United States should resort to force only if there is "strong evidence that the country is in imminent danger of being attacked," thus rejecting the bipartisan consensus on "preemptive war" and adopting the rather conventional interpretation of the UN Charter reiterated by the UN's High-level Panel of December 2004 and the UN World Summit a year later. A small majority of the population even favors giving up Security Council vetoes, so that the United States would follow the UN's lead even if it is not the preference of US state managers. On domestic issues, overwhelming majorities favor expansion of government programs: primarily health care (80 percent), but also funding for education and Social Security. Similar results on domestic issues have long been found in these studies conducted by the Chicago Council on Foreign Relations (CCFR). As noted, other mainstream polls report that large majorities support guaranteed health care, even if it would raise taxes. Not only does the US government stand apart from the rest of the world on many crucial issues, but even from its own population.[44]

One illustration of Washington's international isolation, as discussed earlier, is its having rejected World Court orders. Washington's opposition to the ICC has reached levels that have elicited considerable ridicule abroad, particularly after the passage of what many call the "Netherlands Invasion Act," which authorizes the president to use force to rescue Americans brought to The Hague—a prospect about as likely as an asteroid hitting the earth. Also because of its extreme opposition to any thought, however remote, that ICC jurisdiction might extend to the United States and interfere with its unique ultra-sovereignty, Washington effectively prevented prosecution of crimes in Darfur, even though it insists that literal genocide is under way. Security Council Resolution 1593 (March 31, 2005, under Chapter VII, which permits use of force) authorized referral of the situation in Darfur to the ICC for investigation and prosecution. The United States agreed to abstain instead of the usual veto, it is assumed, only after language was added that prevents UN funding for the investigation, which means that it is unlikely to proceed. Two weeks earlier, the editors of the *Boston Globe* had written that "history will not forgive the powerful people who could have ended yet another genocide but preferred to play their pitiless games," blaming Europe and the United States for delay on a resolution. So it stands, though the generally preferred story is that "China is seen by the US as the main hindrance to passing a UN Security Council resolution that would put pressure on Sudan to halt the mass killings and destruction of villages in its western region of Darfur." Human Rights Watch saw it differently. The director of its International Justice Program, Richard Dicker, said, "As killing and rape continue in Darfur, the United States now proposes further delay [at the Security Council] . . . the Bush administration's rearguard campaign to avert an ICC referral is putting innocent civilians at risk in Darfur."[45]

Washington's isolation extends to other areas too. The United States (and Israel) alone opposed a UN treaty "to protect and promote cultural diversity," debated by UNESCO. The organization had been severely weakened by the Reagan administration and the media twenty years earlier when it sought to allow some Third World participation in international communication systems. The fraudulent grounds for the assault on UNESCO were that these efforts to broaden participation, thereby breaking the virtual Western monopoly, were an attempt to control the media and undermine freedom of the press. The United States also stands almost alone in opposing international supervision of the Internet, insisting that governance must be solely in the hands of the United States.[46]

The United States has fallen off the map in other respects as well. One well-known example is the dramatic increase in incarceration during the past twenty-five years. The United States began the period with incarceration rates resembling Europe's and has ended it with rates five to ten times as high, targeting mainly blacks, and independent of crime rates, which remain mostly at European levels. The US prison population is the highest in the world, far higher than China's or Russia's. It increased again in 2004, particularly among women. Over half of those in federal prisons are there for drug-related crimes. Also familiar is the fact that the United States is virtually alone in the industrial world in granting the state the power to kill prisoners—oddly called a "conservative" position, in fact a radical statist one. Amnesty

International and Human Rights Watch report that the United States is alone in the world in locking up juveniles without possibility of parole. They counted 2,225 such juveniles in the United States and a dozen in the rest of the world combined, restricted to South Africa, Israel, and Tanzania. Some US states permit such sentencing for children as young as ten; the youngest currently serving is thirteen. In many cases, the charge was presence at the scene of a murder, during a robbery. The number of children sentenced to permanent life imprisonment has risen sharply over the past twenty-five years, at an even faster rate than for adult murderers. Such practices are in violation of the UN Convention on the Rights of the Child, ratified by every member state except the United States and Somalia (which has no functioning government).[47]

Popular attitudes toward social programs, stable for a long time, strongly suggest that the public supports the socioeconomic provisions of the Universal Declaration of Human Rights, which affirm that "everyone has the right to a standard of living adequate for the health and well-being of himself and his family, including food, clothing, housing and medical care and necessary social services, and the right to security in the event of unemployment, sickness, disability, widowhood, old age or other lack of livelihood in circumstances beyond his control." This is the wording of Article 25, which has the same status as all other sections of the UD, as recognized once again by the September 2005 UN World Summit, with the United States formally agreeing. The summit "reaffirm[ed] that all human rights are universal, indivisible, interrelated, interdependent and mutually reinforcing and that all human rights must be treated in a fair and equal manner, on the same footing and with the same emphasis." If so, then the public once again firmly opposes the "moral values" of the Bush administration, which has effectively rejected these rights even though formally accepting them, again in April 2005 as "the sole dissenter in separate votes of 52 to 1 on [UN] resolutions on the right to food and the right to the highest attainable standard of physical and mental health."[48]

A month earlier, Undersecretary of State Paula Dobriansky presented the State Department's annual report on human rights around the world, affirming eloquently that "promoting human rights is not just an element of our foreign policy; it is the bedrock of our policy and our foremost concern." Elsewhere Dobriansky has explained the concept of human rights that it is her task to uphold. In her capacity as deputy assistant secretary of state for human rights and humanitarian affairs in the Reagan and Bush I administrations, Dobriansky sought to dispel what she called "myths" about human rights, the most salient being the myth that so-called " 'economic and social rights' constitute human rights." She denounced the efforts to obfuscate human rights discourse by introducing these spurious rights— which are entrenched in the UD, but which the administrations she represented firmly rejected. They are a "letter to Santa Claus" (UN ambassador Jeane Kirkpatrick), "little more than an empty vessel into which vague hopes and inchoate expectations can be poured," "preposterous," and even a "dangerous incitement" (Ambassador Morris Abram, casting the sole vote against the UN Right to Development, a declaration that closely paraphrased Article 25 of the UD).[49]

It is instructive to look more closely into popular attitudes on the war in Iraq against the background of the general opposition to the "preemptive war" doctrines of the bipartisan consensus. A study by the Program on International Policy Attitudes (PIPA) found that on the eve of the 2004 elections, 74 percent of the public felt that the United States should not have gone to war if Iraq did not have weapons of mass destruction or was not providing support to Al Qaeda (58 percent of Bush supporters, 92 percent of Kerry supporters, and 77 percent of the uncommitted). If Saddam only had the intent to develop WMDs, 60 percent opposed going to war. But nearly half favored the decision to go to war. The director of the study, Steven Kull, points out that this is not a contradiction. Despite the official Kay and Duelfer reports undermining the claims about WMDs in Iraq (there was no serious effort to support the claims about ties to Al Qaeda), the decision to go to war was "sustained by persisting beliefs among half of Americans that Iraq provided substantial support to al Qaeda, and had WMD, or at least a major WMD program," and thus they saw the invasion as defense against a severe and imminent threat. The powerful government-media propaganda campaign launched in September 2002, and continuing into 2005, seems to have had a lasting effect in implanting irrational fears, not for the first time.[50]

PIPA studies have shown that by April 2003, a few weeks after the invasion, a large majority of Americans felt that the UN should take the lead in "civil order and economic reconstruction" in Iraq. By December 2003, 70 percent held that the UN should also "take the lead to work with Iraqis to write a new constitution and build a new democratic government." The figures are particularly noteworthy in light of the fact that popular opinion on these matters is scarcely reported, such views receive little articulate support, the issues do not appear on the electoral agenda, and Americans have remarkable misperceptions about the war, probably unique in the world.[51]

As already noted, these figures suggest a simple "exit strategy," if the administration had any interest in pursuing this course: follow the will of the American public, and transfer authority to the UN—assuming, as always, that Iraqis favor this option.

In March 2004, Spanish voters were bitterly condemned for appeasing terror when they voted out of office the government that had gone to war despite overwhelming popular opposition, taking its orders from Crawford, Texas, and winning plaudits for its leadership in the "New Europe" that is the hope for democracy. Few if any commentators noted that Spanish voters in March 2004 were taking about the same position as the large majority of people in the United States: Spanish troops should remain in Iraq only under UN authority. The major differences between the two countries are that in Spain public opinion was known, but not in the United States; and in Spain the issue came to a vote, almost unimaginable in the United States—more evidence of the serious deterioration of functioning democracy even by the standards of similar societies.[52]

What would the results of the 2004 elections have been if either of the political parties had been willing to articulate and represent the concerns of the population on issues they regard as important? Or if these issues could even have entered into public discussion within the mainstream? We can only speculate about that, but we do know that it did not happen.

The aftermath to the elections followed the course one would expect in a failing state. When the Bush administration released its budget in February 2005, PIPA did a study of popular attitudes about what the budget should be. It revealed that popular attitudes are virtually the inverse of policy: with considerable consistency, where the budget was to increase, the public wanted it to decline; where it was to decline, the public wanted it to increase. PIPA's main conclusion was that "the American public would significantly alter the Bush administration's recently proposed federal budget. . . . The most dramatic changes were deep cuts in defense spending, a significant reallocation toward deficit reduction, and increases in spending on education, job training, reducing reliance on oil, and veterans." The deepest cut called for by the public was in the defense budget, on average 31 percent; second largest was cuts in supplementals for Iraq and Afghanistan. That comes as little surprise, with the long-term financial toll of Bush's wars in Iraq and Afghanistan estimated to run "to more than $1.3 trillion, or $11,300 for every household in the United States," and uncountable effects on lost opportunities, not to speak of the human cost.[53]

Furthermore, "a clear majority (63%) favored rolling back the tax cuts for people with incomes over $200,000." Nevertheless, the Bush administration insisted that funding for the victims of Hurricane Katrina must come instead from social spending, because of "the continuing support for tax cuts, including those aimed at the wealthiest Americans," the press reported. "Tax cuts remain politically sacrosanct," much like privatized health care. In contrast, government programs "lack political support," enjoying only popular support. Accordingly, Congress proposed cutting food support for adults and children among the miserably poor to finance the reconstruction of New Orleans, where the victims were also overwhelmingly the miserably poor and are not likely to be the main beneficiaries of the project.[54]

The public also called for spending increases, the largest ones for social spending, including sharp increases for education and job training and for employment. Clear majorities also called for sharp increases in medical research and veterans benefits. "In percentage terms, by far the largest increase [the public wished to see] was for conserving and developing renewable energy—an extraordinary 1090% or $24 billion—which also had the highest percentage of respondents (70 percent) favoring an increase." One of the largest percentage increases in funding proposed (over 200 percent) was for the UN and UN peacekeeping operations.

In brief, the public called for the deepest cuts in the programs that are most rapidly increasing, and for substantial spending increases in areas that are shortchanged. Once again, these results provide very significant information for the population of a functioning democracy. Fortunately, the United States is a very free society, so it is possible to obtain the information. Unfortunately, an individual research project is required to discover it. Media coverage appears to have been zero.[55]

Public preferences on government spending correspond well to the results of public opinion studies. The findings reveal a dramatic divide between public opinion and public policy. The same has been found in many studies of major issues: the "free trade agreements," to take a case already mentioned. Some of the reasons for the divide are occasionally recognized in the professional literature. Reaffirming the general conclusions of earlier studies, in a careful analysis of the sources of US foreign policy, Lawrence Jacob and Benjamin Page find, unsurprisingly, that the major influence is "internationally oriented business corporations," with a secondary effect of "experts (who, however, may themselves be influenced by business)." Public opinion, in contrast, has "little or no significant effect on government officials." As they note, the results would have been welcome to "realists" such as Walter Lippmann, who "considered public opinion to be ill-informed and capricious" and "warned that following public opinion would create a 'morbid derangement of the true functions of power' and produce policies 'deadly to the very survival of the state as a free society.'" The "realism" is scarcely concealed ideological preference. One will search in vain for evidence of the superior acumen of those who have the major influence on policy, apart from their skill in protecting their own interests, much as Adam Smith observed.[56]

For decades, increasing sharply during the Reagan years, polls have shown that people do not feel that the government is responsive to the public will. In the most recent study, "Asked how much influence the views of the majority of Americans have on the decisions of elected officials in Washington, on a scale of 0 to 10 (0 meaning not at all influential and 10 meaning extremely influential), the mean response was 4.5," about half of what was considered acceptable. Confidence in the functioning of democracy was ranked lower for the United States than for Canada and Britain. The analysts suggest that the reservations Americans express about "democracy promotion" abroad may derive from a belief that the project might be needed at home.[57]

INSTITUTIONALIZING STATE-CORPORATE CONTROL

The reactionary statists who have a thin grip on political power are dedicated warriors. With consistency and passion that approach caricature, their policies serve the substantial people—in fact, an unusually narrow sector of them—and disregard or harm the underlying population and future generations. They are also seeking to use their current opportunities to institutionalize these arrangements, so that it will be no small task to reconstruct a more humane and democratic society.

"The Republicans in charge aren't just pro-business," Jeffrey Birnbaum reported accurately, "they are also pro-government." One indication is the 30 percent increase in federal spending from 2000 to 2004, mostly for "programs that are prime lobbying targets" for the corporate system, which feeds on big government. In recognition of the pro-business, pro-government climate, "the number of registered lobbyists in Washington has more than doubled since 2000 to more than 34,750 while the amount that lobbyists charge their new clients has increased by as much as 100 percent."[58]

To institutionalize further their linkage to the corporate sector, the reactionary statists who defame the term *conservative* have initiated what Republican power brokers call the "K Street Project." Longtime Washington correspondent Elizabeth Drew describes this purge of the trade associations and lobbying organizations clustered on K Street in Washington as a "more thorough, ruthless, vindictive and effective attack on Democratic lobbyists and other Democrats who represent business and other organizations than anything Washington has seen before." The aim is to ensure that "all the power centers in Washington," including the corporate world, are loyal to the party line. The effect is to strengthen still further "the connections between those who make policy and those who seek to influence it," the latter over-whelmingly within the corporate sector, as Jacobs and Page recently reaffirmed. One predictable result has been a "new, higher level of cor-ruption." Corruption includes extensive gerrymandering to prevent competition for seats in the House, the most democratic of government institutions and therefore the most worrisome. "The expectation" is that corruption will be "undetected and unenforced," a Republican lobbyist says, unless it becomes so extreme that it harms business in-terests. More generally, there have been "profound" effects on "the way the country is governed. . . . Not only is legislation increasingly skewed to benefit the richest interests, but Congress itself has been changed," becoming a "transactional institution," geared to imple-menting the pro-business policies of the increasingly powerful state.[59]

The same dedication to centralization of power is revealed in the "dramatic increase in overall government secrecy," with a fivefold in-crease in secrets kept from the population, according to the government's Information Security Oversight Office. The pretext is "terrorism"—hardly credible in the light of the administration's lack of concern for preventing terrorism, already reviewed, or in the light of history. If the secrets are ever disclosed, the results are likely to be similar to what the study of declassified documents has generally revealed: for the most part, classification protects state power from scrutiny by the "ill-informed and capricious" public, whose knowledge of what is being done in their name might endanger "freedom." The same is true of the efforts of the radical statist right to prevent declassification. When the Reaganites barred revelations of US overthrow of parliamentary gov-ernments in Iran and Guatemala in the early 1950s, it was not for rea-sons of "security," apart from keeping the powerful state they cherished "secure" from the gaze of the annoying public. The same was true when the incoming Bush II administration intervened in the regular declassification procedures to block revelations of the Johnson administration's actions to undermine Greek democracy in the 1960s, leading to the first restoration of fascism in Europe. Radical rightists had no interest in protecting crimes of Democrats from exposure, but popular understanding of the workings of government is not conducive to instilling proper reverence for powerful leaders and their nobility.[60]

In pursuit of the same commitment to reactionary pro-business statism, the Republican leadership has been reconstructing both Congress and the White House into "top-down systems," with important decisions placed in the hands of "a tight group of West Wing loyalists" in the executive branch and with Congress controlled by "a few leaders [and] conservative loyalists" in a manner that resembles "the flow chart of a Fortune 500 business." In structure, the political counterpart to a corporation is a totalitarian state. There are rewards for loyalists, and quick punishment for those who "cross party leaders." The antidemocratic thrust has precedents, of course, but is reaching new heights. It should surprise no one familiar with history that it is accompanied by the most august missions and visions of democracy.[61]

The educational system is still not a wholly owned subsidiary of the state-corporate system, so it too is under attack by statist reactionaries who are outraged by the "liberal bias" that subjects "conservative students" to punishment and instills anti-American, pro-Palestinian, and other left-liberal dogma, always effusively welcomed by the liberal faculty, we are to understand. As readers of Orwell would have expected, the effort to institute state controls over curricula, hiring, and teaching is carried out under the banner of "academic freedom," another brazen resort to the "Thief, thief!" technique.

Oddly, the takeover of the educational system by the anti-American, pro-Palestinian left is not reflected in academic publications, a fact studiously ignored by the "defenders of academic freedom" in favor of random anecdotes of dubious merit. Also missing is an obvious way to estimate the scale of the anti-Israel extremism that is alleged to have taken over faculties: conduct a poll to see how many believe that Israel should have the same rights as any state in the international system. Easy, but better avoided, for reasons that the organizers of the campaign understand very well.

"Congress is taking the first steps toward pressuring colleges to maintain ideological balance in the classroom," the press reports, "a move that supporters insist is needed to protect conservative students from being graded down by liberal professors," claims that would scarcely merit ridicule among those familiar with the realities of the academic world. In Pennsylvania, the House of Representatives "passed a resolution creating a special committee that is charged with investigating—at public colleges in the state—how faculty members are hired and promoted, whether students are fairly evaluated, and whether students have the right to express their views without fear of being punished for them." The vote is "a tremendous victory for academic freedom," said David Horowitz, author of the "Academic Bill of Rights," which was the source of the legislation. Opposition from faculty groups, he said, "was fierce, and their defeat is that much more bitter as a result." "Academic freedom" wins another victory over academic freedom.

In Ohio, drawing from the same courageous defenders of academic freedom against the onslaught from the left, Senator Larry Mumper introduced legislation to "restrict what university professors could say in their classrooms." His " 'academic bill of rights for higher education' would prohibit instructors at public or private universities from 'persistently' discussing controversial issues in class or from using their classes to push political, ideological, religious or anti-religious views." Many professors, Mumper said, "undermine the values of their students because '80 percent or so of them [professors] are Democrats, liberals or socialists or card-carrying Communists' who attempt to indoctrinate students." Thus one can see why their resistance to academic freedom is so "fierce" and their defeat so "bitter."[62]

The proposal admittedly has merits: it would save substantial sums by eliminating the departments of economics, government, history, and other disciplines concerned with human affairs, which inevitably push political and ideological views and persistently discuss controversial issues—unless they too are reduced to testing on skills and data.

Similar bills have been introduced in many state legislatures. Under particular attack are Middle East departments and peace studies programs. The federal government has also entered the fray. In October 2003, the House of Representatives "unanimously passed a bill that could require university international studies departments to show more support for American foreign policy or risk their federal funding." This bill was aimed particularly at Middle East programs: "Inherent in the act is the assumption that if most established experts believe American Middle East policy is bad, the flaw lies with the experts, not the policy," Michelle Goldberg writes. Faculty feel "the threat that [academic] centers will be punished for not toeing the official line out of Washington, which is an unprecedented degree of federal intrusion into a university-based area studies program," a conclusion that could be debated if we consider more indirect forms of intrusion. In an important review of the scandalous attacks on Middle East and peace studies departments, the eminent Israeli sociologist Baruch Kimmerling warned of the ominous consequences of "this assault on academic freedom by a coalition of neocons and zealous Jewish students supported by some Jewish 'mainstream' organizations," inspired by "Horowitz's crusade." The title of his essay was: "Can a 'Patriotic' Mob Take Over the Universities?" The essay was rejected by the *Chronicle of Higher Education.* Pursuing similar themes, Harvard Middle East scholar Sara Roy quotes Horowitz's attack on 250 peace studies programs in the United States that, he asserts, "teach students to identify with America's terrorist enemies and to identify America as a Great Satan oppressing the world's poor and causing them to go hungry. . . . The question is: how long can a nation at war with ruthless enemies like bin Laden and Zarqawi survive if its educational institutions continue to be suborned in this way?"[63]

Rather different questions come to mind, including those raised by Fritz Stern in *Foreign Affairs* or, from the opposite perspective, the words of the classic guardian of authority Thomas Hobbes, who warned that "the *Universities* have been to this nation as the wooden horse was to the Trojans." They must be "better disciplined," Hobbes continued: "I despair of any lasting peace among ourselves, till the Universities here shall bend and direct their studies to the . . . teaching of absolute obedience to the laws of the King." He denounced the universities for "teaching subversion," for advocating divided sovereignty, and even "spreading the doctrines of ancient liberty and religious refusal," Corey Robin writes.[64]

The campaign of the "patriots" to ensure even tighter control over the educational system is particularly dangerous against the background of the widespread rejection of science, a phenomenon with deep roots in American history that has been cynically exploited for narrow political gain in the past quarter century. The belief system has no counterpart in the industrial societies. About 40 percent of the population believe that "living things have existed in their present form since the beginning of time" and support a ban on the teaching of evolution in favor of creationism. Two-thirds want to have both evolution and creationism taught in the schools, agreeing with the president, who favors teaching evolution as well as "intelligent design"—"so people can understand what the debate is about," in his words.[65] His handlers surely know there is no "debate." As a result of many forms of harassment in recent years, foreign students and faculty, including those in the sciences and technology, have become increasingly unwilling to study and work in the United States. These developments proceed alongside Bush administration hostility to science and their readiness to put the "innovation pipeline at risk" by reducing the university-based research on which the advanced economy relies. A further development is the ongoing corporatization of universities, which tends to foster short-term projects and secrecy, among other effects. The long-term consequences for the society could be severe.

A "CLEAR RUN FOR BUSINESS"

The consequences of the pro-business, pro-government policies became impossible to conceal after the Hurricane Katrina tragedy. The Federal Emergency Management Agency (FEMA) had listed a major hurricane in New Orleans as one of the three most likely catastrophes in the United States. One high official reported that "New Orleans was the No.1 disaster we were talking about. We were obsessed with New Orleans because of the risk." FEMA had carried out drills and made elaborate plans, but they were not implemented. National Guard troops who had been sent to Iraq "took a lot of needed equipment with them, including dozens of high-water vehicles, Humvees, refueling tankers and generators that would be needed in the event a major natural disaster hit the state," the *Wall Street Journal* reported, and "a senior Army official said the service was reluctant to commit the 4th Brigade of the 10th Mountain Division from Fort Polk, because the unit, which numbers several thousand soldiers, is in the midst of preparing for an Afghanistan deployment."[66]

In accord with Bush administration priorities, the hurricane threat had been downgraded just as the threat of terror was. Lack of concern covered a broad range. Take the matter of wetlands, an important factor in reducing the power of hurricanes and storm surges. Wetlands were "largely missing when Katrina struck," Sandra Postel writes, in part because "the Bush administration in 2003 effectively gutted the 'no net loss' of wetlands policy initiated during the administration of the elder Bush." Furthermore, former FEMA officials reported that the agency's capabilities were "effectively marginalized" under Bush as it was folded into the Homeland Security Department, with fewer resources and extra layers of bureaucracy, and a "brain drain" as demoralized employees left, rather like what happened in the CIA when it was punished for disobedience. Formerly a "tier one federal agency," under Bush FEMA isn't "even in the backseat," a high official said: "They are in the trunk of the Department of Homeland Security car." Hence the inability to carry out the successful simulated hurricane drill for New Orleans a year before Katrina hit. Bush funding cuts had compelled the Army Corps of Engineers to reduce flood-control work sharply, including badly needed strengthening of the levees that protected the city. Bush's February 2005 budget called for another sharp reduction, "the largest cut ever proposed," the *Financial Times* reported, a specialty of Bush administration timing, much like the sharp cut in security for public transportation right before the London bombing in July 2005, which targeted public transportation. Relative to size of economy, the FEMA budget declined by almost 9 percent in the preceding three years, economist Dean Baker reported. The poverty rate, which has grown under Bush, reached 28 percent in New Orleans, and the limited welfare safety net was weakened still further. The effects were so dramatic that the media, across the spectrum, were appalled by the scale of the class- and race-based devastation. Reviewing the sorry record, Paul Krugman wrote that Bush's agenda had created a "can't-do government" for the general population, another striking feature of a failing state.[67]

While the media were showing vivid scenes of human misery, Republican leaders wasted no time in "using relief measures for the hurricane-ravaged Gulf coast to achieve a broad range of conservative economic and social policies." Among these are suspending rules that require payment of prevailing wages by the federal contractors who are likely to be the prime players in the next corruption scandal, thereby "lowering costs for doing business"; limiting victims' right to sue; providing children with vouchers rather than supporting schools (with a bonus for private schools); cutting funds for food stamps and school lunch and breakfast programs (while releasing the figures on the increase in hunger in the country); lifting environmental restrictions; "waiving the estate tax for deaths in the storm-affected states"—a great boon for the black population fleeing New Orleans slums—and in general making it clear once again that cynicism knows few bounds.[68]

Although Bush-style extremism doubtless accelerated the tendencies that were savagely revealed in New Orleans, their roots lie much deeper, in militarized state capitalism with corresponding neglect of the needs of cities and human services overall, topics extensively explored by Seymour Melman in particular for many years. "Once again," political economist Tom Reifer observes in an analysis of the Katrina disaster, "National Security ideology proved crucial in the bitter class war not only against the Third World, but against the domestic population at home."[69]

The achievements of the first George W. Bush term included huge corporate profits while wages stagnated or declined, along with huge tax cuts for the rich to redistribute wealth even further upward than before. These were among the many policies benefiting a tiny minority and likely to create a long-term "fiscal train wreck" that will undermine future social spending and transfer to future generations the costs of today's plunder by the very rich.[70]

Bush's second term quickly justified a *Wall Street Journal* headline reading "Bush Starts to Deliver for Big Business." Its first legislative triumph was a bankruptcy law, "crafted with industry help and backed by President Bush," the *Journal* reported. The legislation "takes the firm view that this is the borrower's problem, not the industry's" and thus "would swing the legal pendulum on this long-running issue in favor of creditors." The law seeks to address the problems created by huge credit card industry campaigns to stimulate reckless borrowing by more vulnerable sectors of the population, who then face unpayable debt and are forced to file for bankruptcy to survive. Adopting the priorities of the rich and powerful, the bill "does little to hold the financial-services industry responsible for the easy access to credit they have been offering consumers." Sponsors even rejected an effort "to have the bill put limits on marketing to students under age 18 and cap some credit-card interest rates." The guiding principles are much the same as for international lending. The World Bank and others stimulate borrowing by the rich and powerful in the poor countries, the risky loans yield high returns, and when the system crashes, structural adjustment programs transfer the costs to the poor, who never borrowed the money in the first place and gained little from it, and to the taxpayers of the North. The IMF serves as "the credit community's enforcer," in the apt phrase of its US executive director. Mechanisms to impose costs of risky high-yield loans on the lenders are well known, but ignored.[71]

The problems caused by financial industry avarice are severe. Bankruptcy filings "rose eightfold over the last 30 years, from 200,000 in 1978 to 1.6 million" in 2004; they are expected to reach 1.8 million in 2005. "The overwhelming majority of them are personal, not business," resulting from a steady increase in household debt, "now at record highs relative to disposable income." A primary cause of debt is relentless pressure by the financial industries that now have to be protected from the consequences of their (highly profitable) actions. Studies reveal that "families with children are three times more likely to file as those without, [and] more than 80 percent of them cite job loss, medical problems or family breakup as the reason." About half of the filings in 2001 resulted from health care costs. "Even middle-class insured families often fall prey to financial catastrophe when sick."[72]

"Reduced access to healthcare services is a financial hardship that threatens Americans' quality of life more directly than any other," the Gallup organization found. From January 2005, "healthcare costs have topped the list when Americans were asked to name the most important financial problem their families face." What the directors regard as the most "astounding" finding is that only 6 percent of Americans "reported being satisfied with the total cost of healthcare in the United States," while 71 percent were dissatisfied and 46 percent "not at all" satisfied. A third of respondents reported that they had put off health care during the past year because of costs; as expected, percentages are considerably higher for those with lower incomes or who describe their health as "fair" to "poor." Over half had put off treatment for very serious or somewhat serious conditions, a figure rising to 69 percent among those with incomes under $25,000. The fact that "income has become a serious barrier to accessing needed services" means that those who most need care are not receiving it, Gallup observes. Satisfaction with the health care system is lower than in Britain and Canada, even disregarding the approximately 45 million Americans who lack health insurance altogether.[73]

As noted earlier, substantial majorities favor national health care even if it would lead to higher taxes. It is, however, likely that a national health care system would reduce expenses considerably, avoiding the heavy costs of multiple layers of bureaucracy, close supervision, endless paperwork, and other concomitants of privatization. These costs, along with the unique power of the pharmaceutical corporations and financial institutions, render the US system the most inefficient in the industrial world, with costs far higher than the average for industrial (OECD) societies, and some of the worst health outcomes.

The rapidly escalating costs of health care are threatening a serious fiscal crisis, along with immeasurable human costs. Infant mortality is one major index. The UN *Human Development Report 2005* reveals that "since 2000 a half century of sustained decline in infant death rates [in the United States] first slowed and then reversed." By 2005 the rates had risen to the level of Malaysia, a country where the average income is one-quarter that in the United States. The report also reviews the effects of government programs. In the United Kingdom, for example, the rate of child poverty rose sharply during the Margaret Thatcher years, then reversed after the Labour government adopted policies to halve child poverty by 2010. "Fiscal redistribution has played a central role in strategies for meeting the target," the report concludes: "Large increases in financial support for families with children," as well as other fiscal programs, "boosted the incomes of low-income working families with children," with significant effects on child poverty.[74]

The financial crisis is surely no secret. The press reports that 30 percent of health care costs go for administration, a proportion vastly higher than in government-run systems, including those within the United States, which are far from the most efficient. These estimates are seriously understated because of the ideological decision not to count the costs for individuals—for doctors who waste their own time or are forced to misuse it, or for patients who "enter a world of paperwork so surreal that it belongs in one of Kafka's tales of the triumph of faceless bureaucracies." The complexities of billing have become so outlandish that the National Coordinator for Health Information Technology, the president's senior adviser, says when he gets a bill for his four-year-old child, he "can't figure out what happened, or what I'm supposed to do." Those who want to see government bureaucracy reaching levels that even Kafka might not have imagined should look at the official ninety-eight-page government handbook on the Medicare prescription drug plan, provided to Medicare participants to inform them of their options under the bill passed by Congress in June 2004, with the help of an army of lobbyists from pharmaceutical companies and health maintenance organizations (HMOs). The idea, the *Wall Street Journal* informs its affluent readers, "is that patients will be encouraged to bargain-hunt for medical care" and may even save money, if they can hire enough research assistants to work through the many private options available, and make lucky guesses. Health Savings Accounts, also welcomed by the editors, have similar properties. For the wealthy and the corporate beneficiaries the exciting new programs will be just fine, like health care in general. The rest will get what they deserve for not having ascended to these heights.[75]

The Bush administration response to the health care crisis has been to reduce services to the poor (Medicaid). The timing was again impeccable. "As Republican leaders in Congress move to trim billions of dollars from the Medicaid health program," the *Washington Post* reported, "they are simultaneously intervening to save the life of possibly the highest-profile Medicaid patient: Terri Schiavo." Republican majority leader Tom DeLay, while proclaiming his deep concern for Schiavo and his dedication to ensure that she has the chance "we all deserve," simultaneously shepherded through the House a budget resolution to cut $15 billion to $20 billion from Medicaid for the next five years. As if the exploitation of the tragedy of this poor woman for partisan gain were not disgraceful enough, DeLay and others like him were depriving her, and who knows how many others, of the means of survival. They were also providing more instruction about their actual moral values and concern for the sanctity of life.[76]

The primary method devised to divert attention from the health care crisis was to organize a major PR campaign to "reform" Social Security—meaning dismantle it—on the pretext that it is facing an awesome fiscal crisis. There is no need to review the remarkable deceit of the administration propaganda, and the falsifications and misrepresentations repeated without comment by much of media commentary, which cooperated in making it the "hot topic" in Washington. Exposure has been carried out more than adequately elsewhere. The steady drumbeat of deceit has been so extreme as to drive frustrated analysts to words rarely voiced in restrained journals: that Bush "repeatedly lied about the current [Social Security] system," making claims that "were demonstrably false and that his staff must have known were false."[77]

It is not that the system has no flaws. It surely does. The highly regressive payroll tax is an illustration. More generally, an OECD study found that the US system "is one of the least generous public pension systems in advanced countries," consistent with the comparative weakness of benefits in the United States.[78]

The alleged crisis of Social Security is rooted in demographic facts: the ratio of working people to retired people is declining. The data are accurate, but partial. The relevant figure is the ratio of working people to those they support. According to official statistics, the ratio of working people to dependents (under twenty, over sixty-five) hit its lowest point in 1965 and is not expected to reach that level through the projected period (to 2080). The propaganda image is that the retirement of the "baby boomers" is going to crash the system; as repeatedly pointed out, their retirement had already been financed by the Greenspan-led increase in payroll taxes in 1983. That aside, the boomers were once children, and had to be cared for then as well. And we find that during those years there was a sharp increase in spending for education and other child care needs. There was no crisis. If American society was able to take care of the boomers from ages zero to twenty, there can be no fundamental reason why a much richer society, with far higher output per worker, cannot take care of them from ages sixty-five to ninety. At most, some technical fixes might be needed, but no major crisis looms in the foreseeable future.[79]

Critics of Bush's efforts to chip away at Social Security by various "ownership society" schemes have proclaimed success because public opposition was too high to ram the legislation through. But the celebration is premature. The campaign of deceit achieved a great deal, laying the basis for the next assault on the system. Reacting to the PR campaign, the Gallup poll, for the first time, included Social Security among the choices for "top concerns." Gallup found that only "the availability and affordability of healthcare" is a larger concern for the public than Social Security. About half of Americans worry "a great deal" about it, and another quarter a "fair amount," more than are concerned about such issues as terrorism or oil prices. A Zogby poll found that 61 percent believe the system faces "serious problems" and 14 percent think it's "in crisis," though in fact it is "financially stronger than it has been throughout most of its history, according to the Trustees' [President Bush's] numbers," economist Mark Weisbrot observes. The campaign has been particularly effective among the young. Among students, 70 percent are "concerned that the pension system may not be there when they retire."[80]

These are major victories for those who hope to destroy Social Security, revealing once again the effectiveness of a flood of carefully contrived propaganda amplified by the media in a business-run society where institutionalized deceit has been refined to a high art. The propaganda success compares well with that of the government-media campaign to convince Americans that Saddam Hussein was an imminent threat to their survival, driving them completely off the spectrum of world opinion.

There has been some discussion of the curious fact that the need to reform Social Security became the "hot topic" of the day, while reforming the health care system in accord with public opinion is not even on the agenda, an apparent paradox: the very serious fiscal crisis of the remarkably inefficient and poorly performing health care system is not a crisis, while urgent action is needed to undermine the efficient system that is quite sound for the foreseeable future. Furthermore, to the extent that Social Security might face a crisis some time in the distant future, it would result primarily from exploding health care costs. Government projections predict a sharp increase in total benefits relative to GDP, from under 10 percent in 2000 to almost 25 percent in 2080, which is as far as the projections reach. Through this period Social Security costs are barely expected to increase beyond the 2000 level of 5 percent. A slightly larger increase is predicted for Medicaid, and a huge increase for Medicare, traceable primarily to the extreme inefficiency of the privatized health care system.[81]

Sensible people will seek differences between the Social Security and health care systems that might explain the paradox. And they will quickly find critical differences, which are quite familiar in other domains: the paradox mirrors closely the "schizophrenia" of all administrations that underlies the "strong line of continuity" with regard to "democracy promotion," to take one example. Social Security is of little value for the rich, but is crucial for survival for working people, the poor, their dependents, and the disabled. For the wealthy, it is an irrelevant pittance. But for close to 60 percent of the population it is the "major source" of retirement income, and the most secure. Furthermore, as a government program, it has such low administrative costs that it offers nothing to financial institutions. Social Security helps only the underlying population, not the substantial people. It is therefore natural that it should be dispatched to the flames. The medical system, in contrast, works very well for the substantial people, with health care effectively rationed by wealth, while enormous profits flow to private power for superfluous bureaucracy and supervision, overpriced drugs, and other useful inefficiencies. The underlying population can be treated with lectures on responsibility.[82]

There are other sound reasons to destroy the Social Security system.

It is based on principles that are deeply offensive to the moral values of the political leadership and the sectors they represent—not those who vote for them, a different category of the population. Social Security is based on the idea that it is a community responsibility to ensure that the disabled widow on the other side of town has food to eat, or that the child across the street should be able to go to a decent school. Such evil ideas have to be driven from the mind. They stand in the way of the "New Spirit of the Age" of the 1850s: "Gain Wealth, forgetting all but Self." According to right thinking, it isn't my fault if the widow married the wrong person or if the child's parents made bad investment decisions, so why should I contribute a few cents to a public fund to take care of them? The "ownership society," in contrast, suffers from none of these moral defects.

Returning to the November 2004 elections, we learn little of significance from them about popular attitudes and opinions, though we can learn a lot from the studies that are kept in the shadows. And the whole affair adds more to our understanding of the current state of American democracy—with most of the industrial world trailing not too far behind, as privileged and powerful sectors learn and apply the lessons taught by their leader.

Afterword

No one familiar with history should be surprised that the growing democratic deficit in the United States is accompanied by declaration of messianic missions to bring democracy to a suffering world. Declarations of noble intent by systems of power are rarely complete fabrication, and the same is true in this case. Under some conditions, forms of democracy are indeed acceptable. Abroad, as the leading scholar-advocate of "democracy promotion" concludes, we find a "strong line of continuity": democracy is acceptable *if and only if* it is consistent with strategic and economic interests (Thomas Carothers). In modified form, the doctrine holds at home as well.

The basic dilemma facing policy makers is sometimes candidly recognized at the dovish liberal extreme of the spectrum, for example, by Robert Pastor, President Carter's national security advisor for Latin America. He explained why the administration had to support the murderous and corrupt Somoza regime in Nicaragua, and, when that proved impossible, to try at least to maintain the US-trained National Guard even as it was massacring the population "with a brutality a nation usually reserves for its enemy," killing some forty thousand people. The reason was the familiar one: "The United States did not want to control Nicaragua or the other nations of the region, but it also did not want developments to get out of control. It wanted Nicaraguans to act independently, *except* when doing so would affect U.S. interests adversely."[1]

Similar dilemmas faced Bush administration planners after their invasion of Iraq. They want Iraqis "to act independently, *except* when doing so would affect U.S. interests adversely." Iraq must therefore be sovereign and democratic, but within limits. It must somehow be constructed as an obedient client state, much in the manner of the traditional order in Central America. At a general level, the pattern is familiar, reaching to the opposite extreme of institutional structures. The Kremlin was able to maintain satellites that were run by domestic political and military forces, with the iron fist poised. Germany was able to do much the same in occupied Europe even while it was at war, as did fascist Japan in Manchuria (its Manchukuo). Fascist Italy achieved similar results in North Africa while carrying out virtual genocide that in no way harmed its favorable image in the West and possibly inspired Hitler. Traditional imperial and neocolonial systems illustrate many variations on similar themes.[2]

To achieve the traditional goals in Iraq has proven to be surprisingly difficult, despite unusually favorable circumstances, as already reviewed. The dilemma of combining a measure of independence with firm control arose in a stark form not long after the invasion, as mass nonviolent resistance compelled the invaders to accept far more Iraqi initiative than they had anticipated. The outcome even evoked the nightmarish prospect of a more or less democratic and sovereign Iraq taking its place in a loose Shiite alliance comprising Iran, Shiite Iraq, and possibly the nearby Shiite-dominated regions of Saudi Arabia, controlling most of the world's oil and independent of Washington.

The situation could get worse. Iran might give up on hopes that Europe could become independent of the United States, and turn eastward. Highly relevant background is discussed by Selig Harrison, a leading specialist on these topics. "The nuclear negotiations between Iran and the European Union were based on a bargain that the EU, held back by the US, has failed to honour," Harrison observes. The bargain was that Iran would suspend uranium enrichment, and the EU would undertake security guarantees. The language of the joint declaration was "unambiguous. 'A mutually acceptable agreement,' it said, would not only provide 'objective guarantees' that Iran's nuclear programme is 'exclusively for peaceful purposes' but would 'equally provide firm commitments on security issues.' "[3]

The phrase "security issues" is a thinly veiled reference to the threats by the United States and Israel to bomb Iran, and preparations to do so. The model regularly adduced is Israel's bombing of Iraq's Osirak reactor in 1981, which appears to have initiated Saddam's nuclear weapons programs, another demonstration that violence tends to elicit violence. Any attempt to execute similar plans against Iran could lead to immediate violence, as is surely understood in Washington. During a visit to Teheran, the influential Shiite cleric Muqtada al-Sadr warned that his militia would defend Iran in the case of any attack, "one of the strongest signs yet," the Washington Post reported, "that Iraq could become a battleground in any Western conflict with Iran, raising the specter of Iraqi Shiite militias—or perhaps even the U.S.-trained Shiite-dominated military—taking on American troops here in sympathy with Iran." The Sadrist bloc, which registered substantial gains in the December 2005 elections, may soon become the most powerful single political force in Iraq. It is consciously pursuing the model of other successful Islamist groups, such as Hamas in Palestine, combining strong resistance to military occupation with grassroots social organizing and service to the poor.[4]

Washington's unwillingness to allow regional security issues to be considered is nothing new. It has also arisen repeatedly in the confrontation with Iraq. In the background is the matter of Israeli nuclear weapons, a topic that Washington bars from international consideration. Beyond that lurks what Harrison rightly describes as "the central problem facing the global non-proliferation regime": the failure of the nuclear states to live up to their NPT obligation "to phase out their own nuclear weapons"—and, in Washington's case, formal rejection of the obligation.[5]

Unlike Europe, China refuses to be intimidated by Washington, a primary reason for the growing fear of China on the part of US planners. Much of Iran's oil already goes to China, and China is providing Iran with weapons, presumably considered a deterrent to US threats. Still more uncomfortable for Washington is the fact that "the Sino-Saudi relationship has developed dramatically," including Chinese military aid to Saudi Arabia and gas exploration rights for China. By 2005, Saudi Arabia provided about 17 percent of China's oil imports. Chinese and Saudi oil companies have signed deals for drilling and construction of a huge refinery (with Exxon Mobil as a partner). A January 2006 visit by Saudi king Abdullah to Beijing was expected to lead to a Sino-Saudi memorandum of understanding calling for "increased cooperation and investment between the two countries in oil, natural gas, and minerals."[6]

Indian analyst Aijaz Ahmad observes that Iran could "emerge as the virtual lynchpin in the making, over the next decade or so, of what China and Russia have come to regard as an absolutely indispensable Asian Energy Security Grid, for breaking Western control of the world's energy supplies and securing the great industrial revolution of Asia." South Korea and southeast Asian countries are likely to join, possibly Japan as well. A crucial question is how India will react. It rejected US pressures to withdraw from an oil pipeline deal with Iran. On the other hand, India joined the United States and the EU in voting for an anti-Iranian resolution at the IAEA, joining also in their hypocrisy, since India rejects the NPT regime to which Iran, so far, appears to be largely conforming. Ahmad reports that India may have secretly reversed its stand under Iranian threats to terminate a $20 billion gas deal. Washington later warned India that its "nuclear deal with the US could be ditched" if India did not go along with US demands, eliciting a sharp rejoinder from the Indian foreign ministry and an evasive tempering of the warning by the US embassy.[7]

India too has options. It may choose to be a US client, or it may prefer to join a more independent Asian bloc that is taking shape, with growing ties to Middle East oil producers. In a series of informative commentaries, the deputy editor of the *Hindu* observes that "if the 21st century is to be an 'Asian century,' Asia's passivity in the energy sector has to end." Though it "hosts the world's largest producers and fastest growing consumers of energy," Asia still relies "on institutions, trading frameworks and armed forces from outside the region in order to trade with itself," a debilitating heritage from the imperial era. The key is India-China cooperation. In 2005, he points out, India

and China "managed to confound analysts around the world by turning their much-vaunted rivalry for the acquisition of oil and gas assets
in third countries into a nascent partnership that could alter the basic
dynamics of the global energy market." A January 2006 agreement
signed in Beijing "cleared the way for India and China to collaborate
not only in technology but also in hydrocarbon exploration and production, a partnership that eventually could alter fundamental equa-
tions in the world's oil and natural gas sector." At a meeting in New
Delhi of Asian energy producers and consumers a few months earlier,
India had "unveiled an ambitious $22.4 billion pan-Asian gas grid and
oil security pipeline system" extending throughout all of Asia, from
Siberian fields through central Asia and to the Middle East energy gi-
ants, also integrating the consumer states. Furthermore, Asian countries "hold more than two trillion dollars worth of foreign reserves,"
overwhelmingly denominated in dollars, though prudence suggests di-
versification. A first step, already being contemplated, is an Asian oil
market trading in euros. The impact on the international financial system and the balance of global power could be significant. The United
States "sees India as the weakest link in the emerging Asian chain," he
continues, and is "trying actively to divert New Delhi away from the
task of creating new regional architecture by dangling the nuclear car-
rot and the promise of world power status in alliance with itself." If
the Asian project is to succeed, he warns, "India will have to resist
these allurements." Similar questions arise with regard to the Shanghai Cooperation Organization formed in 2001 as a Russia-China-
based counterweight to the expansion of US power into former Soviet
central Asia, now evolving "rapidly toward a regional security bloc
[that] could soon induct new members such as India, Pakistan, and
Iran," longtime Moscow correspondent Fred Weir reports, perhaps
becoming a "Eurasian military confederacy to rival NATO."[8]

The prospect that Europe and Asia might move toward greater independence has seriously troubled US planners since World War II,
and concerns have significantly increased as the tripolar order has continued to evolve, along with new south-south interactions and rapidly
growing EU engagement with China.[9]

US intelligence has projected that the United States, while controlling

Middle East oil for the traditional reasons, will itself rely mainly on more stable Atlantic Basin resources (West Africa, Western Hemisphere). Control of Middle East oil is now far from a sure thing, and these expectations are also threatened by developments in the Western Hemisphere, accelerated by Bush administration policies that have left the United States remarkably isolated in the global arena. The Bush administration has even succeeded in alienating Canada, an impressive feat. Canada's relations with the United States are more "strained and combative" than ever before as a result of Washington's rejection of NAFTA decisions favoring Canada, Joel Brinkley reports. "Partly as a result, Canada is working hard to build up its relationship with China [and] some officials are saying Canada may shift a significant portion of its trade, particularly oil, from the United States to China." Canada's minister of natural resources said that within a few years one-quarter of the oil that Canada now sends to the United States may go to China instead. In a further blow to Washington's energy policies, the leading oil exporter in the hemisphere, Venezuela, has forged probably the closest relations with China of any Latin American country, and is planning to sell increasing amounts of oil to China as part of its effort to reduce dependence on the openly hostile US government. Latin America as a whole is increasing trade and other relations with China, with some setbacks, but likely expansion, in particular for raw materials exporters like Brazil and Chile.[10]

Meanwhile, Cuba-Venezuela relations are becoming very close, each relying on its comparative advantage. Venezuela is providing low-cost oil while in return Cuba organizes literacy and health programs, sending thousands of highly skilled professionals, teachers, and doctors, who work in the poorest and most neglected areas, as they do elsewhere in the Third World. Cuba-Venezuela projects are extending to the Caribbean countries, where Cuban doctors are providing health care to thousands of people with Venezuelan funding. Operation Miracle, as it is called, is described by Jamaica's ambassador to Cuba as "an example of integration and south-south cooperation," and is generating great enthusiasm among the poor majority. Cuban medical assistance is also being welcomed elsewhere. One of the most horrendous tragedies of recent years was the October

2005 earthquake in Pakistan. In addition to the huge toll, unknown numbers of survivors have to face brutal winter weather with little shelter, food, or medical assistance. One has to turn to the South Asian press to read that "Cuba has provided the largest contingent of doctors and paramedics to Pakistan," paying all the costs (perhaps with Venezuelan funding), and that President Musharraf expressed his "deep gratitude" for the "spirit and compassion" of the Cuban medical teams. These are reported to comprise more than one thousand trained personnel, 44 percent of them women, who remained to work in remote mountain villages, "living in tents in freezing weather and in an alien culture" after the Western aid teams had been withdrawn, setting up nineteen field hospitals and working twelve-hour shifts.[11]

Some analysts have suggested that Cuba and Venezuela might even unite, a step towards further integration of Latin America in a bloc that is more independent from the United States. Venezuela has joined Mercosur, the South American customs union, a move described by Argentine president Néstor Kirchner as "a milestone" in the development of this trading bloc, and welcomed as opening "a new chapter in our integration" by Brazilian president Luiz Inácio Lula da Silva. Independent experts say that "adding Venezuela to the bloc furthers its geopolitical vision of eventually spreading Mercosur to the rest of the region." At a meeting to mark Venezuela's entry into Mercosur, Venezuelan president Chávez said, "We cannot allow this to be purely an economic project, one for the elites and for the transnational companies," a not very oblique reference to the US-sponsored "Free Trade Agreement for the Americas," which has aroused strong public opposition. Venezuela also supplied Argentina with fuel oil to help stave off an energy crisis, and bought almost a third of Argentine debt issued in 2005, one element of a region-wide effort to free the countries from the control of the US-dominated IMF after two decades of disastrous effects of conformity to its rules. The IMF has "acted towards our country as a promoter and a vehicle of policies that caused poverty and pain among the Argentine people," President Kirchner said in announcing his decision to pay almost $1 trillion to rid itself of the IMF forever. Radically violating IMF rules, Argentina enjoyed a substantial recovery from the disaster left by IMF policies.[12]

Steps toward independent regional integration advanced further with the election of Evo Morales in Bolivia in December 2005, the first president from the indigenous majority. Morales moved quickly to reach energy accords with Venezuela. The *Financial Times* reported that these "are expected to underpin forthcoming radical reforms to Bolivia's economy and energy sector" with its huge gas reserves, second only to Venezuela's in South America. Morales too committed himself to reverse the neoliberal policies that Bolivia had pursued rigorously for twenty-five years, leaving the country with lower per capita income than at the outset. Adherence to the neoliberal programs was interrupted during this period only when popular discontent compelled the government to abandon them, as when it followed World Bank advice to privatize water supply and "get prices right"— incidentally, to deprive the poor of access to water.[13]

Venezuelan "subversion," as it is described in Washington, is extending to the United States as well. Perhaps that calls for expansion of the policies of "containment" of Venezuela ordered by Bush in March 2005. In November 2005, the *Washington Post* reported, a group of senators sent a letter "to nine big oil companies: With huge increases in winter heating bills expected, the letter read, we want you to donate some of your record profits to help low-income people cover those costs." They received one response: from CITGO, the Venezuelan-controlled company. CITGO offered to provide low-cost oil to low-income residents of Boston, later elsewhere. Chávez is only doing it "for political gain," the State Department responded; it is "somewhat akin to the government of Cuba offering scholarships to medical school in Cuba to disadvantaged American youth." Quite unlike aid from the United States and other countries, which is purehearted altruism. It is not clear that these subtleties will be appreciated by the recipients of the "12 million gallons of discounted homeheating oil [provided by CITGO] to local charities and 45,000 lowincome families in Massachusetts." The oil is distributed to poor people facing a 30–50 percent rise in oil prices, with fuel assistance "woefully underfunded, so this is a major shot in the arm for people who otherwise wouldn't get through the winter," according to the director of the nonprofit organization that distributes low-cost oil to "homeless shelters, food banks, and low-income housing groups." He also "said he hoped the deal would present 'a friendly challenge' to US oil companies—which recently reported record quarterly profits—to use their windfall to help poor families survive the winter," apparently in vain.[14]

Though Central America was largely disciplined by Reaganite violence and terror, the rest of the hemisphere is falling out of control, particularly from Venezuela to Argentina, which was the poster child of the IMF and the Treasury Department until its economy collapsed under the policies they imposed. Much of the region has left-center governments. The indigenous populations have become much more active and influential, particularly in Bolivia and Ecuador, both major energy producers, where they either want oil and gas to be domestically controlled or, in some cases, oppose production altogether. Many indigenous people apparently do not see any reason why their lives, societies, and cultures should be disrupted or destroyed so that New Yorkers can sit in SUVs in traffic gridlock. Some are even calling for an "Indian nation" in South America. Meanwhile the economic integration that is under way is reversing patterns that trace back to the Spanish conquests, with Latin American elites and economies linked to the imperial powers but not to one another. Along with growing south-south interaction on a broader scale, these developments are strongly influenced by popular organizations that are coming together in the unprecedented international global justice movements, ludicrously called "anti-globalization" because they favor globalization that privileges the interests of people, not investors and financial institutions. For many reasons, the system of US global dominance is fragile, even apart from the damage inflicted by Bush planners.

One consequence is that the Bush administration's pursuit of the traditional policies of deterring democracy faces new obstacles. It is no longer as easy as before to resort to military coups and international terrorism to overthrow democratically elected governments, as Bush planners learned ruefully in 2002 in Venezuela. The "strong line of continuity" must be pursued in other ways, for the most part. In Iraq, as we have seen, mass nonviolent resistance compelled Washington and London to permit the elections they had sought to evade. The

subsequent effort to subvert the elections by providing substantial advantages to the administration's favorite candidate, and expelling the
independent media, also failed. Washington faces further problems.
The Iraqi labor movement is making considerable progress despite
the opposition of the occupation authorities. The situation is rather
like Europe and Japan after World War II, when a primary goal of
the United States and United Kingdom was to undermine independent labor movements—as at home, for similar reasons: organized labor contributes in essential ways to functioning democracy with
popular engagement. Many of the measures adopted at that time—
withholding food, supporting fascist police—are no longer available.
Nor is it possible today to rely on the labor bureaucracy of AIFLD to
help undermine unions. Today, some American unions are supporting
Iraqi workers, just as they do in Colombia, where more union activists
are murdered than anywhere in the world. At least the unions now receive support from the United Steelworkers of America and others,
while Washington continues to provide enormous funding for the government, which bears a large part of the responsibility.[15]

The problem of elections arose in Palestine much in the way it did
in Iraq. As already discussed, the Bush administration refused to permit elections until the death of Yasser Arafat, aware that the wrong
man would win. After his death, the administration agreed to permit
elections, expecting the victory of its favored Palestinian Authority
candidates. To promote this outcome, Washington resorted to much
the same modes of subversion as in Iraq, and often before. Washington used USAID as an "invisible conduit" in an effort to "increase the
popularity of the Palestinian Authority on the eve of crucial elections
in which the governing party faces a serious challenge from the radical
Islamic group Hamas," spending almost $2 million "on dozens of
quick projects before elections this week to bolster the governing Fatah faction's image with voters." In the United States, or any Western
country, even a hint of such foreign interference would destroy a candidate, but deeply rooted imperial mentality legitimates such routine
measures elsewhere. However, the attempt to subvert the elections
again resoundingly failed.[16]

The US and Israeli governments now have to adjust to dealing somehow with a radical Islamic party that approaches their traditional rejectionist stance, though not entirely, at least if Hamas really does mean to agree to an indefinite truce on the international border as its leaders state. The US and Israel, in contrast, insist that Israel must take over substantial parts of the West Bank (and the forgotten Golan Heights). Hamas's refusal to accept Israel's "right to exist" mirrors the refusal of Washington and Jerusalem to accept Palestine's "right to exist"—a concept unknown in international affairs; Mexico accepts the existence of the United States but not its abstract "right to exist" on almost half of Mexico, acquired by conquest. Hamas's formal commitment to "destroy Israel" places it on a par with the United States and Israel, which vowed formally that there could be no "additional Palestinian state" (in addition to Jordan) until they relaxed their extreme rejectionist stand partially in the past few years, in the manner already reviewed. Although Hamas has not said so, it would come as no great surprise if Hamas were to agree that Jews may remain in scattered areas in the present Israel, while Palestine constructs huge settlement and infrastructure projects to take over the valuable land and resources, effectively breaking Israel up into unviable cantons, virtually separated from one another and from some small part of Jerusalem where Jews would also be allowed to remain. And they might agree to call the fragments "a state." If such proposals were made, we would—rightly—regard them as virtually a reversion to Nazism, a fact that might elicit some thoughts. If such proposals were made, Hamas's position would be essentially like that of the United States and Israel for the past five years, after they came to tolerate some impoverished form of "statehood." It is fair to describe Hamas as radical, extremist, and violent, and as a serious threat to peace and a just political settlement. But the organization is hardly alone in this stance.

Elsewhere traditional means of undermining democracy have succeeded. In Haiti, the Bush administration's favorite "democracy-building group, the International Republican Institute," worked assiduously to promote the opposition to President Aristide, helped by the withholding of desperately needed aid on grounds that were dubious at best. When it seemed that Aristide would probably win any genuine election, Washington and the opposition chose to withdraw, a standard device to discredit elections that are going to come out the wrong way: Nicaragua in 1984 and Venezuela in December 2005 are examples that should be familiar. Then followed a military coup, expulsion of the president, and a reign of terror and violence vastly exceeding anything under the elected government.[17]

The persistence of the strong line of continuity to the present again reveals that the United States is very much like other powerful states. It pursues the strategic and economic interests of dominant sectors of the domestic population, to the accompaniment of rhetorical flourishes about its dedication to the highest values. That is practically a historical universal, and the reason why sensible people pay scant attention to declarations of noble intent by leaders, or accolades by their followers.

One commonly hears that carping critics complain about what is wrong, but do not present solutions. There is an accurate translation for that charge: "They present solutions, but I don't like them." In addition to the proposals that should be familiar about dealing with the crises that reach to the level of survival, a few simple suggestions for the United States have already been mentioned: (1) accept the jurisdiction of the International Criminal Court and the World Court; (2) sign and carry forward the Kyoto protocols; (3) let the UN take the lead in international crises; (4) rely on diplomatic and economic measures rather than military ones in confronting terror; (5) keep to the traditional interpretation of the UN Charter; (6) give up the Security Council veto and have "a decent respect for the opinion of mankind," as the Declaration of Independence advises, even if power centers disagree; (7) cut back sharply on military spending and sharply increase social spending. For people who believe in democracy, these are very conservative suggestions: they appear to be the opinions of the majority of the US population, in most cases the overwhelming majority. They are in radical opposition to public policy. To be sure, we cannot be very confident about the state of public opinion on such matters because of another feature of the democratic deficit: the topics scarcely enter into public discussion and the basic facts are little known. In a highly atomized society, the public is therefore largely deprived of the opportunity to form considered opinions.

Another conservative suggestion is that facts, logic, and elementary moral principles should matter. Those who take the trouble to adhere to that suggestion will soon be led to abandon a good part of familiar doctrine, though it is surely much easier to repeat self-serving mantras. Such simple truths carry us some distance toward developing more specific and detailed answers. More important, they open the way to implement them, opportunities that are readily within our grasp if we can free ourselves from the shackles of doctrine and imposed illusion.

Though it is natural for doctrinal systems to seek to induce pessimism, hopelessness, and despair, reality is different. There has been substantial progress in the unending quest for justice and freedom in recent years, leaving a legacy that can be carried forward from a higher plane than before. Opportunities for education and organizing abound. As in the past, rights are not likely to be granted by benevolent authorities, or won by intermittent actions—attending a few demonstrations or pushing a lever in the personalized quadrennial extravaganzas that are depicted as "democratic politics." As always in the past, the tasks require dedicated day-by-day engagement to create—in part re-create—the basis for a functioning democratic culture in which the public plays some role in determining policies, not only in the political arena, from which it is largely excluded, but also in the crucial economic arena, from which it is excluded in principle. There are many ways to promote democracy at home, carrying it to new dimensions. Opportunities are ample, and failure to grasp them is likely to have ominous repercussions: for the country, for the world, and for future generations.

Notes

PREFACE

1. Gar Alperovitz, *America Beyond Capitalism* (Wiley, 2005). The "historic values" are those professed. On the operative values for the powerful, there is, as always, a good deal more to say.
2. Stuart Eizenstat, John Edward Porter, and Jeremy Weinstein, *Foreign Affairs*, January–February 2005.
3. See, especially, my *Hegemony or Survival* (Metropolitan, 2003; updated, Owl, 2004); additional discussion and sources in the electronic edition at www.americanempireproject.com.

Chapter 1: STARK, DREADFUL, INESCAPABLE

1. *New York Times,* 10 July 1955.
2. On the shameful record, see Howard Friel and Richard Falk, *The Record of the Paper* (Verso, 2004).
3. For a brief sample, see my "Simple Truths, Hard Problems," *Philosophy,* January 2005. I know of only one case of explicit rejection, a highly regarded work by international law professor Michael Glennon, *Limits of Law, Prerogatives of Power* (Palgrave, 2001), pp. 171ff. His rejection of the principle, perhaps unwitting, is based on the tacit assumption that responsibility cannot be shared. The remainder of his argument against "objectivist philosophies" fares similarly. For further comment, see my

"Moral Truisms, Empirical Evidence, and Foreign Policy," *Review of International Studies,* October 2003.

4. Philip Zelikow, *National Interest,* Spring 2003. On the realities, see ActionAid, *Real Aid: An Agenda for Making Aid Work,* May 2005. They estimate real aid by the rich at 0.1 percent of national income, with the United States and France the lowest in real aid (close to 90 percent "phantom aid," returning to the donor country), while the United States ranks near the bottom even in official aid.

5. Michael Phillips, *Wall Street Journal,* 27 January 2005. Jeffrey Sachs, *New York Times,* 25 June 2005. Warren Hoge, *New York Times,* 3 September 2005. With the "I'm the boss" image established, Bolton later agreed to some compromises.

6. Alexis de Tocqueville, *Democracy in America* (Everyman's Library, 1994), volume 2, p. 355.

7. Adam Smith, *The Wealth of Nations* (Modern Library, 1994), book 3, p. 444.

8. Probably close to universal practice, usually tacit, but sometimes honesty prevails: for example, the determination by Israel's Defense Ministry that "the law only recognises terrorism as committed by 'organisations hostile to Israel.'" Chris McGreal, *Guardian,* 1 September 2005. Michael Kinsley, *Wall Street Journal,* 26 March 1987.

9. Indira A. R. Lakshmanan, *Boston Globe,* 13 June 2005.

10. Reuters, *New York Times,* 20 July 2005.

11. Reuters, *New York Times,* 28 September 2005. Jimmy Burns, *Financial Times,* 29 September 2005. Ciaran Giles (AP), *Seattle Post-Intelligencer,* 13 October 2005. *El País,* 15 and 16 October 2005. The Ibero-American Summit refused to yield on the call for an end to the economic warfare against Cuba, and again condemned the "blockade" by the United States. On 8 November 2005, the UN General Assembly again called for ending the US embargo against Cuba, 182 to 4 (United States, Israel, Marshall Islands, and Palau; Micronesia abstained). There was scarcely a word in the press. See also Jim Lobe, Inter Press Service, 12 May 2005.

12. Graham Allison, *Foreign Affairs,* January–February 2004. For Mueller, see *Hegemony or Survival,* p. 200.

13. Stockholm International Peace Research Institute (SIPRI), 2005 Year Book. Reuven Pedatzur, *Ha'aretz,* 26 May 2005.

14. Max Boot quoted by Roger Cohen, *New York Times,* 12 June 2005. Program on International Policy Attitudes (PIPA), news release, 6 April 2005. Max Boot, *New York Times,* 13 February 2003.

15. Pedatzur, *Ha'aretz,* 26 May 2005.

16. James Blight and Philip Bremer, *Sad and Luminous Days* (Rowman and Littlefield, 2002). On the facts of the matter, see *Hegemony or Survival,* p. 74.

17. Robert McNamara, *Foreign Policy*, May–June 2005.

18. Graham Allison, *Nuclear Terrorism* (Times Books, 2004). He also cites very close calls.

19. John Steinbruner and Nancy Gallagher, *Daedalus*, Summer 2004.

20. National Intelligence Council, *Global Trends 2015* (Washington, December 2000). US Space Command, *Vision for 2020*, February 1997. Pentagon, *Quadrennial Defense Review*, May 1997. On UN and militarization of space and more detail, see *Hegemony or Survival*, pp. 209, 230, 231–32.

21. STRATCOM, "Essentials of Post–Cold War Deterrence," 1995. For extensive quotes from this important study, and sources, see my *New Military Humanism* (Common Courage, 1999). Harold Brown, Report of Secretary of Defense to Congress on FY 1981 Budget, 29 January 1980. On recognition of the need to delude the public about the "Soviet threat," see p. 103 in the present work.

22. Air Force Space Command, *Strategic Master Plan FY06 and Beyond*, 1 October 2003 (emphasis in original). Tim Weiner, *New York Times*, 18 May 2005.

23. William Arkin, *Washington Post*, 15 May 2005. Walter Pincus, *Washington Post*, 16 March 2005.

24. Tim Weiner, *New York Times*, 18 May 2005. Demetri Sevastopulo, *Financial Times*, 19 and 20 May 2005. Jehangir Pocha, *Boston Globe*, 1 August 2004, citing *Jane's Defence Weekly* editor. Edward Cody, *Washington Post*, 12 April 2005. See also *Hegemony or Survival*, Afterword. On spending, see Simon Collard-Wexler et al., *Space Security 2004* (Northview Press, 2005).

25. David C. Hardesty, *Naval War College Review*, Spring 2005. Chinese physicist, strategic analyst, and Kennedy Institute fellow Hui Zhang, *Financial Times*, 9 June 2005.

26. Neil King, *Wall Street Journal*, 8 September 2005.

27. Michael MccGwire, *International Affairs*, January 2005 (his emphasis).

28. Sam Nunn, *Financial Times*, 6 December 2004. Bruce Blair, *Defense Monitor* (Center for Defense Information, Washington), January–February 2004.

29. Graham Allison, *Nuclear Terrorism*. See also Graham Allison, *Russia in Global Affairs* online, September–October 2004.

30. Bruce Blair, president of the Center for Defense Information and former Minuteman launch officer, *Washington Post*, 19 September 2004. Blair, *Defense Monitor,* January–February 2004. Chalmers Johnson, *The Sorrows of Empire* (Metropolitan, 2004), p. 288.

31. Walsh, see Stephen Fidler, *Financial Times*, 22 May 2005.

32. Science correspondent Mark Henderson, *Times* (London), 7 June 2005. Lead editorial, *Financial Times*, 9 June 2005. Andrew Revkin, *New York Times*, 18 June 2005. Lead editorial, *Financial Times*, 20 June 2005.

33. Clive Cookson, *Financial Times*, 19 February 2005. Andrew Revkin, *New York Times*, 29 September 2005. A database search found reports in three local newspapers. The *Washington Post* ran a brief "sampling of noteworthy presentations" at the AAAS meeting, keeping to a paper on pollution in the northern United States.

34. Chicago Council on Foreign Relations, *Global Views 2004*. PIPA, *The Separate Realities of Bush and Kerry Supporters*, 21 October 2004.

35. George Tenet, letter to Senator Bob Graham, 7 October 2002. For this and many other documents, see John Prados, *Hoodwinked: The Documents That Reveal How Bush Sold Us a War* (New Press, 2004). Reuters, *Boston Globe*, 22 June 2005. Douglas Jehl, *New York Times*, 22 June 2005. Douglas Jehl and David Sanger, *New York Times*, 28 September 2004. NIC 2020 Project, *Mapping the Global Future*, December 2004. Douglas Jehl, *New York Times*, 14 January 2005. Susan Glasser, *Washington Post*, 29 May 2005.

36. Alan Richards, *Middle East Policy*, Summer 2005. Scott Atran, "Lifting the Veil—the Face of Jihad in Southeast Asia," unpublished ms., Jakarta, Indonesia, August 2005. Among many press reports, see Jimmy Burns and Mark Huband, *Financial Times*, 24 January 2003. Douglas Frantz et al., *Los Angeles Times*, 26 September 2004. Dana Priest and Josh White, *Washington Post*, 17 February 2005. Also Peter Spiegel, *Financial Times*, 20 October 2004, on the annual report of the London Institute of Strategic Studies reviewing the effect of the Iraq war on proliferation and reiterating its earlier conclusion that the Iraq war increased recruitment to Al Qaeda and "perversely impelled an already decentralized and evasive transnational terrorist network to become more 'virtual' and protean and, therefore, harder to identify and neutralize." See Scott Atran, "Confounding Terrorist Networks and Rogue States," lecture, Centre Nationale de la Recherche Scientifique, Paris, and University of Michigan, January 2004.

37. Royal Institute of International Affairs (RIIA), *Security, Terrorism and the UK*, July 2005. Richard Norton-Taylor, *Guardian*, 29 July 2005. Gerri Peev, *Scotsman*, 29 July 2005. MI5 website, 19 July 2005.

38. Alan Cowell, *New York Times*, 19 July 2005. Tony Thompson et al., *Guardian*, 31 July 2005.

39. Bryan Bender, *Boston Globe*, 17 July 2005. Greg Miller and Tyler Marshall, *Los Angeles Times*, 16 September 2005. Nawaf Obaid and Anthony Cordesman, *Saudi Militants in Iraq*, Center for Strategic and International Studies, 19 September 2005. Dan Murphy, *Christian Science Monitor*, 27 September 2005. John Ward Anderson, *Washington Post*, 19 October 2005.

40. Bender, *Boston Globe*, 17 July 2005. Peter Bergen and Alec Reynolds, *Foreign Affairs*, November–December 2005.

41. Dan Murphy, *Christian Science Monitor*, 25 July 2005. Reuters, *Boston Globe* and *Sydney Morning Herald*, 2 November 2005.
42. Robert Pape, *New York Times*, 9 July 2005. B. Raman, *Asia Times*, 16 July 2005.
43. Fawaz A. Gerges, *The Far Enemy* (Cambridge, 2005), "Final Thoughts."
44. Anonymous (Michael Scheuer), *Imperial Hubris* (Brasseys, 2004). See also Jonathan Randal, *Osama* (Knopf, 2004); Jason Burke, *Al-Qaeda* (I. B. Tauris, 2003).
45. Thomas Friedman, *New York Times*, 22 July 2005.
46. Jack Synder, *National Interest,* Spring 2003.
47. *New York Times*, 7 March 2003.
48. Sheryl Gay Stolberg and Joel Brinkley, *New York Times*, 26 January 2005.
49. Prados, *Hoodwinked*.
50. Alan Cowell, *New York Times*, 29 April 2005. Memo from *Guardian*, 28 April 2005.
51. *Sunday Times* (London), 1 May 2005. Matthew Clark, *Christian Science Monitor*, 17 May 2005. Mark Danner, *New York Review of Books*, 9 June 2005. Thomas Wagner, AP, *Boston Globe*, 19 June 2005. On the media reaction, see Fairness and Accuracy in Reporting (FAIR), Action Alert, 14 June 2005, quoting Michael Kinsley (*Los Angeles Times*) and Dana Milbank (*Washington Post*), who were far from alone.
52. Michael Smith, *Sunday Times* (London) defense commentator, *New Statesman*, 30 May 2005; *Los Angeles Times*, 23 June 2005; *Sunday Times* (London), 26 June 2005.
53. Ed Harriman, *Sunday Times* (London), 11 January 2004.
54. Michael Smith, *Sunday Times* (London), 1 May 2005. Chris Tudda, *Journal of Cold War Studies*, Fall 2005. For more on Israel and Lebanon, see my *Fateful Triangle* (South End, 1983; updated, 1999). On internal acknowledgment of reasons for the invasion, see my *World Orders Old and New* (Columbia, 1994; updated 1996). On Kosovo, see my *A New Generation Draws the Line* (Verso, 2000). James Risen and David Sanger, *New York Times*, 15 October 2005. Attacks also took place within Syrian territory, as they report.
55. For recent review, see Irene Gendzier, *Middle East Report*, Spring 2005. See also Gendzier, *Dying to Forget* (Rowman and Littlefield, forthcoming). On the BWTC violations and the anthrax strains, see Dominic Kennedy, *Times* (London), 9 August 2005, referring to the study by Geoffrey Holland, "United States Exports of Biological Materials to Iraq: Compromising the Credibility of International Law," available through the Centre for Research on Globalization (www.globalresearch.ca).

56. James Glanz, *New York Times*, 17 April 2005. Associated Press, 3 June 2005. Rami Abdelrahman, personal communication, October 2005.

57. The list of Saddam supporters includes just about every leading figure in the Reagan, Bush I, Bush II, and Thatcher administrations. On the remarkable record of Blair's New Labour, as late as 2001, see *Hegemony or Survival*, p. 30. Allison, *Nuclear Terrorism*.

58. Michael Jansen, *Jordan Times*, 7 July 2005. Javier Blas, Carola Hoyos, and Steve Negus, *Financial Times*, 15 June 2005.

59. This section relies mostly on Stephen Zunes, *Middle East Policy*, Spring 2004. On Syrian intelligence cooperation with the United States in the "war on terror," see also Steven Van Evera, *American Conservative*, 14 March 2005. In 1982, Cuba replaced Iraq on the list of states supporting terror. Shortly before, the terrorist war against Cuba launched by the Kennedy administration had reached a peak of ferocity.

60. Stephen Zunes, *Middle East Policy*, Spring 2004. Zogby International poll, 7 April 2004. PIPA, *Americans on the Israel/Palestinian Conflict*, 8 May 2002. Mark Sappenfield, *Christian Science Monitor*, 15 April 2002. For more information, see *Hegemony or Survival*, chapter 7.

61. Philip Shenon, *New York Times*, 6 June 2005. Shenon, *New York Times*, 21 October 2005.

62. Thomas Oliphant, *Boston Globe*, 10 July 2005.

63. "Treasury Office Has Four Agents Investigating Wealth of Bin Laden, Saddam," *White House Bulletin*, 29 April 2004. Marc Frank and Richard Lapper, *Financial Times*, 10 May 2004. Nancy San Martin, *Miami Herald*, 30 April 2004. Christopher Marquis, *New York Times*, 7 May 2004, quoting Baucus. On the sources of the obsession with Cuba, see pp. 112–14 in the present work.

64. Reuters, 23 July 2005.

65. Robert Dreyfuss, *American Prospect*, 23 November 2005.

66. Stephen Grey and Don Van Natta, *New York Times*, 26 June 2005. On terror and intelligence services in Italy, see Edward Herman and Frank Brodhead, *The Rise and Fall of the Bulgarian Connection* (Sheridan Square, 1986). For new information on the US role, see Daniele Ganser, *NATO's Secret Armies* (Frank Cass, 2005). On retrial, Motassadeq was convicted of "ideological support for the Islamic Jihad," but may appeal. Hugh Williamson et al., *Financial Times*, 29 August 2005.

67. Keith Johnson, *Wall Street Journal*, 20 October 2005. José Calvo, *El País*, 20 October 2004.

68. Bosch, Posada, see pp. 5–6, 35 in the present work. On Constant, see *Hegemony or Survival*, p. 204, and my *9-11* (Seven Stories, 2001).

69. Téllez, see Duncan Campbell, *Guardian*, 4 March 2005. Carla Anne Robbins, *Wall Street Journal*, 27 April 2004. On Negroponte, see p. 151 in the present work.

70. Michael Lind, *Financial Times*, 2 May 2005.

71. Walter Hume Long, cited by Ian Rutledge, *Addicted to Oil* (I. B. Tauris, 2005). Stephen Rabe, *The Road to OPEC* (Texas, 1982).

72. Zbigniew Brzezinski, *National Interest*, Winter 2003–4.

73. On these matters, see *Hegemony or Survival*, chapter 3, and National Intelligence Council 2020 Project. See also Afterword in the present work.

74. Arctic Power, "ANWR Fact of the Day," posted 21 April 2005. Quick access to Arctic reserves should not pose huge difficulties, by developing shut-in-spare capacity for emergencies. See Rutledge, *Addicted to Oil*, p. 43.

75. Energy consultant Alfred Cavallo, *Bulletin of the Atomic Scientists*, May–June 2005. This is not the first time that national security has been sidelined by depletion of domestic reserves for immediate gain. Another case is the fourteen-year program of mandatory quota restrictions on foreign oil initiated in 1959, with the "long-range effect of seriously depleting the nation's [petroleum] reserves" and imposing a "substantial burden on consumers, estimated by [MIT oil expert M. A.] Adelman to amount in the early sixties to $4 billion a year," with no concern for national security, the alleged motive for the legislation. John Blair, *The Control of Oil* (Pantheon 1976), pp. 171ff. Blair directed government inquiries into the industry.

Chapter 2: OUTLAW STATES

1. John Rawls, *The Law of Peoples* (Harvard University Press, 1999). John Mikhail, *Stanford Journal of International Law,* 2000.

2. Report of the International Law Commission on the work of its second session, 5 June–29 July 1950 (Document A/1316).

3. John Murphy, *The United States and the Rule of Law in International Affairs* (Cambridge University Press, 2004), p. 287. Pedatzur, *Ha'aretz,* 26 May 2005.

4. Sanford Levinson, *Daedalus,* Summer 2004.

5. Michael Isikoff, *Newsweek,* online edition (MSNBC.com), 19 May 2004. Alberto R. Gonzales, Memorandum for the President: Decision re Application of the Geneva Convention on Prisoners of War to the Conflict with Al Qaeda and the Taliban, 25 January 2002. Available at www.washingtonpost.com.

6. Levinson, *Daedalus,* Summer 2004. Burke, *Observer,* 13 June 2004. Dana Priest, *Washington Post,* 2 November 2005. On the criminal behavior of the 82nd Airborne, traceable to "the administration's refusal to insist on adherence to a lawful, long-recognized, and well-defined standard of treatment" of detainees, see Human Rights Watch, "Leadership Failure," 25 September 2005.

7. Paust, *Columbia Journal of Transnational Law* 43, no. 3 (2005).

8. Human Rights Watch press release, 24 April 2005, and report, "Getting Away with Torture? Command Responsibility for the US Abuse of Detainees," April 2005. Amnesty International, press conference, 25 May 2005. Farah Stockman, *Boston Globe*, 26 May 2005. Alan Cowell, *New York Times,* 26 May 2005.

9. Casey and Rivkin, *National Interest,* Spring 2005.

10. MccGwire, *International Affairs* 81, no. 1 (January 2005); Philippe Sands, *Lawless World* (Viking, 2005). Peter Weiss, *Arab Studies Quarterly,* Spring–Summer 2002. Wayne Smith, *South Florida Sun-Sentinel,* 28 November 2003. Charles Lane, *Washington Post,* 29 June 2004. Eric Schmitt, *New York Times,* 11 November 2005.

11. "Declaration of Judge Buergenthal," International Court of Justice, 15 September 2005. "The Judgment on the Fence Surrounding Alfei Menashe," HCJ 7957/04, 15 September 2005. "Report on Israeli Settlement in the Occupied Territories," Foundation for Middle East Peace, November–December 2005. For detailed analysis of the ICJ conclusions and the conflicting HCJ decision, see Norman Finkelstein, "Reconciling Irreconcilables," *Georgetown Journal of International Law,* forthcoming.

12. Zunes, *Middle East Policy,* Winter 2004.

13. Harald Frederiksen, *Middle East Policy,* Spring 2005.

14. Michael Byers, *War Law: An Introduction to International Law and Armed Conflict* (Atlantic Books, 2005), p. 85. Nermeen Al-Mufti, *Al-Ahram Weekly,* 21–27 October 2004.

15. Al-Mufti, *Al-Ahram Weekly,* 21–27 October 2004.

16. Richard Oppel, *New York Times,* 8 November 2004. Eric Schmitt, *New York Times,* 15 November 2004. Robert Worth, *New York Times,* 17 November 2004. Dexter Filkins and James Glanz, *New York Times,* 15 November 2004.

17. Schmitt, *New York Times,* 15 November 2004. Filkins and Glanz, *New York Times,* 15 November 2004.

18. Dexter Filkins, *New York Times,* 15 November 2004. On what residents called "the Murderous Maniacs" of the 82nd Airborne, and executive responsibility for their actions, see note 6 above.

19. Steven Weisman, *New York Times,* 30 January 2005. See additional discussion, p. 161 in the present work.

20. Dr. Miles Schuman, medical network of the Canadian Centre for Victims of Torture, *Nation,* 24 November 2004. Annie Kelly and Alison Benjamin, *Guardian,* 15 December 2004. Annie Kelly, *Guardian,* 15 December 2004.

21. Fadhil, *Guardian,* 22 December 2004. Erik Eckholm, *New York Times,* 6 January 2005. Edmund Sanders, *Los Angeles Times,* 29 December 2004.

22. Carr, *National Catholic Reporter,* 17 June 2005.

23. Reuters, 15 October 2005. A database search found reports in the *Los Angeles Times* and *Boston Globe,* 15 October 2005. On the same date, an Associated Press report by Bradley Klapper appeared in the London *Independent.*

24. Ahmed Hashim, *Current History,* January 2005. Aamer Madhani, *Chicago Tribune,* 5 October 2005. Farnaz Fassihi, *Wall Street Journal,* 13 October 2005. See also Dan Murphy and Jill Carroll, *Christian Science Monitor,* 12 October 2005, for similar reports.

25. Luttwak, *Foreign Affairs,* January–February 2005.

26. Mark Danner, *New York Times,* 6 January 2005. For one remarkable example, completely ignored with lethal consequences, see my *Necessary Illusions* (South End, 1989), p. 138. On the long record of torture, see Alfred McCoy, *A Question of Torture* (Metropolitan, 2006). Les Roberts et al., "Mortality Before and After the 2003 Invasion of Iraq," *Lancet,* online, 29 October 2004. Geneva-based Graduate Institute of International Studies annual small arms survey, 2005. Hamit Dardagan et al., *Iraq Body Count,* July 2005. The study by the *Lancet* eliminated Falluja. Had it been included, as the random sampling method required, the most probable estimate of deaths would have been 268,000, according to Iraq specialist Andrew Cockburn. *Los Angeles Times,* 17 December 2005.

27. Milan Rai, "Iraq Mortality," 14 October 2005 (iraqmortality.org/iraqmortality). Sabrina Tavernise, *New York Times,* 30 October 2005.

28. Robert Worth, *New York Times,* 24 October 2005.

29. Louise Roug, *Los Angeles Times,* 19 June 2005. Karl Vick, *Washington Post,* 21 November 2004. Peter Feuilherade, *Middle East International,* 15 April 2005.

30. Anthony Shadid and Steve Fainaru, *Washington Post,* 20 August 2005. Bill Spindle, *Wall Street Journal,* 1 April 2005.

31. For a response to the British government reaction, see Les Roberts et al., *Independent,* 12 December 2004, excerpted from Open Letter to Jack Straw. See Lila Gluterman, *Chronicle of Higher Education,* 27 January 2005, comparing endorsements from scientists with media dismissal.

32. Sut Jhally et al., "The Gulf War: A Study of the Media, Public Opinion, and Public Knowledge," February 1991 (available online at www.sutjhally.com). Justin Lewis, *Constructing Public Opinion* (Columbia, 2001), p. 210. The sample was students at the University of Massachusetts at Amherst, who are likely to be better informed than the general public. On the chemical warfare attacks initiated by Kennedy in 1962, see *Necessary Illusions,* chapter 2; *Hegemony or Survival* (e-edition), chapter 2. For a shattering graphic portrayal, see the study by photojournalist Philip Jones Griffiths, *Agent Orange* (Trolley, 2003), reviewed in England but virtually ignored in the United States. A

curious feature of commentary on the 2004 presidential election was puzzlement over "the Media's Vietnam Obsession" (the title of a CNN panel of leading commentators moderated by Howard Kurtz, 12 September 2004). In reality, the Vietnam war was virtually absent from the electoral campaign, which kept scrupulously to the extremely marginal question of John Kerry's service record in 1969 in the Mekong Delta, deep in the south, seven years after Kennedy launched the direct US attack against South Vietnam, two years after the highly respected military historian and Vietnam specialist Bernard Fall warned that "Vietnam as a cultural and historic entity . . . is threatened with extinction . . . [as] . . . the countryside literally dies under the blows of the largest military machine ever unleashed on an area of this size." Bernard Fall, *Last Reflections on a War* (Doubleday, 1967).

33. For discussion of Ignatieff's views on these and other matters of international law, see Friel and Falk, *The Record of the Paper*; Michael Walzer, *Arguing About War* (Yale University Press, 2004). On the practices of the "decent left" (*Dissent, American Prospect*), see Paul Street, *Empire and Inequality* (Paradigm, 2004), chapter 4, and *Z magazine,* May 2005.

34. See Harriman, *Sunday Times* (London) 11 January 2004, and p. 27 in the present work, on the elaborate preinvasion bribery and spying operations. For one example of the extraordinary incompetence, see the report of the special inspector-general for Iraq reconstruction, concluding that the Pentagon civilians in charge had "no comprehensive policy or regulatory guidelines in place for staffing the management of postwar Iraq." Stephanie Kirchgaessner, *Financial Times,* 30 October 2005. See Carl Kaysen et al., *War with Iraq* (American Academy of Arts and Sciences, 2002). Patrick Cockburn, *Counterpunch,* 16–31 March 2004.

35. The reasons, frankly explained at the time but since deeply hidden, were that Washington preferred an "iron-fisted Iraqi junta without Saddam Hussein" (Thomas Friedman, *New York Times,* 7 June 1991), but short of that, Hussein would have to do, because Washington and its allies held the "strikingly unanimous view [that] whatever the sins of the Iraqi leader, he offered the West and the region a better hope for his country's stability than did those who have suffered his repression" (Alan Cowell, *New York Times,* 11 April 1991).

36. John Mueller and Karl Mueller, *Foreign Affairs,* May–June 1999. Anthony Shadid, *Night Draws Near* (Holt, 2005), pp. 39ff. On the effects of the sanctions, and the fraudulent justifications, see, among others, International Committee of the Red Cross, "Iraq: 1989–1999, a Decade of Sanctions," 14 December 1999; Eric Herring, *Review of International Studies,* January 2002; Anthony Arnove, ed., *Iraq Under Siege,* 2nd ed. (South End, 2002); Joy Gordon, *Harper's,* November 2002. UNICEF, see Frances Williams, *Financial Times,* 12 December 2002.

37. Kamil Mahdi, *Middle East International,* 24 December 1999.

38. See *Hegemony or Survival,* pp. 127, 190. See also Hans von Sponeck, *Spokesman* 86, 2005.

39. Warren Hoge, *New York Times,* 7 January 2005. Judith Miller, *New York Times,* 10 January 2005. Claudio Gatti, *Financial Times,* 13 January 2005. Joy Gordon, *Harper's,* December 2004.

40. Mark Turner, *Financial Times,* 14 and 19 January 2005.

41. *Financial Times,* 9 December 2004. Gareth Smyth and Thomas Cattan, *Financial Times,* 21 June 2004. Claudio Gatti and Mark Turner, *Financial Times,* 30 November 2004. Julia Preston and Judith Miller, *New York Times,* 15 April 2005. Yochi Dreazen, *Wall Street Journal,* 26 July 2005. Julia Preston and Simon Romero, *New York Times,* 22 October 2005.

42. Ed Harriman, *London Review of Books,* 7 July 2005. Stuart Bowen, in Stephanie Kirchgaessner, *Financial Times,* 19 October 2005. See also Pratap Chatterjee, *Iraq, Inc.: A Profitable Occupation* (Seven Stories, 2004).

43. Alan Cullison and Yochi Dreazen, *Wall Street Journal,* 14 June 2005. Judith Miller, *New York Times,* 14 June 2005. Todd Purdum, *New York Times,* 14 June 2005. Howard LaFranchi, *Christian Science Monitor,* 2 August 2005.

44. Warren Hoge, *New York Times,* 7 September 2005. UN correspondent Ian Williams, *Middle East International,* September 2005.

45. Richard Thornburgh (Bush I), Christopher Burnham, a major campaign contributor (Bush II). Editorial, *Wall Street Journal,* 9 September 2005. See also Williams, *Middle East International,* September 2005.

46. Warren Hoge, *New York Times,* 27 and 28 October 2005. Doreen Carvajal and Andrew Kramer, *New York Times,* 28 October 2005.

47. Carola Hoyos, *Financial Times,* 29 and 30 October 2005. For Spain, see my *American Power and the New Mandarins* (Pantheon, 1969; New Press, 2002), pp. 121–22 and notes. For Haiti, see pp. 153–55 in the present work.

48. Eric Herring, *Review of International Studies,* March 2002.

49. Gareth Smyth, *Financial Times,* 20 July 2005. South Africa, see *Hegemony or Survival,* p. 110.

50. Edward Alden, *Financial Times,* 10 June 2004.

51. John Murphy, *The United States and the Rule of Law in International Affairs* (Cambridge, 2004), who adds that the torture convention was also ratified as non-self-executing, giving further legal justification for Bush-Rumsfeld practices; Michael Mandel, *How America Gets Away with Murder* (Pluto, 2004).

52. Friel and Falk, *The Record of the Paper.* Murphy, *The United States and the Rule of Law in International Affairs.*

53. Robert H. Jackson, *The Nürnberg Case* (Knopf, 1947), p. 86. UN General Assembly Resolution 3314, "Definition of Aggression," adopted

without a vote, December 1974. Carsten Stahn, *American Journal of International Law,* October 2003.

54. Telford Taylor, *The Anatomy of the Nuremberg Trials* (Knopf, 1992), pp. 50, 66, 627.

55. Abram Sofaer, US Department of State, *Current Policy,* No. 769 (December 1985). Colter Paulson, *American Journal of International Law,* July 2004. Howard N. Meyer, *The World Court in Action* (Rowman & Littlefield, 2002), chapter 9.

56. *El Universal Online,* 20 March 2005. Also Fred Rosen, NACLA's *Report on the Hemisphere,* May–June 2005.

57. Charles Lane, *Boston Globe* and *Washington Post,* 10 March 2005.

58. Murphy, *The United States and the Rule of Law in International Affairs,* p. 117.

59. Sands, *Lawless World,* pp. 132ff., 162.

60. Dean Acheson, *Proceedings,* ASIL, 13, 14 (1963). Acheson was referring specifically to US economic war, but surely knew about the international terrorism.

61. MccGwire, *International Affairs,* January 2005 (emphasis in original).

62. MccGwire, *International Affairs,* January 2005.

63. Mohamed ElBaradei, *Economist,* 16 October 2003. Frank von Hippel, in Rakesh Sood, Frank von Hippel, and Morton Halperin, "The Road to Nuclear Zero: Three Approaches" (Center for Advanced Study of India, 1998).

64. Allison, *Nuclear Terrorism.* John Deutsch, Arnold Kanter, Ernest Moniz, and Daniel Poneman, *Survival,* Winter 2004–5.

65. David Sanger et al., *New York Times,* 1 and 3 May 2005.

66. *Australian,* 1 May 2005. Dow Jones Newswires, 9 March 2005, referring to what appears to be the same article in the *Washington Post* the day before. The *Post* reports that Kissinger refuses to have his articles archived. Dafna Linzer, *Washington Post,* 27 March 2005. She dates Kissinger's article 9 March 2005.

67. Martin van Creveld, *International Herald Tribune,* 21 August 2004. See *Hegemony or Survival,* Afterword. Dan Williams, Reuters, 23 September 2004.

68. Matthew Karnitschnigg, *Wall Street Journal,* 28 January 2005. Dilip Hiro, *Middle East International,* 21 January 2005.

69. Robert Norris and Hans Kristensen, *Bulletin of the Atomic Scientists,* May–June 2005. See Afterword in the present work for more discussion.

70. John Mearsheimer, *New York Times,* 24 March 2000. Lawrence Korb, *Defense Monitor,* July–August 2005. On options in 1990–91, see my *Deterring Democracy* (Hill & Wang, 1991). On 1999, see *New Military Humanism* and *A New Generation Draws the Line.*

71. Ambassador Jackie Sanders, US Mission to the UN, Statement to the

NPT Conference, 20 May 2005. Nick Wadhams, Associated Press, 21 May 2005. *Boston Globe,* 21 May 2005. Farah Stockman and Joe Lauria, *Boston Globe,* 28 May 2005. *Bulletin of the Atomic Scientists,* July–August 2002, reviewing a series of such departures from treaties. Farah Stockman, *Boston Globe,* 9 May 2005. See also Guy Dinmore, *Financial Times,* 5 February 2005. The administration had already made clear that it "no longer support[s] some of the Article VI conclusions," and had informed other countries in preparatory meetings for the 2005 review that it regarded previous commitments as nonbinding, refusing to sign a conference agenda referring to them—a stand that is "unprecedented," according to a Dutch delegation adviser who had attended every review conference. Preliminary discussions were "stalled, in part because of the US refusal to reaffirm the '13 steps' adopted at the 2000 conference [including] a broad commitment to undertake nuclear disarmament and not to resume testing." Again, quite in accord with the "new thinking" of the president and his advisers. See *Bulletin of the Atomic Scientists,* July–August 2002, reviewing a series of such departures from treaties.

72. John Burrough (executive director of the Lawyers' Committee on Nuclear Policy), *News at Home,* 27 January 2003. Thomas Graham, *Current History,* April 2005. Ambassador Jackie W. Sanders, "Remarks to the Conference on Disarmament" (UN), 29 July 2004. US Department of State, "Fissile Material Cut-Off Treaty Policy," July 2004. Press release, 11 April 2004, GA/DIS/3291, General Assembly, First Committee. Jean du Preez, "The Fissban," *Disarmament Diplomacy,* April–May 2005. On the general background, see Nicole Deller et al., *Rule of Power or Rule of Law?* (Apex, 2003).

73. Resolution adopted by the UN General Assembly, Prevention of an arms race in outer space, A/Res/59/65, 3 December 2004.

74. MccGwire, *International Affairs,* January 2005. The 1981 resolution was passed in response to Israel's bombing of Iraq's nuclear reactor, which, it was quickly learned, had no nuclear weapons capacity, an act of aggression that appears to have initiated Saddam Hussein's nuclear weapons program in reaction. See *Hegemony or Survival,* p. 25.

75. Charles Hanley, Associated Press, 28 May 2005. Stockman and Lauria, *Boston Globe,* 28 May 2005. Maggie Farley, *Los Angeles Times,* 28 May 2005. Jimmy Carter, *The Advertiser* (Australia), 28 May 2005.

76. Robin Cook, *Guardian,* 27 May 2005. Under strong pressure, the administration may have dropped, or delayed, its plans to develop nuclear deep-penetration weapons. Associated Press, 26 October 2005.

77. Graham, *Current History,* April 2005.

Chapter 3: ILLEGAL BUT LEGITIMATE

1. Report of the UN High-level Panel on Threats, Challenges, and Change, UN General Assembly, 3 December 2004, A/59/565.
2. UN General Assembly, 20 September 2005 (A/60/L.1).
3. Report of the UN High-level Panel, 3 December 2004.
4. For these and many other such pronouncements, see *New Military Humanism* and *A New Generation Draws the Line.*
5. Mark Curtis, *Unpeople: Britain's Secret Human Rights Abuses* (Vintage, 2004).
6. Bruce Cumings, "American Airpower and Nuclear Strategy in Northeast Asia," in M. Selden and A.Y. So, eds., *War and State Terrorism* (Rowman & Littlefield, 2004), citing the *New York Times* (emphasis added).
7. Telford Taylor, *Nuremberg and Vietnam* (Times Books, 1970). Taylor, *Anatomy*, pp. 325–26, 592–93, 640.
8. Jonathan Steele, Ewen MacAskill, Richard Norton-Taylor, and Ed Harriman, *Guardian*, 22 September 2001.
9. Michael Sherry, *The Rise of American Airpower* (Yale, 1987), p. 102. Bruce Franklin, *War Stars* (Oxford, 1988), on the backgrounds in popular American culture.
10. Friel and Falk, *The Record of the Paper* (their emphasis).
11. Condoleezza Rice, *Foreign Affairs,* January–February 2000.
12. Report of the Quadrennial Defense Review (QDR), US Department of Defense, May 1997. G. John Ikenberry, *Foreign Affairs,* September–October 2002. Madeleine K. Albright, *Foreign Affairs,* September–October 2003. John Bolton, quoted in Phyllis Bennis, *Calling the Shots* (Olive Branch, 1996), p. xv.
13. Condoleezza Rice quoted in Steven Weisman, *New York Times,* 8 March 2005. Jacob Weisberg, *New York Times Magazine.* James Traub, *New York Times Magazine,* 16 September 1990.
14. For recent review, see Joseph Nevins, *A Not-So-Distant Honor* (Cornell, 2005); Ben Kiernan, "War, Genocide, and Resistance in East Timor, 1975–99," in Selden and So, *War and State Terrorism.*
15. Henry Kissinger, *Chicago Tribune,* 11 August 2002. Kissinger was commenting on Bush's West Point address where the National Security Strategy was presented in outline.
16. Elizabeth Becker, *New York Times,* 27 May 2004 (emphasis added).
17. Cees Wiebes, cited by Chris Stephens, *Observer,* 10 October 2004. See Wiebes, *Intelligence and the War in Bosnia, 1992–1995* (Transaction, 2003), p. 388.
18. John Lewis Gaddis, *Surprise, Security, and the American Experience* (Harvard, 2004). Matt Bai, *New York Times Magazine,* 10 October 2004.
19. William Weeks, *John Quincy Adams and the American Global Empire*

(Kentucky, 1992). The source, here and below, except where noted. Richard Immerman and Regina Gramer, *Passport* (newsletter of the Society for Historians of American Foreign Relations), August 2005. In his response, Gaddis does not take issue with these observations.

20. William Weeks, *Building the Continental Empire* (Ivan Dee, 1996), pp. 44ff.

21. Worthington Chauncey Ford, ed., *Writings of John Quincy Adams* (Macmillan, 1916), volume 6, p. 385n. This was brought to my attention by Kelly Gerling.

22. The phrase is that of Ernest May and Philip Zelikow, *The Kennedy Tapes* (Harvard, 1998). See Louis Pérez, *The War of 1898* (North Carolina, 1998). Weeks, *Building the Continental Empire*, p. 144.

23. Thomas Hietala, *Manifest Design: Anxious Aggrandizement in Late Jacksonian America* (Cornell, 1985). Weeks, *Building the Continental Empire*, p. 112.

24. Independent International Commission on Kosovo, *Kosovo Report*, (Oxford, 2001). Goldstone, "Kosovo: An Assessment in the Context of International Law," Nineteenth Morgenthau Memorial Lecture, Carnegie Council on Ethics and International Affairs, 2000.

25. See *New Military Humanism* and *A New Generation Draws the Line* for details and for reactions outside NATO. See *Hegemony or Survival*, pp. 56ff., for more recent information.

26. Frank C. Carlucci, *New York Times*, 22 February 2005. Niall Ferguson, *Colossus* (Penguin, 2004), p. 146. David Rieff, "Kosovo: the End of an Era?," in Fabrice Weissman, ed., *In the Shadow of "Just Wars"* (Cornell, 2004). Karl-Heinz Kamp, *Bulletin of the Atomic Scientists*, March–April 2005.

27. James Traub, *New York Times Magazine*, 30 October 2005. Andrew Bacevich, *American Empire* (Harvard, 2003), pp. 104ff., 196. See also John Norris, *Collision Course: NATO, Russia, and Kosovo* (Praeger, 2005), p. xxiii. Presenting the position of the Clinton Administration, he writes that "it was Yugoslavia's resistance to the broader trends of political and economic reform—not the plight of Kosovar Albanians—that best explains NATO's war." Norris was director of communications during the war for Deputy Secretary of State Strobe Talbott (now president of the Brookings Institute), who was a leading figure in State Department and Pentagon planning concerning the war. Talbott writes in his foreword that "thanks to John Norris," anyone interested in the war in Kosovo "will know . . . how events looked and felt at the time to those of us who were involved" in the war. Hence Norris's evaluation is of particular significance for determining the motivation for the war.

28. See, for example, "Essentials of Post-Cold War Deterrence." See also chapter 1, note 21.

29. I cited the British government claim at the time but added that it is not credible because of the balance of forces, if nothing else. However, it has been confirmed by the British parliamentary inquiry, from the highest sources. See *Hegemony or Survival*, p. 56, for discussion. Nicholas Wheeler, *Saving Strangers: Humanitarian Intervention and International Society* (Oxford, 2000).

30. For citations, see *New Military Humanism* and *A New Generation Draws the Line*. Bacevich, *American Empire*. Drake Bennett, *Boston Globe*, 16 October 2005. Bennett adds the defeat of Milošević by Vojislav Kostunica in a later election as another triumph of military humanism. The claim would be irrelevant if true, but the evidence is to the contrary. See, among others, Martin Sieff, senior analyst for UPI, "Kostunica Not Clinton Man," UPI Analysis, September 2000; Simon Jenkins, *Times* (London), 7 October 2000, explaining why "Yugoslavia's democracy deserves the credit, not Nato's Tomahawk missiles"; John Simpson (world affairs editor of BBC) drew the same conclusion in the *Sunday Telegraph*, 8 October 2000. Also Steven Erlanger and Carlotta Gall, *New York Times*, 21 September 2000, on Kostunica's denunciation of "NATO's criminal bombing of Yugoslavia" and denunciation of the International Criminal Tribunal on Yugoslavia (ICTY) as "an American tribunal—not a court, but a political instrument."

31. Anne-Marie Slaughter (*New York Times*, 18 March 2003, and *American Society of International Law Newsletter*, March–April 2004), cited by Sands, *Lawless World*, pp. 174–75.

32. Sean Murphy, *Humanitarian Intervention: The United Nations in an Evolving World Order* (Pennsylvania, 1996).

33. International Court of Justice, judgment of 9 April 1949, on Corfu.

Chapter 4: DEMOCRACY PROMOTION ABROAD

1. Jonathan Monten, *International Security*, Spring 2005. Eva Bellin, *Political Science Quarterly*, Winter 2004–5. Katarina Dalacoura, "US Democracy Promotion in the Arab Middle East Since 11 September 2001: A Critique," *International Affairs*, October 2005; the critique has to do with implementation. I will return to the evidence provided. This appears to be a fair sample of the most careful scholarship on this topic.

2. Huntington, *International Security*, Summer 1981; *National Interest*, Fall 1989.

3. George Orwell, "The Freedom of the Press," unpublished preface to the first edition of *Animal Farm* (1946).

4. Hirohito cited in Tsuyoshi Hasegawa, *Racing the Enemy* (Harvard University Press, 2005), the most highly regarded scholarly study of the

Japanese surrender. Hasegawa attributes the surrender largely to the Soviet invasion of Manchuria, which dashed the hopes of Japanese hawks for a last defense of the homeland. Martin Heidegger, *Introduction to Metaphysics* (1935; Yale University Press, 1959).

5. For Mill, see *Hegemony or Survival* and, for more detail, my *Peering into the Abyss of the Future* (Fifth Lakdawala Memorial Lecture; Institute of Social Sciences [New Delhi], 2002).

6. Adam Smith, *The Wealth of Nations,* book 4, chapters 4 and 7.

7. Center for Defense Information, *Defense Monitor,* January 1980.

8. Colette Youngers and Eileen Rosin, eds., *Drugs and Democracy in Latin America* (Washington Office on Latin America, Lynne Rienner, 2005), pp. 15, 26. On the striking continuity of policy as "defense against Communism" morphed into the "drug war," see particularly Doug Stokes, *America's Other War: Terrorizing Colombia* (Zed, 2004). On the reality of the "drug war" for the victims, a topic ignored by the perpetrators, see Hugh O'Shaughnessy and Sue Branford, *Chemical Warfare in Colombia* (Latin American Bureau, 2005).

9. Youngers and Rosin, eds., *Drugs and Democracy in Latin America,* p. 190. Adam Isacson, Jay Olson, and Lisa Haugard, *Blurring the Lines* (Latin America Working Group, Center for International Policy and Washington Office on Latin America, 2004).

10. Petra Minnerop, *German Law Journal,* 1 September 2002.

11. Arno Mayer, *Daily Princetonian,* 5 October 2001, cited by Mark Selden and Alvin So, "Introduction," in Selden and So, *War and State Terrorism.* On US terror (as officially defined by Washington), see, among others, Edward Herman, *The Real Terror Network* (South End, 1982); my *Pirates and Emperors* (1986; updated edition, South End, 2002); Alexander George, ed., *Western State Terrorism* (Polity/Blackwell, 1991).

12. Samuel Huntington, *Foreign Affairs,* March–April 1999; Robert Jervis (then president of the American Political Science Association), *Foreign Affairs,* July–August 2001; Robert Tucker and David Hendrickson, *Foreign Affairs,* November–December 2004. On difficulties of denial, see William Blum, *Rogue State* (Common Courage, 2000), and my *Rogue States* (South End, 2000).

13. Alfred McCoy, *The Politics of Heroin* (Lawrence Hill, 2003; revision of 1972 edition). Peter Dale Scott and Jonathan Marshall, *Cocaine Politics* (California, 1991). Scott, "Drugs and Oil," in Selden and So, *War and State Terrorism.*

14. Stuart Eizenstat et al., *Foreign Affairs,* January–February 2005. Thomas Carothers, *Critical Mission: Essays on Democracy Promotion* (Carnegie Endowment for International Peace, 2004), p. 230. See particularly Paul Farmer, *The Uses of Haiti* (Common Courage, 2003). On the March 2004 debacle, see Farmer's essay and others in *Getting Haiti Right This*

Time (Common Courage, 2004). My "Democracy Restored," *Z Magazine,* November 1994.

15. Gaddis, *Surprise, Security, and the American Experience.* The nineteenth-century project is quoted from Thomas Bailey, *A Diplomatic History of the American People* (Appleton-Century-Crofts, 1969), a standard work.

16. Daniel Thürer, *International Review of the Red Cross* 836, 31 December 1999.

17. Byers, *War Law,* pp. 107, 111.

18. Charles Bergquist, *Labor and the Course of American Democracy* (Verso, 1996), p. 100.

19. Seymour Hersh, *The Price of Power* (Simon & Schuster, 1983), p. 270, quoting Roger Morris; *New York Times,* 11 September 1974, cited by Morton Halperin et. al., *The Lawless State* (Penguin, 1976), p. 17.

20. John Dinges, *The Condor Years* (New Press, 2004), p. 65. See Kenneth Maxwell, *The Case of the Missing Letter in Foreign Affairs: Kissinger, Pinochet and Operation Condor* (David Rockefeller Center for Latin American Studies, Working Paper No. 04/05–3, 2004), on the efforts to "cut off a discussion about the role of the United States and Henry Kissinger in Chile, and of the accountability of public officials in highly controversial foreign policy actions in the principal foreign affairs journal of the nation."

21. Dinges, *The Condor Years.* Peter Kornbluh, ed., *The Pinochet File* (National Security Archive, New Press, 2004).

22. See p. 33 in the present work. On "successful defiance," see *Hegemony or Survival,* pp. 89ff. Other quotes from Louis Pérez, *Journal of Latin American Studies,* May 2002.

23. Curtis, *Unpeople,* p. 137. On Cuba, see my *Hegemony or Survival,* chapter 4. Eisenhower cited by Pérez, *Journal of Latin American Studies,* May 2002.

24. For a detailed account, see Laurent Dubois, *Avengers of the New World* (Harvard University Press, 2004).

25. John Lewis Gaddis, *The Long Peace* (Oxford University Press, 1987).

26. For review of scholarly sources and declassified documents, see *Deterring Democracy,* chapter 11. Mario Del Pero, *Diplomatic History,* June 2004. See chapter 1, note 66.

27. For numerous sources, see my *Year 501* (South End, 1993), chapter 5; *Powers and Prospects* (South End, 1996), chapters 7 and 8; and *Rogue States,* p. 38. See, particularly, Audrey Kahin and George Kahin, *Subversion as Foreign Policy* (New Press, 1995). On Wolfowitz, see pp. 133ff. in the present work.

28. In the rich scholarly literature, George Kahin's *Intervention* (Knopf, 1986) remains indispensable. For review of the relevant documentary

record, including recently released State Department history, see my *Rethinking Camelot* (South End, 1993).

29. My *Rethinking Camelot*. More recent material adds only further confirmation, leaving the defense of the doves of Camelot to amateur psychology about "multiple levels of deception" and "recollections" after the war became unpopular.

30. Gareth Porter, *Perils of Dominance* (University of California Press, 2005), p. 158. Bryan Bender, *Boston Globe*, 6 June 2005.

31. Melvin Leffler, *A Preponderance of Power* (Stanford University Press, 1992), p. 339. On the prewar diplomacy, see my *American Power and the New Mandarins*. On the war aims, see my *At War with Asia* (Pantheon, 1970) and *For Reasons of State* (Pantheon, 1973), the latter using documentation from the Pentagon Papers. John Dower, "The Super-domino [Japan] in Postwar Asia," in Chomsky and Howard Zinn, eds., *Critical Essays*, volume 5 of *The Pentagon Papers* (Beacon, 1972). There has been extensive new material since, but primarily extending the basic conclusions. On postwar planning there is substantial literature. For review and sources, see *Deterring Democracy* and *Year 501*.

32. See references of note 27, above.

33. Cited by David Fromkin and James Chace, *Foreign Affairs*, Spring 1985.

34. For serious analysis of the NLF, see Kahin, *Intervention*, and the highly illuminating studies of province advisers; see my *Rethinking Camelot* for review and sources. On intelligence and the Pentagon Papers, see my *For Reasons of State*, pp. 51ff.

35. Richard Aldrich, *The Hidden Hand* (John Murray, 2001), p. 19, an invaluable source on British secret intelligence, with documentation from the United States too. For Grand Area planning, see Larry Shoup and William Minter, *Imperial Brain Trust* (Monthly Review, 1977).

36. Omer Bartov, *Diplomatic History*, Summer 2001. A general estimate is that the Red Army killed fifteen to twenty times as many German soldiers as the British and Americans did. At the D-day landings the Allied forces faced fifty-eight German divisions; Soviet forces continued to face four times that many. Andrew Bacevich, *American Conservative*, 20 June 2005; Geoffrey Wheatcroft, *Boston Globe*, 8 May 2005; Jonathan Steele, *Guardian Weekly*, 13–19 May 2005.

37. John Price, "Casualties of War," unpublished ms., referring to the unilateral US-run San Francisco Peace Conference. See *Hegemony or Survival*, chapter 6, largely based on his earlier work. Kimball, *The Juggler* (Princeton University Press, 1991), pp. 34ff. Gaddis, *Surprise*, p. 50.

38. Timothy Crawford, *Political Science Quarterly*, 22 December 2001. Alonzo Hamby, *Man of the People* (Oxford, 1995), pp. 329ff., 443. Leffler, *Preponderance of Power*, p. 15.

39. Aldrich, *The Hidden Hand*, pp. 25, 36ff., 43, 48, 57.

40. Aldrich, *The Hidden Hand*, pp. 48, 57ff.

41. Robert McNamara, *In Retrospect* (Times Books, 1995). See my "Hamlet Without the Prince of Denmark," *Diplomatic History,* Summer 1996.

42. Henry Kissinger, *American Foreign Policy* (Norton, 1969). On the astonishing pronouncements in his scholarly essays, see my *Towards a New Cold War* (Pantheon, 1982).

43. Aldrich, *The Hidden Hand*, p. 327.

44. For extensive quotes, see *Deterring Democracy,* chapter 1.

45. Stephen Kurkjian and Adam Pertman, *Boston Globe,* 5 January 1990. For further discussion, see my *Deterring Democracy,* chapter 5.

46. For discussion and sources, see *Hegemony or Survival* (e-edition), chapter 9.

47. See *Rogue States,* pp. 192–93, for a review of Greenspan's chosen illustrations, all textbook examples refuting his claims—which are, however, conventional ideology.

48. For further details and sources, see *Deterring Democracy,* chapter 1.

49. A. M. Gray, *Marine Corps Gazette,* May 1990.

50. See Barbara Harriss-White, *India Working* (Cambridge, 2003), an in-depth study of the black and informal economies, which involve about 80–90 percent of the population, she estimates. On the disastrous impact of the reforms on the rural majority, see Utsa Patnaik, "Full Liberalisation of Agricultural Trade Jeopardises Food Security," International Workshop: Policies Against Hunger III, Berlin, 20–22 October 2004; "The Republic of Hunger," Public Lecture, New Delhi, 10 April 2004; and the remarkable journalism of P. Sainath, mostly in the *Hindu,* recording in vivid detail the deterioration in the lives of the rural majority. See also Alexander Cockburn, *Counterpunch,* 16 April 2005. A graphic illustration is the sharp rise in peasant suicides in Andhra Pradesh, not far from the high-tech miracles in Bangalore and Hyderabad, all resulting from the same neoliberal policies—for the rural population, withdrawal of essential state services and pressures to shift to economically very hazardous export crops. See Robert Pollin, *Contours of Descent* (Verso, 2003), pp. 138ff. *Frontline* (India), 2 July 2004. The situation in China is probably similar, but much less investigated in that far more closed and repressive society.

51. National Intelligence Council, *Mapping the Global Future,* December 2004 (NIC 2004–13).

52. Kamal Kharrazi, *Middle East Policy,* Spring 2005. Augustus Richard Norton, *Middle East Policy,* Spring 2005. Prados, *Hoodwinked.*

53. Dana Milbank and Mike Allen, *Washington Post,* 1 August 2003. On the many equivocations, see *Hegemony or Survival,* pp. 33–34. But the "single question" prevailed throughout.

54. Sam Allis, *Boston Globe,* 29 April 2004. David Ignatius (veteran *Wash-*

ington Post correspondent and former editor of the *International Herald Tribune*), *Washington Post,* 2 November 2003.

55. Steven Weisman, *New York Times,* 29 November 2003. David Brooks, *New York Times,* 7 October 2003.

56. Walter Pincus, *Washington Post,* 12 November 2003. Richard Burkholder, "Gallup Poll of Baghdad: Gauging US Intent," *Government & Public Affairs,* 28 October 2003.

57. Steven Weisman, *New York Times,* 30 September 2005. Special, *Daily Star* (Lebanon), 14 October 2005.

58. Byers, *War Law.*

59. On other criteria of great geopolitical significance, see *Hegemony or Survival,* chapter 6.

60. Elcano Royal Institute poll, February 2003: 27 percent said they would support a war if it was authorized by a new UN resolution. Charles Powell, *Current History,* November 2004. For poll details throughout Europe, see *Hegemony or Survival,* chapter 5.

61. Marc Lacey, *New York Times,* 8 May 2003. Ignatius, *Washington* Post, 2 November 2003.

62. Sebastian Mallaby, *Washington Post,* 28 March 2005. Andrew Balls, *Financial Times Weekend,* 25 September 2005. See also the admiring articles by Todd Purdum and Eric Schmitt, *New York Times,* 17 March 2005, also singularly devoid of evidence.

63. Jeffrey Winters, "Wolfowitz's Track Record on Economic Policy and Human Rights Is Poor," Joyo Exclusive (online news service on Indonesia), 29 March 2005. "Indonesia's Suharto Tops 'Worst Ever' Corruption Charts," Agence France-Presse (London), 26 March 2004. Alan Beattie, *Financial Times,* 17 March 2005.

64. Winters, "Wolfowitz's Track Record," 29 March 2005.

65. "Indonesian Activists Slam Wolfowitz' World Bank Candidacy," Dow Jones Newswires, 22 March 2005. Shawn Donnan, *Financial Times,* 30 March 2005—the favorable ones from "Indonesia's political elite." For more details from the early 1980s, and Wolfowitz's support for Suharto's crimes well after his overthrow, see *Hegemony or Survival,* Afterword.

66. Joseph Nevins, *National Catholic Reporter,* 11 February 2005.

67. Steven Dudley and Pablo Bachelet, *Miami Herald,* 16 September 2005.

68. Argentine political scientist Atilio Boron, "The Truth About Capitalist Democracy," in Leo Panitch and Colin Leys, eds., *Socialist Register* (Merlin, 2006). For popularity rating, see Alma Guillermoprieto, *New York Review of Books,* 6 October 2005.

69. Chicago Council on Foreign Relations and Program on International Policy Attitudes, "Americans on Promoting Democracy—Poll," 29 September 2005.

70. Colum Lynch, *Washington Post,* 18 September 2005; see wire services

for reporting on his speech. Hugh O'Shaughnessy, *Irish Times*, 17 September 2005. See also p. 256 in the present work.

71. Tim Weiner, *New York Times*, 22 March 2004. Thomas Walker, "El Salvador and Iraq: The Wrong Lesson from Flawed History," *Athens News*, 18 November 2004. On elections, see Edward Herman and Frank Brodhead, *Demonstration Elections* (South End, 1984); Herman and Chomsky, *Manufacturing Consent* (Pantheon, 1988; updated 2002).

72. Walker, "El Salvador and Iraq." On media commentary, see my article in Morris Morley and James Petras, *The Reagan Administration and Nicaragua* (Institute for Media Analysis, 1987). On Figueres and the press, see *Necessary Illusions* and *Deterring Democracy*. See also p. 139 in the present work.

73. Danna Harman, *Christian Science Monitor*, 3 March 2005. El Salvador may help provide the United States with the kind of foreign legion that has been a staple of European empires, though still not coming close to the scale of the South Korean mercenaries employed by the United States in South Vietnam, no longer available after the overthrow of the US-backed dictatorship in 1987, just as Washington lost its Argentine killers after the fall of the military dictatorship there.

74. Philip Shishkin, *Wall Street Journal*, 19 May 2005. Craig Murray, *Guardian*, 16 May 2005. Alan Cowell, *New York Times*, 31 December 2005.

75. Craig Murray, *Guardian*, 3 August 2005.

76. David Wall, *Financial Times*, 26 May 2005. Ann Scott Tyson and Robin Wright, *Washington Post*, 4 June 2005.

77. David E. Sanger, *New York Times*, 29 May 2005. Human Rights Watch, "Turkmenistan: Human Rights Update," 14 May 2004.

78. Sanger, *New York Times*, 29 May 2005, unarchived insert.

79. Sarah Mendelson and Theodore Gerber, *Foreign Affairs*, January–February 2006. On Japan, see my *Year 501*, chapter 10.

80. Cited by Curtis, *Unpeople*, p. 81.

81. On the US and UK reaction in 1958, see *Deterring Democracy*, chapter 6, Afterword.

82. Curtis, *Unpeople*, p. 82.

83. Nasser's plans: Douglas Little, *Diplomatic History*, November 2004. Salim Yaqub, *Containing Arab Nationalism* (University of North Carolina Press, 2004), pp. 225, 228, 240ff. State Department memorandum, cited by John M. Blair, *Control of Oil* (Pantheon, 1976), p. 85.

84. Roger Morris, *New York Times*, 14 March 2003. Washington's ally King Hussein of Jordan, on the CIA payroll since 1957, reported that he knew "for a certainty" that American intelligence supported the coup and provided the names of Communists to be executed, about five thousand of them in the first days; Hanna Batatu, *The Old Social Classes and the Revolutionary Movements of Iraq* (Prince-

ton, 1978), pp. 985–86, the classic scholarly study. Curtis, *Unpeople*, pp. 80ff.

85. See *Deterring Democracy*, Afterword.

86. Neil MacFarquhar, *New York Times*, 2 March 2005. Scott Wilson, *Washington Post*, 28 February 2005.

87. See pp. 254ff. in the present work.

88. Neil MacDonald and Najmeh Bozorgmehr, *Financial Times*, 8 July 2005. Edward Wong, *New York Times*, 7 July 2005.

89. Peter Galbraith, *New York Review of Books*, 11 August 2005.

90. On the rise and nature of the family dictatorship and the US alliance, and Saudi society and its travail and struggles for freedom, see As'ad Abukhalil, *The Battle for Saudi Arabia* (Seven Stories, 2004).

91. Alan Richards, *Middle East Policy*, Summer 2005.

92. For example, Robert Kuttner, *American Prospect*, August 2005.

93. On these matters, see *Hegemony or Survival*, Afterword and sources cited.

94. Carothers, *Critical Mission*, pp. 7, 42.

95. See p. 102 in the present work. Thomas Carothers, in Abraham Lowenthal, ed., *Exporting Democracy* (Johns Hopkins, 1991); Thomas Carothers, *In the Name of Democracy* (California, 1991), pp. 29, 249.

96. Peter Kornbluh, interview with Scott Harris, ZNet, 1 March 2005. Gary Cohn and Ginger Thompson, *Baltimore Sun*, 15 June 1995. For fuller details of Honduran state crimes and US involvement, see Gary Cohn and Ginger Thompson, *Baltimore Sun*, 11–18 June 1985. Michael Dobbs, *Washington Post*, 12 April 2005. Larry Rohter, *New York Times*, 21 December 1995. Carla Anne Robbins, *Wall Street Journal*, 27 April 2004.

97. Charles Bergquist, *Labor and the Course of American Democracy*, p. 5. Gordon Connell-Smith, *The Inter-American System* (Oxford, Royal Institute of International Affairs, 1966), pp. 23ff., 343.

98. Carothers, *Critical Mission*, p. 262.

99. See references of note 14, above. See my "Democracy Restored" for details from OFAC and other government sources.

100. Thomas Griffin, *Haiti Human Rights Investigation*, Center for the Study of Human Rights, University of Miami School of Law, December 2004.

101. Daniel Grann, *Atlantic Monthly*, June 2001, among others.

102. Warren Strobel, Knight-Ridder, *San Diego Union-Tribune*, 5 November 2003. Indira Lakshmanan, *Boston Globe*, 27 October 2005.

103. Stephen Rabe, *Diplomatic History*, November 2004.

104. Thomas Walker, *Nicaragua: Living in the Shadow of the Eagle*, 4th edition (Westview, 2003). Carothers, *Exporting Democracy*.

105. *Envío* (Universidad Centroamericana [UCA], Jesuit University, Managua), November 2003. Study financed by the German branch of Bread

for the World, *Nicaragua News Service*, 23 August 2005. "2004 Public Health Sector Summary," *La Prensa*, December 2004; Nicaragua News Service, Nicaragua Network 12.3, 21–27 December 2004. Economist Adolfo Acevedo, *Envío*, March 2005. On the Costa Rican exception, see my *Necessary Illusions*, pp. 111ff., Appendix 5; *Deterring Democracy*, pp. 221ff., 273ff.

106. Adolfo Acevedo, *Envío*, June 2005.

107. Editorial, *Boston Globe*, 15 March 2005; Thomas Gagen, *Boston Globe*, 15 March 2005. See p. 51 in the present work.

108. Warren Strobel, Knight-Ridder, *San Diego Union-Tribune*, 5 November 2003.

109. Larry Rohter, *New York Times*, 10 June 2003.

110. James Dobbins, *Foreign Policy*, January–February 2005.

111. Carothers, *Critical Missions*, p. 51. Leader, *Financial Times*, 5 March 2005. Richards, *Middle East Policy*, Summer 2005. Farnaz Fassihi, *Wall Street Journal*, 22 January 2004. Patrick Cockburn, *Counterpunch*, 21 July 2005. For a review of US efforts through mid-2004 to evade elections, drawn from the mainstream press, see *Hegemony or Survival*, Afterword.

112. John Burns, *New York Times*, 24 July 2005. Elaine Sciolino and Don Van Natta, *New York Times*, 25 July 2005.

113. Steven Weisman, *New York Times*, 30 January 2005. Bombing, see Anthony Shadid, *Night Draws Near* (Holt, 2005), p. 114.

114. Weisman, *New York Times*, 30 January 2005.

115. Steve Lee Myers, *New York Times*, 3 August 2005. See my *Necessary Illusions*, pp. 123ff., Appendix 5.

116. Marc Danner, *New York Review of Books*, 28 April 2005. Robert Fisk, *Independent*, 31 January 2005.

117. Scott Peterson and Dan Murphy, *Christian Science Monitor*, 28 January 2005. Yochi Dreazen, *Wall Street Journal*, 25 January 2005. Farnaz Fassihi, Philip Shishkin, and Greg Jaffe, *Wall Street Journal*, 17 October 2005.

118. Andrew Gowers, Philip Stephens, and James Blitz, *Financial Times*, 26 January 2005. Richard Burkholder, Gallup Organization, 28 April 2004.

119. Zogby International poll, released 28 January 2005. Oxford Research International, December 2003. Andrew Cordesman, "Playing the Course," Center for Strategic and International Studies, 22 November 2004. Nancy Youssef, Knight-Ridder, *San Jose Mercury News*, 13 September 2005. Gareth Smyth, *Financial Times*, 28 September 2005. IslamOnline.net, 17 November 2005 (Arabic), translated by Gilbert Achcar. Hassan Fatah, *New York Times*, 22 November 2005.

120. Bill Danvers (Clinton National Security Council official) and Michael O'Hanlon (Brookings), *Christian Science Monitor*, 2 November 2005.

Steven Kull, director of the Program on International Policy Attitudes (PIPA), Institute for Public Accuracy, 23 September 2005. Sean Rayment, *Sunday Telegraph*, 23 October 2005. Ned Temko, *Observer*, 23 October 2005. Nina Kamp, Michael O'Hanlon, and Amy Unikewicz, *New York Times*, 14 December 2005.

Chapter 5: SUPPORTING EVIDENCE: THE MIDDLE EAST

1. See Douglas Little, *Diplomatic History*, November 2004, for recent comment. For more detail, see *Pirates and Emperors* and my article in George, ed., *Western State Terrorism.*
2. See *Pirates and Emperors* and my article in George, ed., *Western State Terrorism.*
3. Justin Huggler and Phil Reeves, *Independent*, 25 April 2002. Amira Hass, *Ha'aretz*, 19 April 2002, reprinted in Hass, *Reporting from Ramallah* (Semiotext, 2003, distributed by MIT Press).
4. Michael Bohn, *The Achille Lauro Hijacking* (Brassey's, 2004).
5. Ian Williams, *Middle East International*, 29 April 2005.
6. Stephen Zunes, *National Catholic Reporter*, 1 July 2005. On the record until final withdrawal, see my *Fateful Triangle.*
7. For background and review on Kifaya, see *Al-Ahram Weekly*, 23–29 June 2005. For the Intifada, see my *Hegemony or Survival*, pp. 180ff.
8. See p. 63 in the present work.
9. Ian Williams, *Middle East International*, 13 May 2005.
10. Adeed Dawaisha, *Middle East Journal*, Winter 2005. See Batatu, *The Old Social Classes and the Revolutionary Movements of Iraq*, for in-depth analysis.
11. Steven Erlanger, *New York Times*, 14 November 2004.
12. Joel Brinkley, *New York Times*, 17 September 2005. Subsequently Israel backed away on grounds that it would be "impractical," a senior official said. Steven Erlanger, *New York Times*, 24 October 2005.
13. Gilbert Achcar, *Le Monde diplomatique* (English edition), July 2005.
14. James Bennet, *New York Times*, 17 March 2003.
15. Steven Erlanger, *New York Times,* 12 and 13 November 2004.
16. Shlomo Gazit, *Trapped Fools* (Frank Cass, 2003), chapter 15.
17. Harald Frederiksen, *Middle East Policy*, Spring 2005. David Ratner, *Ha'aretz*, 4 April 2005.
18. Benny Morris, *Righteous Victims* (Vintage, 2001), p. 341. For recent accounts by soldiers of barbaric behavior, see Yonatan Geffen, *Ma'ariv*, 23 September 2005, reported by the soldiers' organization Shovrim Shtika (Breaking Silence). *Middle East International*, 29 September 2005. The record goes far back.

19. See my essays in those years reprinted in *Peace in the Middle East?* (Pantheon, 1975); republished with additional essays in *Middle East Illusions* (Rowman and Littlefield, 2003).

20. David Kretzmer, *American Journal of International Law*, January 2005. See also Michael Galchinsky, *Israel Studies* (Ben-Gurion University), Fall 2004. Buergenthal, see p. 45 in the present work.

21. Elaine Sciolino, *New York Times*, 2 December 2002.

22. Judith Miller, *New York Times*, 11 November 2004. See *Necessary Illusions*, Appendix 5.

23. See my *Letters from Lexington: Reflections on Propaganda* (Common Courage, 1992; reprinted and extended, Paradigm, 2003), chapter 1. On the Israeli coalition and the Baker Plan, also the scanty and falsified news reporting, see *World Orders Old and New*, pp. 231–32.

24. UN General Assembly Resolution 44/42, 6 December 1989.

25. David Bar-Illan, interview with Victor Cygielman, *Palestine-Israel Journal*, Summer–Autumn 1996. Norman Finkelstein, *Beyond Chutzpah* (California, 2005), p. 296.

26. Shlomo Ben-Ami, *A Place for All* (Hebrew) (Hakibbutz Hameuchad, 1998). Cited by Efraim Davidi, *Palestine-Israel Journal,* volume 7, nos. 1 and 2, 2000. Barak is described by Israeli historian Benny Morris as "one of Israel's leading doves." Benny Morris, *New Republic*, 8 November 2004, review of Dennis Ross, *The Missing Peace* (Farrar, Straus and Giroux, 2004).

27. Ron Pundak and Shaul Arieli, *The Territorial Aspect of the Israeli-Palestinian Final Status Negotiation* (Peres Center, September 2004) (Hebrew). Maps in Ron Pundak, "From Oslo to Taba: What Went Wrong," *Survival* (International Institute for Strategic Studies), Autumn 2001. Pundak is director general of the Shimon Peres Center for Peace (Tel Aviv), and was closely involved in negotiations leading to the Oslo agreements and subsequently.

28. Jeremy Pressman, *International Security*, Fall 2003. He adds that "Barak gave Clinton a 20-page letter outlining Israel's reservations, some of them quite significant": "Lost Opportunities," review of Dennis Ross, *The Missing Peace*, in *Boston Review*, December 2004.

29. Pundak and Arieli, *The Territorial Aspect of the Israeli-Palestinian Final Status Negotiation*. Akiva Eldar, *Ha'aretz*, 15 and 18 February 2002. Amos Oz, *Guardian*, 5 January 2001 (pre-Taba).

30. David Matz, *Palestine-Israel Journal,* volume 10, nos. 3 and 4, 2003 (citing the press conference and Barak). Ahron Bregman, *Elusive Peace: How the Holy Land Defeated America* (Penguin, 2005), p. 145 (citing Barak). Pundak, *Survival*, Autumn 2001. On the Moratinos document, and Barak's order to terminate the negotiations, see Akiva Eldar, *Ha'aretz*, 15 and 18 February 2002, who shares the optimistic projections.

31. Pundak, *Survival*, Autumn 2001.

32. Ross, *The Missing Peace*. Jerome Slater, *Tikkun*, May–June 2005.

33. Akiva Eldar, *Ha'aretz*, 11 June 2004.

34. Benny Morris, *New York Times*, 12 November 2004.

35. Benny Morris, "Revisiting the Palestinian Exodus of 1948," in Eugene Rogin and Avi Shlaim, eds., *The War for Palestine* (Cambridge, 2001); Benny Morris, *Israel's Border Wars, 1949–1956* (Oxford, 1993), p. 410. Ari Shavit, interview with Morris, *Ha'aretz*, 8 January 2004. See letters in following issues.

36. Of some interest are the tales presented to children: "to create a Palestinian homeland [Arafat] needed land that is now part of Israel" and he "carried out attacks against the Israeli people that made many people hate him." Inversion of the scale of atrocities of friends and enemies is routine, but recognition of the occupied territories as part of Israel breaks some new ground. *KidsPost, Washington Post*, 12 November 2004.

37. *Ha'aretz*, 14 November 2003; Molly Moore, *Boston Globe*, 15 November 2003; Greg Myre, *New York Times*, 15 November 2003, with a photo of the four chiefs standing before a poster reading "We are on the road to catastrophe" (Hebrew). Moshe Negbi, *Kisdom Hayinu* (*We have become like Sodom*) (Keter, 2004). On the economic costs (and gains) of the occupation to Israel, see Shlomo Swirski, *Palestine-Israel Journal* 12.1 (2005). On the record of the courts, see David Kretzmer, *The Occupation of Justice* (SUNY, 2002); Lisa Hajjar, *Courting Conflict* (California, 2005).

38. Reuven Pedatzur, *Ha'aretz*, 21 February 2005 (Hebrew), review of Akiva Eldar and Idit Zartel, *Adonei Ha'aretz* (*Lords of the Land*) (Kinneret, 2005). The Eldar and Zartel quotations are from the review.

39. Pedatzur, *Ha'aretz*, 21 February 2005. Morris, *Righteous Victims*, p. 341.

40. Amira Hass, *Ha'aretz*, 6 July 2005.

41. Amira Hass, *Ha'aretz*, 22 September 2005.

42. Amir Oren, *Ha'aretz*, 29 November 2002. Ze'ev Schiff, *Ha'aretz*, 27 and 29 July 2005.

43. On the consequences of the assassination, see p. 23 in the present work.

44. Elizabeth Bumiller, *New York Times*, 15 April 2004. Meron Benvenisti, *Ha'aretz*, 22 April 2004. Saree Makdisi, *London Review of Books*, 3 March 2005.

45. B'Tselem, released October 2005. Moshe Dayan, quoted in Yossi Beilin, *Mehiro shel Ihud* (Revivim, 1985), p. 42. These words express Dayan's general conception "as the architect and then the arbiter of policy in the territories," with the goal of "creeping annexation" and "creeping transfer" of "as many of the territories' remaining population as possible" by making their lives difficult. Morris, *Righteous*

Victims, pp. 337ff. Among Labor Party leaders, Dayan was one of those most sympathetic to the plight of the population.

46. Amira Hass, *Ha'aretz*, 30 October 2005, with maps. Ariel Sharon quoted in Reuters, 1 December 2005. *Report on Israeli Settlement*, November–December 2004.

47. Chris McGreal, *Guardian*, 20 October 2005.

48. Gideon Levy, *Ha'aretz*, 24 October 2005.

49. John Ward Anderson, *Washington Post*, 7 February 2005. On the Rabin-Peres plans, see *World Orders Old and New*, Epilogue; *Pirates and Emperors*, chapter 7; *Middle East Illusions*, chapter 6. On Ma'aleh Adumim, see my essay and others in Roane Carey, ed., *The New Intifada* (Verso, 2001).

50. Maskit Bendel, *The Disengagement Plan and Its Repercussions on the Right to Health in the Gaza Strip* (Physicians for Human Rights–Israel, 2005), p. 9. See the report on the eve of the disengagement by B'Tselem, *One Big Prison*, March 2005.

51. Ravi Nessman, AP, 19 April 2004. Aluf Benn, *Ha'aretz*, 11 August 2004. On the timing of disengagement and the separation wall, and the short- and long-term goals, see Tanya Reinhart's epilogue in her *Israel/Palestine: How to End the War of 1948* (Seven Stories, 2005). On the general logic, see also Baruch Kimmerling, *Politicide: Ariel Sharon's War Against the Palestinians* (Verso, 2003).

52. Sara Roy, *Journal of Palestine Studies*, Summer 2005.

53. Bendel, *The Disengagement Plan and Its Repercussions*. Amira Hass, *Ha'aretz*, 28 August 2005.

54. *Ha'aretz*, 27 April 1982. Amnon Kapeliouk, *New Statesman*, 7 May 1982. See *Fateful Triangle*, chapter 4.3.

55. Orit Shohat, *Ha'aretz*, 26 August 2005.

56. Baruch Kimmerling, *Ha'aretz*, 21 August 2005.

57. Joel Brinkley, *New York Times*, 17 September 2005.

58. Amira Hass, *Ha'aretz*, 14 August 2005.

59. AP, *Boston Globe*, 12 July 2005. *Ha'aretz*, 4 December 2003. *Jerusalem Post*, 4 December 2003. Bush's 2002 vote was reported by AP and Agence France-Presse (December 3). See *Hegemony or Survival*, chapter 7, for more detail on resolutions blocked by Bush. On Barak, see Yoaz Yuval, *Ha'aretz*, 7 July 2005.

60. Meron Benvenisti, *Ha'aretz*, 14 July 2005. Rubinstein, *Ha'aretz*, 31 March 2005.

61. Greg Myre, *New York Times*, 25 August 2005. Karin Laub, AP, 2 September 2005 (*Boston Globe*, 3 September 2005, unarchived). *Ha'aretz* Service and AP, 19 September 2005.

62. *Report on Israeli Settlement in the Occupied Territories*, Foundation for Middle East Peace, March 1996, January 1996. For more extensive detail, see *World Orders Old and New*, Epilogue. Jerusalem and

Ramallah Heads of Mission (European Union), *Report on East Jerusalem*, November 2005. Chris McGreal, *Guardian*, 25 November 2005. Steven Erlanger, *New York Times*, 25 November 2005.

63. Chris McGreal, *Guardian*, 18 October 2005.
64. Benedict Carey, *New York Times Week in Review*, 10 July 2005.
65. Jeane Kirkpatrick, *Commentary*, November 1979.
66. Thom Shanker, *New York Times*, 24 November 2004.
67. On Eisenhower and the National Security Council, see *World Orders Old and New*, pp. 79, 201ff. Yaqub, *Containing Arab Nationalism*, pp. 225ff., 228, 240ff.
68. Peter Waldman et al., *Wall Street Journal*, 14 September 2001.
69. David Gardner, *Financial Times*, 8 July 2005. See p. 145 in the present work.

Chapter 6: DEMOCRACY PROMOTION AT HOME

1. On the Bush administration's shameful record of abuse of presidential power and civil rights, see among others Barbara Olshansky, *Democracy Detained* (Seven Stories, forthcoming).
2. Robert Dahl, *How Democratic Is the American Constitution?* (Yale, 2002). Thomas Ferguson, *Golden Rule* (Chicago, 1995). Robert McChesney, *The Problem of the Media* (Monthly Review, 2004). Robert Reich, *New York Times*, 18 March 2001, cited by McChesney. Woodrow Wilson quoted in John Manley, "Theorizing the Unexceptional," 2005 ms., citing R. Baker and W. Dodd, eds., *The Public Papers of Woodrow Wilson* (Harper and Brothers, 1925–27), volume 1, p. 78. Robert Westbrook, *John Dewey and American Democracy* (Cornell, 1991). For a more far-reaching critique and proposals, see Stephen Shalom, *Z Magazine*, October 2004.
3. Morton Horwitz, *The Transformation of American Law, 1870–1960* (Oxford, 1992). Many more rights were added through judicial decisions in the 1970s. See also the classic study by Robert Brady, *Business as a System of Power* (1943; reprinted by Transaction, 2001). Delaware Court, see Scott Bowman, *The Modern Corporation and American Political Thought* (Pennsylvania State University, 1996), p. 133. For an expert and accessible introduction to these topics, see Joel Bakan, *The Corporation* (Free Press, 2004).
4. For sources, see my "Consent Without Consent: Reflections on the Theory and Practice of Democracy," *Cleveland State Law Review*, Fall 1996. Adam Smith, *The Wealth of Nations* (Chicago, 1976), volume 2, p. 236.
5. Aristotle, *Politica (Politics)*, book 4, chapters 2, 11; book 5, chapter 8; book 6, chapter 5; book 7, chapter 10. Richard McKeon, ed., *The Basic Works of Aristotle* (Random House, 1941).

6. Robert Wiebe, *Self-Rule* (Chicago, 1996), pp. 96ff. Norman Ware, *The Industrial Worker, 1840–1860* (Chicago: Ivan Dee, 1990; reprint of 1924 edition).

7. Woodrow Wilson cited in Martin Sklar, *The Corporate Reconstruction of American Capitalism, 1890–1918* (Cambridge, 1988), pp. 413–14. Wiebe, *Self-Rule*, p. 134.

8. See pp. 9, 41 in the present work. For Schlesinger, see *Hegemony or Survival*, pp. 12–13. Fritz Stern, *Foreign Affairs*, May–June 2005.

9. Amos Elon, interview with Ari Shavit, *Ha'aretz*, 23 December 2004.

10. Peter Cromwell, "The Propaganda Problem," *Horizon*, January 1941.

11. See the biennial studies of the Economic Policy Institute, *The State of Working America*; the most recent, by Lawrence Mishel, Jared Bernstein, and Sylvia Allegretto, covers 2004–2005. Marc and Marque-Luisa Miringoff, *The Social Health of the Nation* (Oxford, 1999), Index of Social Health report of the Fordham Institute for Innovation in Social Policy, which monitors social indicators (as is done by government agencies in other industrial societies).

12. Edward Wolff, *Milken Institute Review*, 3rd quarter, 2001. Eduardo Porter, *New York Times*, Business section, 14 July 2005. Census Bureau, see David Leonhardt, *New York Times*, 31 August 2005; Robert Guy Matthews, *Wall Street Journal*, 31 August 2005. Jessica Vascellaro, *Wall Street Journal*, 13 September 2005. Dean Baker, Center for Economic and Policy Research, 17 October 2005.

13. Libby Quaid, AP, 29 October 2005.

14. Alan Greenspan, testimony, Senate Banking Committee, February 1997, cited in *Multinational Monitor*, March 1997. Edward Herman, *Z Magazine*, March 2005.

15. On the "comparative peculiarity" of "religious cognitions," see Walter Dean Burnham, in Thomas Ferguson and Joel Rogers, eds., *The Hidden Election* (Pantheon, 1981), and p. 223 in the present work. For a review of the earlier period, partially shared with England, see Clifford Langley, *Global Dialogue*, Winter–Spring 2003.

16. Bruce Franklin, *War Stars* (Oxford 1988).

17. See, e.g., Ferguson, *Golden Rule*, pp. 389–90. See chapter 1, note 34, on the studies of the Chicago Council on Foreign Relations (CCFR) and the Program on International Policy Attitudes (PIPA) at the University of Maryland.

18. Guy Dinmore, *Finanical Times*, 9 November 2004. Gallup cited by Paul Abramson, John Aldrich, and David Rohde, *Political Science Quarterly*, Spring 2005.

19. Ferguson and Rogers, eds., *Hidden Election*.

20. For sources, see my *Turning the Tide* (South End, 1985), chapter 5. On

the 1984 elections, see more generally Thomas Ferguson and Joel Rogers, *Right Turn* (Hill & Wang, 1986).

21. Samuel Huntington, in M. J. Crozier, S. P. Huntington, and J. Watanuki, *The Crisis of Democracy* (New York, 1975). See Alex Carey, *Taking the Risks out of Democracy* (New South Wales, 1995; Illinois, 1997), and Elizabeth Fones-Wolf, *Selling Free Enterprise* (Illinois, 1995), on corporate propaganda.

22. José Antonio Ocampo, "Rethinking the Development Agenda," 2001 ms., based on paper presented at the American Economic Association annual meeting, January 2001. Marc Weisbrot, Dean Baker, and David Rosnik, Centre for Economic Policy Research, September 2005. Robert Pollin, *Contours of Descent*, chapter 5. Robert Wade, *Challenge*, September–October 2005.

23. On the measures used by the government and press to ram NAFTA through, see my *World Orders Old and New*, chapter 2.5.

24. International political economist Robert Wade, *Challenge*, January–February 2004.

25. Barry Eichengreen, *Globalizing Capital: A History of the International Monetary System* (Princeton, 1996).

26. Gary Jacobson, *Political Science Quarterly*, Summer 2005.

27. Thorstein Veblen cited by Michael Dawson, *The Consumer Trap* (Illinois, 2003), p. 154, an important contribution to a substantial literature. On advertising as a reflection of market decline, and the impact on media, see McChesney, *The Problem of the Media*, chapter 4. Smith, *Wealth of Nations*, book 1, chapter 11, p. 278.

28. K. Lokuge and R. Denniss, *Trading In Our Health System?* Australia Institute, Discussion Paper no. 55, May 2003.

29. Dean Baker, "The High Cost of Protectionism: The Case of Intellectual Property Claims," ms., Economic Policy Institute, 1996; for summary, see Dean Baker, *In These Times*, 22 August 1999. Lokuge and Denniss, *Trading In Our Health System?*.

30. Lokuge and Denniss, *Trading In Our Health System?*.

31. Thomas Patterson, *New York Times*, 8 November 2000; *Boston Globe*, 15 December 2000.

32. Gallup poll, released 16 December 2004, available at www.gallup.com.

33. Jacob Schlesinger and Jackie Calmes, *Wall Street Journal*, 8 October 2004; Liz Marlantes, *Christian Science Monitor*, 22 September 2004; Daniel Yankelovich, *Foreign Affairs*, September–October 2005; the poll keeps largely to superficial questions, such as is the United States "generally doing the right thing with plenty to be proud of?"

34. Seth Jacobs, "Sink or Swim with Ngo Dinh Diem," 81st University of Connecticut Foreign Policy Seminar, 2005. Walter Burnham, in Ferguson

and Rogers, *Right Turn*. Chris Hedges, "The Christian Right and the Rise of American Fascism," available at www.theocracywatch.org, citing Adams. Stern, see pp. 209–10 in the present work. Chris McGreal, *Guardian*, 20 October 2005.

35. Program on International Policy Attitudes (PIPA), "Public Perceptions of the Foreign Policy Positions of the Presidential Candidates," 29 September 2004; "The Separate Realities of Bush and Kerry Supporters," 21 October 2004. Gardiner Harris, *New York Times*, 31 October 2004.

36. Albert Hunt, *Wall Street Journal*, 26 June 1998. Ceci Connolly and Claudia Deane, *Washington Post*, 20 October 2003. Lee Walczak et al., *Business Week*, 16 May 2005. Pew Research Center, *Public Divided on Origins of Life*, 30 August 2005. Wiebe, *Self-Rule*, p. 239. On the record over a longer period, see Vicente Navarro, *Why the United States Does Not Have a National Health Program* (Baywood, 1992); *Dangerous to Your Health* (Monthly Review, 1993); *The Politics of Health Policy* (Blackwell, 1994), pp. 210ff.

37. Harris, *New York Times*, 31 October 2004. Adam Clymer, *New York Times*, 17 October 1993.

38. Frank Newport, Gallup News Service, "Americans Want Leaders to Pay Attention to Public Opinion," 12 October 2005.

39. Dan Roberts and Edward Alden, *Financial Times*, 4 November 2004.

40. Chris Giles, *Financial Times*, 1 December 2004. Jon Hilsenrath, *Wall Street Journal*, 4 April 2005.

41. Edward Lazowska and David Patterson, *Science*, 6 May 2005. As they note, IT funding, like most of electronics, has been under a Pentagon cover, with DARPA at the cutting edge.

42. Glen Johnson, *Boston Globe*, 27 November 2004, citing polls conducted for Pax Christi and by Zogby International. Peter Steinfels, *New York Times*, 2 August 2003.

43. Fareed Zakaria, *Newsweek*, 11 October 2004. See Gerald Seib and Carla Anne Robbins, *Wall Street Journal*, 2 November 2004, lead story, referring to the CCFR study but not conveying its contents accurately. Sources, see chapter 1, note 34.

44. Chicago Council on Foreign Relations (CCFR), *Global Views 2004*.

45. John Crook, *American Journal of International Law*, July 2005. Editor Michael Reisman notes that the added wording may be in violation of the UN Charter and the Rome Statute setting up the ICC. Chicago Council on Foreign Relations (CCFR), *Global Views 2004*. *Boston Globe*, 18 March 2005. Victor Mallet and Guy Dinmore, *Financial Times*, 17 March 2005. Human Rights Watch, news release, 7 March 2005.

46. Frances Williams, *Financial Times*, 20 October 2005. Tom Wright, *International Herald Tribune*, 30 September 2005. On the government-

media campaign against UNESCO, and the remarkable record of falsification and deceit, see William Preston, Edward Herman, and Herbert Schiller, *Hope and Folly* (Minnesota, 1989), apparently ignored.

47. AP, 23 October 2005; Agence France-Presse, 23 October 2005. *Independent* (London), 12 October 2005.

48. Ian Seiderman (legal adviser to the International Commission of Jurists), letter, *New York Times*, 21 April 2005. World Summit, see p. 80 in the present work.

49. Farah Stockman, *Boston Globe*, 1 March 2005. Paula Dobriansky, US Department of State, *Current Policy* No. 1091, 1988; for comment, see Philip Alston, *American Journal of International Law*, April 1990. Jeane Kirkpatrick cited in Joseph Wronka, "Human Rights," in R. Edwards, ed., *Encyclopedia of Social Work* (National Association of Social Workers, 1995). Morris Abram, statement, UN Commission on Human Rights, on "The Right to Development," 11 February 1991.

50. Program on International Policy Attitutes (PIPA), "The Separate Realities of Bush and Kerry Supporters," 21 October 2004. PIPA, "Saddam's Intent to Build WMD Not Seen as Sufficient Reason," online reports, 28 October 2004. See p. 25 in the present work.

51. PIPA, "Americans on America's Role in the World After the Iraq War," 29 April 2003; "7 in 10 Now Say UN Should Take Lead," 3 December 2003. On misperceptions, and their correlation with news sources, see Steven Kull, Clay Ramsay, and Evan Lewis, "Misperceptions, the Media, and the Iraq War," *Political Science Quarterly*, Winter 2003–4.

52. On the Iraq programs of the elected Zapatero government, see *El Mundo*, 19 April 2004.

53. PIPA, "Public Would Significantly Alter Administration's Budget," media release, 7 March 2005. On estimated war costs, see Linda Bilmes, *New York Times*, 20 August 2005.

54. Jason DeParle, *New York Times*, 11 October 2005. Jonathan Weisman, *Washington Post*, 21 September 2005. See also p. 212 in the present work.

55. Media search for March 2005 by David Peterson found no mention of the report and its findings.

56. Jacobs and Page, *American Political Science Review*, February 2005.

57. Chicago Council on Foreign Relations, Program on International Policy Attitudes, *Americans on Promoting Democracy*, 29 September 2005. See also p. 137 in the present work.

58. Jeffrey Birnbaum, *Washington Post Weekly*, 27 June–10 July 2005.

59. Elizabeth Drew, *New York Review of Books*, 23 June 2005.

60. George Lardner, *Washington Post*, 17 August 2001.

61. Jim VandeHei, *Washington Post Weekly*, 30 May–5 June 2005.

62. Kaitlin Bell, *Boston Globe*, 8 August 2005. "A Win for 'Academic Bill of Rights,'" *InsideHigherEd*, 7 July 2005. Kathy Lynn Gray, *Columbus Dispatch*, 27 January 2005.

63. Michelle Goldberg, Salon.com, 6 November 2003. Baruch Kimmerling, www.dissidentvoice.org, 29 March 2005. Sara Roy, *London Review of Books*, 17 February 2005.

64. Corey Robin, *Fear: The History of a Political Idea* (Oxford, 2004), p. 40.

65. Laurie Goodstein, *New York Times*, 31 August 2005.

66. Frank James and Andrew Martin, *Chicago Tribune*, 3 September 2005. Thom Shanker et al., *New York Times*, 2 September 2005. Robert Block et al., *Wall Street Journal*, 6 September 2005.

67. Sandra Postel (a specialist on water policy and ecosystems), *Christian Science Monitor*, 7 September 2005. Edward Alden, *Financial Times*, 4 September 2005; Edward Alden et al., *Financial Times*, 2 September 2005. Dean Baker, Center for Economic and Policy Research, Economic Reporting Review (online), 12 September 2005. Paul Krugman, *New York Times*, 2 September 2005.

68. John Wilke and Brody Mullins, "Marketplace" column, *Wall Street Journal*, 15 September 2005. Dean Baker calculates the private school bonus to be close to 50 percent; Center for Economic and Policy Research, Economic Reporting Review (online), 26 September 2005; see also 12 September 2005. Food support and hunger, see p. 212 in the present work.

69. Tom Reifer, *Focus on Trade,* no. 113 (Focus on the Global South), September 2005. Seymour Melman, *After Capitalism* (Knopf, 2001), summarizing and extending a great deal of his earlier work along with guidelines for a very different and more democratic future.

70. See p. 226 in the present work.

71. Alan Murray, *Wall Street Journal*, 3 August 2005. Michael Schroeder and Suein Hwang, *Wall Street Journal*, 6 April 2005. For discussion and many sources, see Robin Hahnel, *Panic Rules!* (South End, 1999); my *Rogue States*, chapter 8. On alternatives, see Robert Blecker, *Taming Global Finance* (Economic Policy Institute, 1999).

72. Timothy Egan, *New York Times*, 21 August 2005. David Himmelstein et al., *Health Affairs*, 2 February 2005. For summary, see Kayty Himmelstein, *Dollars & Sense*, July–August 2005. See also David Himmelstein and Steffie Woolhandler, "Mayhem in the Medical Marketplace," *Monthly Review*, December 2004.

73. Gallup polls, "Costs Hurt Those Who Need Healthcare Most," 3 May 2005; "U.S. Trails Canada, Britain in Healthcare Ratings," 8 June 2004, available at www.gallup.com.

74. For data, see Phineas Baxandall, *Dollars & Sense*, May–June 2001.

Public Citizen, 14 January 2004, reporting a study in the *International Journal of Health Services*. UN Development Report 2005, chapter 2, available online from the United Nations Development Program.

75. Katie Hafner, *New York Times*, 13 October 2005. Vanessa Fuhrmans, *Wall Street Journal*, 27 and 28 October 2005. Centers for Medicare and Medicaid Services, "Medicare & You" (handbook), 2006.

76. Jonathan Weisman and Ceci Connolly, *Washington Post Weekly*, 26 March–3 April 2005.

77. Paul Krugman, *New York Times*, 15 August 2005. For analysis and exposure, see particularly Dean Baker's weekly analyses published by the Center for Economic and Policy Research, and many columns by Paul Krugman in the *New York Times*. Among many others, see Alicia Munnell, *Challenge*, March–April 2005. For background, see Dean Baker and Mark Weisbrot, *Social Security: The Phony Crisis* (Chicago, 2001).

78. Chris Giles, *Financial Times*, 2 May 2005.

79. 2004 Annual Report of the Board of Trustees of the Federal Old-Age and Survivors Insurance and Disability Insurance Trust Funds, Table V.A2, Dependency Ratios.

80. Gallup poll, "Americans Insecure About Social Security," 5 April 2005, available at www.gallup.com. Mark Weisbrot, Center for Economic and Policy Research release, 3 February 2005. Holly Yeager, *Finanical Times*, 20 April 2005.

81. The chart of GAO analysis is based on data from government actuaries and the Congressional Budget Office, accompanying Linda Feldman, *Christian Science Monitor*, 5 January 2006.

82. Gallup poll, "American Public Opinion About Retirement," 21 June 2005, available at www.gallup.com.

AFTERWORD

1. Robert Pastor, *Condemned to Repetition* (Princeton, 1987), his emphasis.

2. Ali Abdullatif Ahmida, *Forgotten Voice* (Routledge, 2005).

3. Selig Harrison, *Financial Times*, 18 January 2006.

4. Ellen Knickmeyer and Omar Fekeiki, *Washington Post*, 24 January 2006. Charles Levinson, *Christian Science Monitor*, 30 January 2006. For Osirak, see *Hegemony or Survival*, p. 25.

5. See p. 77 in the present work and *Hegemony or Survival*, pp. 157–58.

6. Anthony Bubalo, *Financial Times*, 6 October 2005. Shai Oster, *Wall Street Journal*, 23 January 2006.

7. Aijaz Ahmad, *Frontline* (India), 8 October 2005. Katrin Bennhold, *International Herald Tribune*, 5 October 2004. Also Victor Mallet and

Guy Dinmore, *Financial Times*, 17 March 2005. Daniel Dombey et al., *Financial Times*, 26 January 2006. David Sanger and Elaine Sciolino, *New York Times*, 27 January 2006.

8. Siddharth Varadarajan, *Hindu*, 24 January 2006; *Hindu*, 25 January 2006; *International Herald Tribune*, 25 January 2006. Fred Weir, *Christian Science Monitor*, 26 October 2005. See "Declaration of Heads of Member-States of Shanghai Cooperation Organisation" (China, Russian Federation, Kazakhstan, Kyrgyz Republic, Tajikistan, Uzbekistan), 5 July 2005, Astana, Kazakhstan; *World Affairs* (New Delhi), Autumn 2005.

9. For background see *Hegemony or Survival*, chapter 6.

10. NIC, *Global Trends*. Joel Brinkley, *New York Times*, 25 October 2005. Dan Molinski, AP, 24 October 2005. Bush policies have even alienated Australians, traditionally supportive of the United States. A 2005 survey found that a majority regarded "the external threat posed by both US foreign policy and Islamic extremism" as primary and equivalent concerns, compared with one-third concerned about China. Only 58 percent "viewed the US positively, compared with 94 per cent for New Zealand, 86 per cent for Britain, 84 per cent for Japan, and 69 per cent for China." Half favored a free trade agreement with China, only a third with the United States. Tom Allard and Louise Williams, *Sydney Morning Herald*, 29 March 2005.

11. Marc Frank, *Financial Times*, 21 October 2005. John Cherian, *Frontline* (India), 30 December 2005, citing Pakistan's leading daily *Dawn*.

12. Gwynne Dyer, *Guardian*, 25 October 2005. Adam Thomson, *Financial Times*, 11 December 2005. Economist Mark Weisbrot, codirector of the Center for Economic and Policy Research (Washington), CEPR release, 28 January 2006.

13. Andy Webb-Vidal, *Financial Times*, 3 January 2005. Diego Cevallos, IPS, 19 December 2005. Weisbrot, CEPR release 28 January 2006. Water, *Rogue States*, pp. 77–78.

14. Andy Webb-Vidal, *Financial Times*, 13 March 2005. Justin Blum, *Washington Post*, 22 November 2005. Michael Levenson and Susan Milligan, *Boston Globe*, 20 November 2005.

15. David Bacon, *Z magazine*, January 2006; *Multinational Monitor*, September–October 2005.

16. Scott Wilson and Glenn Kessler, *Washington Post*, 22 January 2006. Steven Erlanger, *New York Times*, 23 January 2006.

17. Walt Bogdanich and Jenny Nordberg, *New York Times*, 29 January 2006. See references of chapter 4, note 14, and p. 154 in the present work. Gregory Wilpert, Znet commentary, December 2005.

Index